Succeeding with Your Doctorate

Succeeding with Your Doctorate

Jerry Wellington, Ann-Marie Bathmaker,
Cheryl Hunt, Gary McCulloch, Pat Sikes

SAGE Publications
London • Thousand Oaks • New Delhi

SAGE Publications Ltd
1 Oliver's Yard
55 City Road
London EC1Y 1SP

SAGE Publications Inc
2455 Teller Road
Thousand Oaks, California 91320

SAGE Publications India Pvt Ltd
B-42, Panchsheel Enclave
Post Box 4109
New Delhi 110 017

Library of Congress Control Number 2004116091

A catalogue record for this book is available from the British Library

ISBN 1-4129-0115-4
ISBN 1-4129-0116-2 (pbk)

Typeset by Pantek Arts Ltd, Maidstone, Kent.
Printed in Great Britain by T.J. International, Padstow, Cornwall.

Contents

Preface   vii
About the authors   x
Acknowledgements   xii

Part 1: EMBARKING ON A DOCTORATE   1

1: What is a doctorate and why do people do them?   3

2: How did I get here? An Auto/ biographical Approach   16

Cameo 1: The long and winding road that led me to an EdD course –   24
Jean Clarkson

Cameo 2: How our experiences influence the research topics we choose –   28
Alan Hearsum

3: Learning on the doctoral journey   30

Cameo: Spiralling into control: a research journey – *Tracy Marshall*   48

Part 2: CONCEPTUALISING AND FOCUSING THE STUDY   53

4: Framing the research   55

Cameo: How I theorised my thesis – my story – *Carolyn Mason*   68

5: Reviewing the literature   72

Cameo: Reviewing the literature – *John O'Neill*   88

PART 3: THINKING ABOUT METHODOLOGIES   93

6: Doing research: reflecting on methods, methodology and ethics   95

Cameo: Methodology and methods – *Bernard Longden*   106

7: Approaching research as lived experience   112

Cameo: Queer matters in methodology – *Mark Vicars*   131

PART 4: WRITING THE THESIS   135

8: Writing and the writing process in a
    doctoral programme   137

Cameo: Me and my writing process – *Kathryn Roberts*   162

9: Production values in the doctoral thesis   165

Cameo: Writing the thesis – a personal account from which it might   175
be hard to generalise much – *Paul Machon*

PART 5: PRESENTING AND SHARING RESEARCH   177

10: Presenting your work at the viva   179

Cameo: Surviving the viva – *Maxine Burton*   195

11: Whatever next? Spreading the word and
     becoming part of the research community   198

Cameo: The doctoral experience – bearing fruit – *Marion Jones*   204

Further reading   207
Useful organisations and websites   209
References   215
Index   224

Preface

The aim of this book is to support, inform and guide students (and by implication their supervisors) through a doctoral programme. The book is intended for students working towards either a 'taught' doctorate (such as an EdD) or a course of study leading to a PhD.

We recognise that doctoral programmes have changed and these changes are described and discussed in Chapter 1. The traditional model of a doctorate based on the concept of three years of independent (but supervised) full-time research is no longer the norm. Thus in writing the book we have had in mind not simply those students who may wish to become professional researchers in education, the social sciences or related fields, but also, and perhaps most especially, those who aspire to being a 'researching professional': a professional, probably already established in a career, who wishes to reflect upon, and research into, her or his own practice and/or the political, social and theoretical contexts in which it is located. Because we are well aware that students who are also working in demanding jobs have to perform complex juggling acts in order to balance the demands of work, study and other aspects of their lives, each chapter of the book contains cameos of students who have struggled to maintain this fine balance – and survived to tell the tale.

Thus the book includes the voices and the stories of past and present students on doctoral programmes – but we do not wish to give the impression that this selection exhausts the range of students' individual lived experiences. There are as many rich, personal stories to be told by doctoral students as there are doctoral students. Some of these may well be uncomfortable and discordant at times, but they are always challenging and we find them an endless source of fascination, and continue to learn from them as we try to improve our own craft.

The book is soundly based on research, theory and practice. It draws on our own, and others', research and writing over many years, and on our extensive experience of working with postgraduate students and examining doctoral theses (both as internal and external examiners – see Chapter 10). Even though the five authors writing this book have a great deal in common, we know that we approach research, supervision and writing in different ways. This is partly because we come from different disciplinary backgrounds – history, science, sociology, psychology and social-psychology – but it is mainly because we are, simply, different people. You will undoubtedly be able to identify our individual 'voices' at various points in the text. You will also notice that different chapters have different styles and tones. Some are of a more procedural, 'how-to-do-it' nature; others are more critical and discursive. This mirrors the way that doctoral studies actually proceed in practice.

We have tried to write this book in an accessible style which is consistent with our approach to teaching and working with our own students – so we often speak directly to you, the reader, in a 'conversational' style, using 'you' and 'we' as appropriate. However, the term 'we' sometimes encompasses different groups: it may refer to us, the authors; or it may refer to us, as part of the 'research community', into which, as a doctoral student, you will be gradually inducted and included. Our hope is that the book will facilitate your entry into, and understanding of, that community as well as your enjoyment in undertaking doctoral research.

Some of the questions and issues covered by the book include:

- **What is a doctorate? Why do people do them?**
- **Learning and studying – what are the implications of 'being a student' again?**
- **How can critical reflective practice, auto/biographical and life history work help you to better understand your research related interests, orientations, assumptions and biases, that is, your 'researcher positionality'?**
- **Relationships with supervisors: what should you expect from them and what should they expect of you?**
- **Reading critically.**
- **Doing and writing a literature review.**
- **Making best use of documentary resources, including on-line material.**
- **Choosing your topic and clarifying the focus of your study.**
- **Considering an appropriate methodology and understanding its practical and ethical implications.**
- **Writing and the writing process.**
- **Producing a thesis at doctoral level.**
- **Preparing for and surviving the viva.**
- **What to do next? (For example, getting published in journals? Conference presenting? Writing your first book?)**

We should also explain what we are *not* trying to do in this book. We do not go into detail about any specific research methods or strategies; there are already plenty of books that do this and which offer very good advice of this kind. Also, although we hope that we provide a handy and accessible guide on how to study at doctoral level, we do not simply give tips and hints to improve your efficiency, but encourage you to think and work in a reflexive and self-aware fashion that is itself an appropriate approach for a doctoral student.

Viewing the contents and chapter headings in this book (and many others) would seem to imply that the process of working for a doctorate is a linear, mechanistic one. This is far from the truth – in reality the doctoral 'journey' is likely to be non-linear, messy, cyclical and always unpredictable. The book should be read with this in mind, and used accordingly. Despite the book's title, we cannot guarantee complete 'success' to readers in pursuit of a doctorate. We emphasise that a successful outcome at doctoral level can be hazardous and unpredictable. We hope that the chapters in this book will make your journey a little less difficult even though it will still be challenging. We think that the journey itself matters as much as the arrival.

The book mainly addresses the situation in Britain, sometimes with references that are specific to this country. However, it includes within its remit doctoral students from both Britain and the European Community and international students from around the world who are preparing their doctorates for a British university.

We welcome your comments on this book (negative or positive). Please send them to: j.wellington@sheffield.ac.uk

About the Authors

Ann-Marie Bathmaker: Ann-Marie is director of the MA in Educational Research at the University of Sheffield, which prepares students for PhD study. She is also a member of the EdD teaching team. Her work focuses on the interrelationship between policy and practice. Her areas of research and publication include education policy in post-compulsory education and training, the changing nature of professionalism in these contexts, teacher and learner identity, youth transitions, and qualifications and training for teaching and learning professionals.

Cheryl Hunt: having been extensively involved in the Sheffield EdD programme for several years, Cheryl now directs the EdD in Professional Studies at the University of Exeter. She has designed and taught on a range of Masters programmes focusing especially on learning and teaching in professional settings. Her research interests and publications include the facilitation of critical reflective practice; policy and practice in adult and community education; and understandings of spirituality. She is currently co-ordinator of an ESRC Seminar Series entitled Researching Spirituality as a Dimension of Lifelong Learning and is an executive editor of *Teaching in Higher Education*.

Gary McCulloch: Gary is Brian Simon professor in the history of education at the Institute of Education, University of London. He has extensive experience of a range of doctoral supervision at Sheffield, London and in his previous posts at the Universities of Auckland and Lancaster. His research interests are in the history of education and in related aspects of the school curriculum, education policy and teacher professionalism. He has published widely in these fields, including several books and numerous journal articles. Gary is former editor of *History of Education*, and has recently published books on historical research in education and documentary methods in research. He is currently president of the History of Education Society (UK).

Pat Sikes: Pat directs Sheffield's EdD programme and has supervised many doctoral theses. Throughout her academic career, the study of aspects of teachers' lives and careers through qualitative research methodologies in general and life history/narrative approaches in particular, have been the central strand of Pat's research interest and activity. This work has focused on four main interrelated areas: teachers' lives and life cycles; life history methodology; social justice issues, and qualitative research method-ology. She has published extensively in all of these fields, and is Series Editor of an Open University Press series entitled *Doing Research in Educational Settings*. Pat is an editor of BERJ (British Educational Research Journal).

Jerry Wellington: Jerry is head of research degrees and a professor in the School of Education at the University of Sheffield. He has supervised a large number of PhD and EdD theses. His main interests are in research methods, science education and the use of information and communication technology (ICT) in education. He has writ-ten many journal articles and books on science education, methods and methodology, and the role of new technology in education and employment.

Acknowledgements

First, we would like to thank all the students who have contributed 'cameos': Maxine Burton, Jean Clarkson, Alan Hearsum, Marion Jones, Bernard Longden, Paul Machon, Tracy Marshall, Carolyn Mason, John O'Neill, Kathryn Roberts and Mark Vicars.

We would also like to thank all the colleagues and students who have contributed to our thinking, teaching and writing. Parts of this book draw upon course materials and *Student Handbooks* developed for use in the School of Education, University of Sheffield. These have been adapted and rewritten over the years but the voices of many colleagues remain embedded in them; we would especially like to acknowledge those of: Felicity Armstrong, Colin Beard, Catherine Edwards, Hazel Hampton, William Hampton, David Hyatt, Elaine Millard and Rita Johnston.

The authors and publisher are grateful for permission to use part of the poem on page 154, by Dr Zar: Candidate for a Pullet Suprise, from The Journal of Irreproducible Results, www.jir.com (http://www.jir.com)

Part I
Embarking on a Doctorate

1 What Is a Doctorate and Why Do People Do Them?

CHAPTER CONTENTS

We start our book by looking at what a doctorate is and why people do them. Although you are probably reading this book because you have already embarked on doctoral study, it can be helpful to take stock of what this means as the process gets under way. The question of what counts as a doctoral degree and the issue of why or when the rather clumsy adjective of 'doctorateness' should be attributed to a thesis are recurrent. The debate occupies, and will continue to occupy, students, supervisors and examiners at various stages of a doctoral programme and we return to it in different chapters of the book.

This chapter traces some of the history of doctoral degrees, considers the recent changes in their structure and organisation, and discusses the notion of the 'professional doctorate'. We have included the personal viewpoints of a small sample of students on why they chose to undertake a doctorate, and the reasons why some choose the so-called professional route whilst others favour the PhD.

What are 'doctoral degrees'?

What do we think of when we think of a doctoral degree? The image that comes into our heads might well be a detailed study of a particular topic, supervised by an established academic with experience of the area; a sustained piece of original research that will hopefully make a difference to our understanding of the field. This would be the basic model of the established Doctor of Philosophy, or PhD degree, which hinges on the production of an extended written work, or thesis. Other images arising from this might also occur to us. In terms of the purpose of the study, it might well be about initiating the student into academic life just as much as it is about enhancing our knowledge of the subject, and indeed the PhD has come to be regarded as a 'union card' for the intending academic. In terms of the process of the study, we might think of it as rather lonely and solitary, with the supervisor as the only contact and support. So far as the topic is concerned we might have the impression that it should be very narrow – finding out more and more about less and less. Perhaps we might assume it to follow on immediately from an undergraduate or Masters degree, something to be done full time when one is young, if at all. We will have the nasty feeling that it will be very hard work, and may well wonder whether it is worth it, and whether we are up to it.

Many of these impressions are entirely accurate, especially the bit about the hard work. In other ways they amount to a familiar stereotype that still holds good in many cases, but which is also under challenge, and undergoing change. Compared to 30, or even 10 years ago, the doctorate is developing in new and interesting ways. There is still a great deal of mystique about it, but also pressure of different kinds that is making it more accountable, to the institution, to the society, to the government, and also to the student. Cutting-edge research is still the key rationale for the study, but there are growing expectations about making use of the study for other social purposes, and about what is often styled 'transfer of skills'. There continues to be a great deal of variety and individuality and even idiosyncrasy in doctoral study, but alongside this can be seen movement towards common standards, and towards a measure of collegiality. Depth of understanding is still treasured, but breadth of coverage is also increasingly promoted.

A significant sign of change in the doctoral degree is its spread in terms of numbers over the past few decades. A relatively uncommon phenomenon before the 1950s, the doctorate today remains a substantial achievement but is no longer so unusual. The type of students taking doctoral degrees is also changing. They are not simply youngsters fresh from undergraduate study, but are in many cases experienced mid-career professionals, often already senior people in their own right, working on their degrees part time. These latter also include what we might describe as global professionals – established in different parts of the world but enabled because of the development of rapid transport links and the information and communications revolution to contemplate taking a doctoral degree based half a world away.

Many among this new, mature clientele are attracted to the established brand of doctoral study, the PhD model and what it stands for. This is the established gold standard, and it often provides the motivation and incentive even for many who would not wish to go into an academic career. Others are looking for something more clearly relevant to their own career development, and are receptive to the appeal of new professionally oriented doctorates.

In this book, we are interested in looking at what the doctorate means in the early twenty-first century, at how far and in what ways its nature and appeal are changing, and in particular at what its appeal is to the new kind of doctoral student – the part-time, mid-career professional, perhaps a school teacher or based in a university but just as likely to be working in industry or commerce or elsewhere. What are they looking for and where do they find it?

FROM BACHELORS TO MASTERS

If you have already participated in a degree ceremony, you will almost certainly have seen an array of academic staff – wearing colourful robes and medieval-style hats – sitting behind the Chancellor or Vice-Chancellor as she or he presented the awards. In the twelfth century, as part of a small, licensed body of teachers qualified to teach the true doctrine of the church, they would all have been called 'Masters' or MAs. The word 'Master' derives from roots in Sanskrit, Greek and Latin; these are variously associated with notions of 'greatness', 'nourishing' and 'leading'. In late Latin, these ideas became linked in the term *magisterium*, meaning 'a body of teachers'. (Partridge, 1979).

The Masters eventually broke free from the authority of the church and formed themselves into a guild, or union (which is what *universitas* originally meant), and were thus able to decide for themselves who was worthy enough to be admitted to their number. It was subsequently decreed that the Chancellor should be obliged to confer degrees upon all those nominated by the Masters – which is why the present-day 'Masters' continue to examine students; why the Dean, acting as their spokesperson, reads out the names of those who are to receive degrees; and why the 'Masters' on the platform watch to see that the Chancellor does what is required of him or her.

The form of words used by the Chancellor as the graduands are presented is: 'I *admit* you to the degree of …'. The word 'degree' comes from the Latin *gradus*, meaning 'a step'. Thus, when a student is admitted to the degree of Bachelor, she or he moves one step up towards the Mastership. When she or he is admitted to the degree of Master, she or he climbs up a further step to reach the level of the Masters, who then receive her or him into their guild or universitas. In the Middle Ages, the newly admitted Master (men only at that time) would have stayed on the platform so that his old Master could invest him with the symbols of his office. The new Master then had to deliver an inaugural lecture, entertain the whole guild of Masters to dinner, and preside over disputations (academic debates) for 40 days continuously. (Fortunately, most of this particular tradition no longer survives, though new Masters' families and friends often preserve the celebratory dinner aspect!)

Taking one's MA was called 'inception', or the beginning of one's career as a Master. It meant that the new Master was responsible for teaching the truth, as it was understood at that time. No longer could he expect his own Master to point out mistakes and correct them – he now had to ensure that what he taught was true, no matter how awkward or inconvenient that might be (as long as this suited the prevailing faith).

Thus, the pursuit of a Masters degree today follows a very long and honourable tradition set by those who have sought to steep themselves in the knowledge, and understand the truth(s), of their particular age and academic discipline – and to pass this on to others in ways best suited to their own time and place.

Masters degree students are not expected merely to assimilate knowledge in order to 'regurgitate' it. Rather, it is expected that, in a variety of ways, they will explore the parameters of their particular subject area in order to obtain a 'mastery' of it (in the sense that they can speak and write authoritatively about it). It has also become increasingly important in our vocationally oriented times that Masters degree students should be able to bring their mastery to bear on their professional practice by seeking constantly to locate practice within a wider theoretical framework, and to identify and hone the skills which will help to improve their performance. In this respect, there is perhaps a closer relationship between many of today's Masters degrees and professional doctorates, like the EdD, than there is between the modern Masters degree and the PhD.

THE DOCTORATE AND ITS HISTORY

Noble (1994) identifies 1150 as the year of the first PhD, in Paris. From the twelfth century until the early part of the nineteenth, professional doctorates could be obtained in theology, law and medicine. The modern Doctor of Philosophy (PhD) degree originated in nineteenth-century Germany and swiftly attracted students from other countries, including the USA. The first American PhD was awarded at Yale in 1861 but it was not until 1920, and after some resistance, that the PhD arrived in Britain – at Oxford (just to complicate the issue, the Oxford PhD is called a DPhil, as is that at the University of Sussex for example).

By that time, the USA had already taken up the idea of a doctorate in education (EdD): the first one was awarded at Harvard in 1921. It was another 70 years before that idea also crossed the Atlantic and the University of Bristol launched the first British EdD in 1992. Just six years later, 29 British universities were offering EdD programmes (Bourner et al., 2000; for a full account of the historical background, see Simpson, 1983).

Over the past 20 years, in the British context, the Research Councils have become increasingly prominent in regulating procedures and standards in doctoral degrees. This has taken place partly in an effort to improve the quality of doctoral theses, for example through systematic research training. Whereas a generation ago doctoral students might be expected to 'sink or swim', with the (variable) support of their supervisors, now they are entitled to take advantage of a wide range of training courses. Also, the Research Councils fund scholarships in approved institutions of higher education on a competitive annual basis, and they monitor these carefully to ensure a successful outcome in the specified time.

Changing concepts of the doctorate

The traditional model of a doctorate had been based on the concept of three years of independent (but supervised) full-time research. This route was and is often considered suitable for those who know exactly what they want to do (or are told by their department what to do). The part-time traditional model consists of four to six years or more of part-time research, with similar features. Why change?

First, the traditional model had (and still has) its critics. One of the most useful but critical pieces of research on the doctorate in a range of countries (including the UK, Canada, USA and Australia) was conducted by Noble in 1994. His evidence, or at least his interpretation of it, painted a very negative portrait of the PhD at that time. He reported poor attrition rates, sex discrimination, extended completion times and poor preparation for employment (p. 32). He identified several problems with PhD programmes including low quality and lack of purpose of research training programmes, poor supervision and low quality of writing in PhD theses – not an encouraging picture.

In the same era, the 1990s, calls came from government and other bodies for two connected and typically utilitarian changes:

1. **For greater 'employability' of graduates from doctoral programmes, targeted to individual career development needs.**
2. **That doctorates should equip students with generic, transferable research skills, for example management, entrepreneurial, teaching. Hence, the need developed, or more accurately calls were made, for more explicit and accountable formal training (often called research training programmes – RTPs).**

More practical and internal points, such as the realisation that not every student knows what subject to focus on from day one supported these extrinsic pressures for change. One of the results was the creation of 'new route' PhD programmes, and these were supported by much rhetoric. For example, the Tony Blair quote that the new routes were 'designed to give students a competitive edge in the knowledge economy of the Twenty First Century' can be found at www.newroutephd.ac.uk.

Two of the models to emerge, both very similar, are:

- **the 'one + three model': one year of training (and deciding on title and focus)** *plus* **three years of researching; and**
- **the four-year doctoral programme, integrating academic supervision with group work, lectures, tutorials and perhaps an annual Graduate Research Conference.**

It is worth noting in passing that the new models have come in for some criticism. For example, some critics have complained about an overloaded agenda for the new PhD, especially if it includes teaching and training for teaching, for example the postgraduate certificate in higher education (PCHE).

As the new models were emerging, professional doctorates were appearing alongside. As we note in the next section, one of the catchphrases in the rise of the professional doctorate has become: the 'scholarly professional not the professional scholar'; or phrased another way, it is the route to professionals gaining doctorates (researching professionals) as opposed to the development of researchers (professional researchers). The utilitarian thrust that contributed to changes in the concept of a PhD was also a contributory factor in the growth of professional doctorates.

The rise of the professional doctorate

Bourner et al. (2000) conducted a survey of professional doctorates in a range of subjects in English universities. They noted that the rapid development of these degrees seems to have been prompted by a government White Paper in 1993 which expressed concern that 'the traditional PhD is not well-matched to the needs of careers outside research in academia or an industrial research laboratory' (p. 218). Bourner et al. conclude: 'if the traditional PhD is intended to develop professional researchers, then the professional doctorate appears to be designed to develop researching professionals' (p. 219).

Taught doctorates, for example the EdD, might typically be two years of part-time study with assignments leading to part two, the thesis stage. Thesis length might be 40,000 to 50,000 words as opposed to perhaps 80,000 for a 'typical' PhD (but total word length when assignments are added might be more, for example 6 x 6,000 plus 50,000).

PROFESSIONAL DOCTORATES: ISSUES FOR DISCUSSION

The professional doctorate is relatively new as compared with the PhD (one century rather than nine). Inevitably there is still considerable debate about the notion and it remains an essentially contested concept (Gallie, 1955). Some of the issues and questions that seem to recur are:

1. The term 'professional doctorate' does raise the issue of what 'professional knowledge' might be, as compared to (say) 'academic knowledge'. A full and helpful discussion of this distinction has yet to be written.
2. The professional doctorate is sometimes referred to as the 'taught' doctorate – obviously this is a misnomer, as the more recent PhDs will all contain a taught or a 'training' component.
3. These supposed distinctions between 'types of knowledge' also raise the centuries-old debate over parity of esteem, commonly between vocational and academic knowledge. Often, academics with experience of the 'pure' established PhD can be rather suspicious of the 'applied' and relatively unproven professional doctorate, even though their institutions are trying hard to assert their parity with each other.

4. Forms of assessment and modes of teaching seem to be very conservative in doctoral programmes (see Chapter 10 on the viva). Perhaps it is time to examine and question these: for example, should all doctoral students have to produce a thesis? Should all students undergo an oral examination on completion of their written submission? Could or should the assessment process be different for the professional doctorate?

5. One of the strong features of the professional doctorate is often called the 'cohort effect', that is, a group of students start together and build up a sense of community, with peer group support and group identity, thus avoiding the social and intellectual isolation that a part-time PhD student might experience (but really should not). Again, this distinction may not always hold, given the new models and routes for PhDs that are now more prevalent.

Why do people do a doctorate?

There are probably as many reasons for doing a doctorate as there are people doing them. We asked a range of our own part-time and full-time students, many of whom could be described as 'mature', for their own reasons. The responses included:

I wanted to give myself 'permission' to take time out to learn more about the theory behind education – I had simply been doing it for about 15 years but had no qualification in it or theoretical knowledge of it as such. I already have two professional qualifications (effectively the equivalent of Masters degrees) and reckoned if I was going to take three years out for an MA I might as well take four years out and aim for the top! Having originally failed two out of three of my A levels, I really wanted to prove that I could cope with education at the highest level. To me it will represent a huge personal achievement.

I decided to do a doctorate because I teach in a university and it has become the basic qualification for university teaching.

The doctorate is my 'Everest'; I have always wanted to climb cogitatively to the highest academic peak so that I can prove to myself that starting my formal education in a secondary modern school was not a disadvantage to me.

I decided to do a doctorate to prove to myself that I could. I did not have a positive school experience and always felt that I could do better.

I decided to do a doctorate because I had recently completed my first degree and felt (for the first time ever!) confident that I could achieve more.

I feel I need to be more knowledgeable and be able to reason and inference at a higher level than the Masters. I am hungry for more knowledge and wish to develop my insight more and believe that a doctorate will get me there.

To be entirely honest a number of people came into our department with PhDs and made it quite clear to the rest of us that they were superior to us because they had PhDs. Furthermore, the Head of School told a number of us that we were virtually unemployable because we didn't have doctorates. At first I decided to ignore such comments, but they must have had an effect because I started looking at advertisements relating to part-time doctorates. There is also a part of me that has always wanted to do it, but I still think the comments within the department spurred me on.

I chose to undertake a doctorate because I am at heart a frustrated academic. I had been meaning to complete further research for something like 20 years, following the completion of my Masters degree. (The latter was felt necessary after a disappointing result in my first degree.) I am passionate about education from an historical/political/philosophical and sociological point of view.

Why choose a professional doctorate?

Many students deliberately choose to take a professional doctorate rather than a PhD. Some of the reasons given for this choice from our own part-time students taking the four-year (minimum) professional doctorate are given below. Clearly, this is a biased sample as they are all people who deliberately chose this route on the basis of their perceptions and in some cases hearsay.

I suppose at 54 years of age I saw it as presenting a focus and a challenge to see if I could achieve something like this. Apart from the personal satisfaction of hopefully completing the EdD was the feeling that, unlike a PhD in mathematics or statistics, I might be able to contribute a piece of research which might, in some small way, make a difference to someone in either my Institute or in education generally. It also helps to be a little bit mad.

I embarked on a PhD (part time) many years ago but found it a lonely business and both the timing and topic weren't right. (Dropped out after 18 months or so). I wanted a degree of structure – which the professional doctorate offers. I also wanted to engage with people from beyond my own institution and subject area. This is of key importance to me.

I chose a professional doctorate because I needed to be taught how to research. I needed to produce a number of different pieces of written work that had a beginning and end so I could build up an experience of writing that had to come up to a standard and be assessed on a longitudinal basis. I suppose if I could have guaranteed getting a good supervisor from the outset then I may have chosen the PhD route. The EdD provides a kind of 'beauty parade' of professors and doctors who could be my supervisor. I also liked the collegial nature of the EdD where I could test my ideas and have others critique my contribution. Lave and Wenger call this a community of practice – you see how my reading has forced me to rethink how learning really does take place in life?

The cohort approach seemed to me important as it promised interaction with other professionals.

I chose a 'professional' degree because it was described as 'taught'. I know that I learn best when I'm with others and learn from and with them, so imagining that a PhD would involve a fairly high degree of doing it alone, I opted for what I hoped would be a more gregarious model.

Having looked at the structure of ordinary PhD's, the Loneliness of the Long Distance Runner springs to mind! I have a very low value of my own worth and I need to have plenty of input and support along the way. I like the breakdown of the modules as I find this easier to work with and less daunting too. It also gives a slight urgency of time – if one relies on doing a dissertation, rather than intermediate papers, there is a false sense of security in the length of time available to work in! Most of us are in jobs which are full of work-related activities I'm sure, and with the best will in the world, we all would find reasons for putting off those things which do not have interim deadlines.

Clearly, the most common reasons given were around the perceived structure and support offered by this route; they also centred around the cohort effect, peer learning and the community of practice that developed as a result of a group all commencing a programme at the same time and meeting on a regular basis. Another factor related to the belief that a wider range of staff, with varying interests and expertise, would be encountered in a professional, taught doctorate.

Why do some choose a PhD rather than a professional doctorate?

From those who specifically chose a PhD, there seem to be a range of reasons, many of them very personal:

> I wanted to extend my research interests based on my postgraduate studies. Another factor was that my career prospects – if I was to go back to work in my home country eventually – would be enhanced if I was to successfully complete my PhD thesis.

> There is always the motivation to try to excel and to achieve the highest level of education that you can. You learn a lot every time you study. And, you just get the feeling that you could better do the things that you really want to do if you study. Studying for the PhD promises much in terms of self-actualisation and community development, particularly if you want that on the basis of evidence rather than on just gut feeling.

> I was just finishing a Masters when friends and colleagues asked whether I was going to do a PhD next – the thought had never occurred to me. My family background is not academic, and a PhD was certainly not 'expected' from me. As soon as the thought had come up, though, I couldn't stop thinking about it – it wasn't so much the letters added to my name, more the thought of the ultimate learning adventure. I enjoy learning new things, and a PhD lends me the cloak of respectability – nobody queries weird tendencies to read around a subject when you say you have to write a thesis on it at the end. In truth, I just thoroughly enjoy getting my teeth into a problem and a PhD gives me the time to do this on a bigger scale than any other 'project' I could think of at the time.

For some international students, the reasons may relate to their own background, and their own country and its attitudes:

> I was not sure whether another doctoral programme would be as well respected as the PhD is in my country – I had never heard of any other doctorate.

> I am attached to one of the universities in my country and it is a requirement that we have to have at least a PhD in order for us to become a permanent staff member and teach the postgrad. students. So that's one of the reasons of doing a PhD, but most importantly I do it because of the encouragement that I get from my mom who wants me to go on learning. I think at least one of her kids should make her proud through learning and teaching.

It was my wish and dream after attending my first degree graduation ceremony and saw these wonderful women and men in red robes and hats; and so that policy-makers can respect me as a doctoral graduate when making recommendations, since I intend to be a consultant in this area. Last but not least, I want to extend my stay in UK since things are not rosy back home due to highest ever rate of inflation and political instability.

For another student, the PhD was the favoured route as he knew exactly what he wanted to research in his field, and he knew his supervisor from his Masters degree:

I chose the PhD route because I knew what I wanted to research and felt comfortable with the supervisor. I felt that it would be a good working experience and that I would learn more from having prolonged close supervision.

So, what is a doctorate?

There is, and there probably always will be, some debate about what counts as 'doctorateness'. Noble (1994) at least makes a start by saying that a doctoral degree is 'an academic university qualification that requires a research thesis above the Master degree level' (p. 1). Later, he describes the three main components of all doctorates as 'lengthy study, original research and thesis preparation'. This connects with the traditional view that a doctorate makes a 'substantial and original contribution to knowledge'. However, that begs the question of what is to be considered as 'original'. Some have also questioned whether the notion of 'originality' should differ for the professional doctorate. For example, the criteria for the professional doctorate are sometimes modified so that they involve more to do with researching, reflecting upon and improving practice.

The publishability criterion is also commonly invoked for the doctorate: 'is worthy of publication either in full or in abridged form'. Should this be the same for all doctorates? The latter seems slightly strange in that a thesis in the library is in a sense a published document anyway; and it is unlikely that any book publisher, in the current commercial climate, will publish a thesis as it stands. The only realistic option is amendment for a book, or carefully selected articles from the thesis (for example, perhaps one on its content and findings; one on any original methodology or methods). We discuss this in a later chapter.

The distinction between a professional doctorate and a PhD is still a matter for debate. Physically, we can often point to the word length of the former (typically 40,000 to

50,000 words in some disciplines) compared with over 75,000 words for many PhD theses. But this contrast in 'volume' breaks down when the prior assignments written and assessed for the professional route are put into the calculation. There can surely be no difference in quality for the two routes, if both are doctoral programmes. It would have to be a matter of scope or extent that would distinguish the two types of thesis. The distinction should also hinge on the view expressed above that one route aims to produce professionals who can reflect upon and research their own practice, while the goal of the other is often to develop professional researchers – but even this does not always apply in practice.

The debate on the doctorate and its distinctive features is certain to continue. Many people (especially experienced examiners of doctoral theses) claim to possess tacit or intuitive knowledge of what constitutes doctorateness – but few have committed their intuition to the written word. Perhaps the viewpoint that our understanding of the notion is essentially tacit and intuitive is a ploy for cutting short the debate or avoiding making it explicit.

Through the different chapters of this book we aim to show what doctoral study might be (including, for example, the literature review, the methodology and the writing of the thesis) even if we do not succeed in providing a succinct definition of it. The next chapter stresses the importance of examining how you reached the point of embarking on a doctorate – and the value of this reflection in approaching your own doctoral research.

2 How Did I Get Here? An Auto/biographical Approach

CHAPTER CONTENTS

In Chapter 1 the focus was on the historical development of the doctorate. In this chapter we shift the focus to the student. The story of how a person comes to be a doctoral student is a significant factor in shaping how they will perceive and experience their studies and for how they will approach all aspects of their research. Reflecting on your own story can be an extremely valuable activity to undertake at the start of your doctoral studies thus, in this chapter our aim is to consider how reflective and reflexive auto/biography, specifically life history, can:

◆ help you to explore and make sense of your experiences to date with a view to getting the best personal and professional benefits from a doctoral programme;
◆ help you to investigate and understand your research related beliefs, values and practices; and
◆ be a valuable research approach.

We do this under the headings of:

◆ Why am I here?
◆ Why life history?
◆ Researcher positionality

Finally, we suggest *a framework for a personal life history* which you can use for your own private self-exploration and which could also provide a basis for a reflexive section in your dissertation. The chapter closes with two auto/biographical cameos written by past doctoral students.

Why am I here?

Enrolling for a doctorate is rarely a snap decision and, given the amount of time, effort, energy and commitment that will be required on the part of the student and, often their family and friends, nor should it be. This is not something to take up on a whim, since most doctorates take a *minimum* of three or four years study to complete (depending on whether they are full- or part-time programmes) and a substantial number of people are finishing off into subsequent years.

Although it might sound something of a truism, in order to be successful on a doctoral programme, you have really got to want to do it. Some people sign up because they want a career in academia, because they love studying, or have an area of interest they want to pursue, or because they no longer find their job as fulfilling and demanding as they once did and are consequently seeking extra intellectual stimulation or a challenge. Others use starting a doctorate as an obvious and explicit indication that this is the beginning of a new phase of their professional and/or personal life. They may, for instance have had a significant life change such as divorce, bereavement or children leaving home, and starting doctoral studies may signal to themselves, and to the world, that they are moving on and doing something for themselves.

Those choosing professional doctorates usually wish to continue working either within or close to their particular field, in contrast to those who want to become career researchers ('researching professionals' rather than 'professional researchers'). These students may, therefore, be looking to these programmes to advance their professionally related theoretical and practical knowledge and are wanting to do research with a view to development and improvement and in order to make things better in some way. Indeed, it is this orientation towards *praxis* (that is, committed informed practice) that characterises most, if not all, professional doctorates (see Lunt et al., 2003). Furthermore, having the opportunity that many such courses provide, to shape assignments to address professional concerns is a big plus because it can allow you to kill more than one bird with one stone and this, together with the actual award of a doctorate, can help when it comes to bids for promotion. This last is, perhaps, particularly the case for people who work in certain higher education (HE) institutions and who may be ineligible for senior posts unless they have a doctorate (although we have also met headteachers who believe that school appointment panels look more favourably on candidates with a professional doctorate).

In many cases, and particularly with regard to EdDs (Lunt et al., 2003; Scott et al., 2004), students on professional doctoral courses are often in middle- or senior-level positions and will have been working for a number of years. They therefore have considerable experience, expertise and knowledge relating to their field and it can be quite a change, and even a challenge, to be in a situation where, in many respects, they are relative beginners and starting out afresh. Having assignments or draft chapters returned to be developed and improved can be quite a shock too if, so far in your educational career, you have never had such an experience, and confidence in your academic ability can be shaken. However, it is worth remembering that, in most cases, you have not been required to work at this level before either. It is also useful to bear in mind that it is very unusual for papers to be accepted for publication in peer reviewed journals on first submission and in many respects work assessed for doctoral qualification can be seen in much the same light. Indeed, it is a good idea to think of all your writing as potentially publishable. Taking this perspective can help when reworking is requested!

Studying whilst doing a job obviously entails a great deal of extra work. For some people, the structure provided by a professional doctorate – that is, taught sessions, work to be submitted by deadlines, assignments that can also address work-based concerns, being part of a cohort with the peer support that that usually entails – is what makes them believe it's possible for them.

The reasons you have for joining a programme will influence what you are looking for in, and hoping to get out of, it. Being clear about your hopes and aims can help in deciding if a doctorate is, indeed, the most appropriate course for you, and can also be a useful touchstone and motivator to refer to if enthusiasm saps. Of course, this is not to suggest that your aspirations and interests will necessarily stay the same during your time on the course and it may well be that the actual experiences that you have as part of it will lead to changes. Accepting this possibility and being willing to go with it can in itself be helpful.

So, however and why ever you have joined a doctoral programme it is worthwhile spending some time thinking about what you are hoping to get out of the experience. Be honest with yourself about your own motivations, aspirations, strengths and insecurities, and be honest too about your strengths and weaknesses when it comes to coping with situations and challenges similar to those you are likely to face on the programme. Think, also, about the impact that being on a course that stretches over a minimum of four years might have on your relationships. If you live with other people – partners, children, parents, whoever – the simple fact that you are likely to need time to study may well impinge on them in practical and physical, as well as in affective and emotional, ways. You need to take them into consideration and consult with them about how best to meet their needs as you proceed through the course. As well as reflecting on your reasons for, and the immediate implications of, starting a doctorate, it will also be worth your while exploring in some detail your life history as it impacts upon you as a student and a researcher.

Why life history?

When you are in the middle of a story it isn't a story at all, but only a confusion; a dark roaring, a blindness, a wreckage of shattered glass and splintered wood; like a house in a whirlwind, or else a boat crushed by the icebergs or swept over the rapids, and all aboard powerless to stop it. It's only afterwards that it becomes a story at all. When you are telling it to yourself or someone else. (Attwood, 1996, p. 298)

Human beings are storying beings. We make sense of our lives and the things that happen to us through narratives which provide links, connections and coherence in ways that we find meaningful. As Donald Polkinghorne puts it, 'narrative descriptions exhibit human activity as purposeful engagement in the world. Narrative is the type of discourse that draws together diverse events, happenings and actions of human lives' (Polkinghorne, 1995, p. 5).

In the hurly-burly of everyday life we rarely have the space to reflect on our experiences or to consider where we are in terms of our beliefs and values, hopes and aspirations. As Margaret Attwood's character, Grace observes, 'when you are in the middle of a story, it isn't a story at all, but only a confusion'. We are recommending that you, as doctoral students, take time to step back from your own personal confusion, from your story in progress (as it were) and consider how you have got to where you are. In other words, we suggest that you spend some time on constructing the story to date. In our view, undertaking an auto/biographical life history type of investigation is one of the most productive ways of doing this. This is because, as well as enabling you to gain critical insights regarding the influence your life experiences may have had upon your perspectives, interests, assumptions, orientations and biases, it can also provide you with the basis for a section in your thesis where you make your researcher positionality clear (see Goodson and Sikes, 2001, for a comprehensive review of life history research). At the end of the chapter we offer 'A framework for a personal life history' which you might like to use for a guide and a starting point.

As an approach, life history recognises that lives cannot be compartmentalised. The things that happen to us in one aspect of our life potentially can have an impact upon, and implications for, other areas too. For instance, we may try to put the breakfast-time argument with our partner out of our minds whilst we are at work and, to a greater or lesser extent, we might succeed. The chances are, though, that it will stay there, affecting in some way, however slight, what we do throughout the day. At a more significant level perhaps, life history acknowledges that there is a crucial inter-active relationship between individuals' lives, perceptions, experiences, beliefs, values and the various identities they negotiate for themselves, and the social, cultural and historical contexts in which those lives are lived. As Michael Erben puts it, 'individual motivations and social influences have no easy demarcation' (1998, p. 1). We, you, everybody, come to everything we do with 'baggage', with histories that are at one and the same time, our own and those of the societies and cultural groups in which we live. Karl Marx's much quoted comment to the effect that, 'men *[sic]* make their own history, but they do not make it just as they please; they do not make it under circum-stances chosen by themselves, but under circumstances directly encountered, given and transmitted from the past' (1969 [1845], p. 389) is pertinent here. Thus, whilst we might have some say over the things that happen to us, it is difficult, if not impossi-ble, to escape totally the influence of our own personal histories and the histories that have shaped the societies in which we live. In order to understand this, C. Wright Mills advocated the use of 'the sociological imagination' (1959) to connect the private and personal to the public and social: life historians fully embrace this injunction.

Essentially, life history research starts from and focuses on the personal and subjective perceptions and experiences of individual people. Where it goes next and what forms it then takes depends on the particular variant being employed. We follow the line taken by Ivor Goodson who, in writing about life history work with teachers, stresses that,

> the crucial focus for life history work is to locate the teacher's own life story alongside a broader contextual analysis, to tell in Stenhouse's words 'a story of action within a theory of context'. The distinction between the life story and the life history is therefore absolutely basic. The life story is the 'story we tell about our life' … The life history is the life story located within its historical context. (1992, p. 6)

This contextualisation is essential because it is that which gives life history its analyt-ical power. So, when you are reflecting on how you have come to be enrolled on a doctoral programme you will need to be thinking about the ways in which your life course has been affected by, for instance, social class, gender, ethnicity, faith, sexuality, where you lived, the times you have lived in, educational policy, ideology, and so on. The type of analysis you make will, inevitably, depend to some extent upon your interests, your philosophical positions, beliefs and values, and upon your awareness of various theoretical models (all of which, of course, are consequent upon your life history). Most importantly, though, is your openness to asking critical questions and challenging your own taken for granted assumptions. Do not assume anything happened 'just because'. It may be the case that you failed the 11+ 'just because you were thick', though that is unlikely given that you are now a doctoral student. Think, rather, about the ways in which your experiences had not fitted you to pass it. You do not need to be familiar with Bourdieu's theory of cultural capital to work out that, if you were a working-class child, you were at a disadvantage!

So, life history can help you to come to a sociologically informed and critical under-standing of your experience in the world. It also offers a useful strategy for investi-gating and articulating the ways in which the beliefs and values you hold have an impact upon you as a researcher – your 'researcher positionality'.

Researcher positionality

In recent years it has come to be widely accepted that research cannot be disembod-ied (see Sikes and Goodson, 2003, p. 32). It is impossible to take the researcher out of any type of research or of any stage of the research process. The biography of researchers, how and where they are socially positioned, the consequent perspectives they hold and the assumptions which inform the sense they make of the world, have implications for their research interests, how they frame research questions, the para-digms, methodologies and methods they prefer, and the styles that they adopt when writing up their research. Engaging in reflective and reflexive auto/biographical life history study of the type we are advocating can help you to understand 'where you are coming from' as a student on a doctoral course *and* as a researcher. It can also be used in a research paper or thesis to give readers information that can enable them to locate and, thereby, make better sense of the work. In itself this information can help counter charges of bias and partisanship which are often levelled at qualitative research in general and particularly that which is explicitly concerned with social justice issues (see Tooley, 1998). Indeed, reflexivity should be an inherent and ubiqui-tous part of the research endeavour (see Hertz, 1997) regardless of which methodolo-gies and paradigms are employed.

Kuhn (1962) argued that there is no way to distinguish between what is out there in the world and what is subjective and perceived and in people's heads. And we would agree with this. Unfortunately a legacy of what Christians refers to as 'the dominant Enlightenment worldview' (2000, p. 134) is the notion that good research practice is neutral, value-free and uncontaminated by the presence of the researcher in any way, shape or form. We would want to challenge this view on the grounds that moral research practice requires us to reject the tradition of hiding ourselves by using discourse that seeks to minimise, neutralise, standardise, control, distance or disengage our subjective and personal experiences or the subjective and personal experiences of the people with whom our research may be concerned (see Fine et al., 2000).

In reflecting reflexively on your positionality as a researcher and how that might affect how you approach research, whether doing your own or reading other people's research accounts, it is a good idea to start by interrogating your philosophical position and your fundamental assumptions concerning:

● **the nature of social reality and the extent to which it is constructed or given – your ontological assumptions;**
● **the nature of knowledge, where knowledge comes from and how and by whom it is created – your epistemological assumptions; and**
● **human nature and agency – specifically, your assumptions about the ways in which human beings relate to and interact with their environment.**

These assumptions are coloured by values and beliefs that are based in, for instance, political allegiance, religious faith, and experiences that are consequent upon social class, ethnicity, gender, sexuality, historical and geographical location, and so on. As we have said, these assumptions affect how people conceive of and conduct their research and we will be returning to them in greater depth in Chapter 6. For now, though, we want you to be aware that positionality is central to the research endeavour and particularly when the research involves other people as research 'subjects' since they come with positions too. As a note of caution we also want to add that we recognise that where people are positioned is rarely clear cut, they may hold views at different points on any continuum and may, indeed, sometimes contradict themselves. Nor do we want to suggest that we believe views to be fixed and immutable. What we think at any one time is dependent upon the conditions and circumstances and experiences relevant to that time, and these may well change. Indeed, the sorts of experiences you are likely to have as a student working towards a doctorate should be leading you constantly to question and, maybe, alter your views.

A framework for a personal life history

Throughout this chapter we have emphasised that understanding the influences that have shaped you as a researcher and as a student on a doctoral programme can be illuminative and valuable, and even liberatory in that it may reveal that the way in which particular aspects of your life have worked out is less to do with you and more the consequence of social positioning or historical events.

There is no one right way to 'do' life history, but an approach that people often find useful involves starting with a time line. The sort of information this could touch on includes:

- Place and date of birth.
- Family background and history including ethnicity and religious affiliation.
- Parents' occupations and level of formal education; their general character and interests.
- Siblings: place and dates of birth; occupations and level of formal education; their general character and interests.
- Extended family: occupations and level of formal education; their general character and interests.
- Your childhood: description of home and general discussion of experiences
- Community and context: general character and feel.
- Educational experience: pre-school, schooling; courses taken, subjects favoured, qualifications attained or not; general character of school experience; peer relations; teachers; good and bad experiences.
- Higher education and professional preparation.
- Occupation: general work history; particular interests; highs and lows; successes and failures.
- How you came to enrol on a doctoral programme.
- Personal relationships: partners, children.
- Interests and pursuits.

When you have compiled the basic information, you should begin to think about how your life fits in to the historical contexts through which it was lived. Depending on your interests, you may want to consider how attitudes and expectations relating to gender, social class, ethnicity or sexuality, or changes in work-related policy or organisation, or being involved in particular innovations and developments, might have influenced the things that have happened to you. If you are thinking about your 'research career' you should look at how paradigm fashions and shifts in thinking might have had an impact on your research-related beliefs and values. You should also explore how beliefs and values arising from upbringing and experience could have played a part in shaping your interests and concerns, and so on.

Having undertaken this exercise, not only should you have an informed understanding of how you got to be on your doctoral programme and of your own positionality as a researcher, but you will also have gained an experiential awareness of an important and valuable research methodology.

In the two auto/biographical cameos that follow, two students who have followed doctoral programmes at Sheffield, Jean Clarkson and Alan Hearsum, reflect upon how their personal experiences have influenced them as researchers.

Cameo 1: The long and winding road that led me to an EdD course

Jean Clarkson

I began my own teacher education course in 1969 in Liverpool after the birth of my son. It seemed like a wise career for a woman who had children and although I had a place at university to study economics, the choice was prudent and the field of education has sustained a fascination for me for over thirty years. Education is a reflection of society, some say it shapes society therefore much of the structure of education has changed and modernised in line with society's needs. In the thirty years of my involvement and interest in the education of children some of the changes have come full circle, or rather spiralled, as Bruner would say.

Most of my first sixteen years as a teacher in the classroom were supported by further academic study. This was to enhance the enjoyable practical aspects of being with children and permit me to reach a better understanding of education and not just be a bystander in the educational game. It allowed me to enjoy education from an adult's perspective. As a teacher I began a part-time Masters degree at the University of North Wales. Educationalists from different settings met together at weekends to hear inspiring lectures from Wilf Carr, Anthony Hartnett, David Naish and others. These weekends challenged the new Education Reforms and allowed practising teachers to think about the effects of education and policy changes.

My Master's research was 'Teacher Appraisal' conducted during the time when teachers were required to become more accountable and the National Curriculum was introduced as part of the Education Reform Act. The higher degree provided a forum to investigate teachers' views and fears and the requirement to be liable to the general public for the educational standards of children. Teachers were moving away from the 'secret garden' and into a transparent role where children's achievements were presented through comparable statistics.

The evolution of the appraisal process led to a thesis entitled 'Teacher Appraisal — is the torch about to scorch?' referring to one of the first studies on the appraisal of teachers by Suffolk Education Department — Those having torches.

After sixteen years in the classroom and with a Masters degree pending, I joined Liverpool Hope University College as a senior lecturer. This is an ecumenical college with a teacher training focus that comprised of three colleges S. Katharine's, an Anglican college founded for women's education, and two Catholic colleges, Christ's and Notre Dame. The colleges had 150 years of teacher education between them and a strong network of schools where education had evolved and changed dramatically over the centuries.

At this stage in my career, further education became even more important, to keep abreast of the changes in education and to ensure that the BEd courses I was teaching and organising reflected recent research. The Teacher Training Agency determines what teacher education consists of yet there is room for challenge and a theoretical base. The psychology, sociology, philosophy and history of education that had formed the foundation of my own training was presented in a 'weakened form' but we were still able to deal with the fundamentals of how children learn. Giving papers at conferences both nationally and internationally with educationalists across the globe based on the research I've undertaken during the years of further study has enabled me to understand and challenge some of the changes to educational policy.

The winding road to the EdD has not been a smooth ride and I have stumbled in potholes on several occasions. In 1994 I began a PhD with a university that for a time completely took away my confidence as a writer and researcher. I had three supervisors over the time (only one of whom had a doctorate) and each one had a different understanding of what should be emphasised in the study. It became difficult to reach a clear understanding of my aims. Indeed the more my confidence diminished, the less able I was to determine the proposed outcomes of the degree. Conceptualisation was impossible for me to grasp since it was defined by three different people, all emphasising different philosophers including Bourdieu and Foucault. Ultimately, I have discovered, one has to determine one's own conceptual stance as this is unique and the basis of understanding the research.

Not surprisingly, perhaps, I ran out of time. I was confused and not clear in my objectives and although I believed I could create a good thesis with the data I had collected in the time I had left, I was offered an MPhil instead of going on to gain a PhD.

My world came to an end.

I cannot be less dramatic than this. It had been a lot of my life for six years. It had taken on such proportions that the rejection was too hard to bear.

The professor who eventually decided that I could not continue to PhD level laughed and said 'It's only a PhD, nothing more', without any understanding or, on the other hand, maybe with complete understanding of the importance of the degree. This unimportance seems a common sentiment to those who already hold a doctorate. Maybe once you have one, it seems to reduce in significance. However when a whole room full of research notes, questionnaires, reference books, journal papers, articles, interview transcripts, library cards, tapes of interviews etc. is all condensed into one small book, concentrated, concise and in perfect detail, the satisfaction must be immense.

Perhaps those with doctorates have forgotten the glorious feeling of reaching their goal. To someone who does not hold a doctorate, failure is traumatic. We soon forget how hungry we were to reach our objective when we have grasped it.

To be rejected from the PhD was devastating; it had become the goal I wanted most, the unattainable, the doctorate that four in my family held already and a major ambition. How much more did I admire them now?

After this rebuff, I ran out of the university leaving all my notes in the department. I could not bring myself to go back to collect them. Everything associated with the research was thrown into a wardrobe and there it remained until, two years later, when a friend, during a walk in the Lake District asked my husband if he could discuss the PhD again with me. My husband said, 'Watch out' but that conversation with a friend at the side of Ullswater, was a turning point.

Tentatively I applied to study for a taught doctorate. The interview was invigorating and when I mentioned that I was dazed and confused by my last experience and how difficult it was to relate to Foucault the two interviewers exchanged smiles and confidently said 'We'll sort that'.

I was accepted and they did; and the years I have spent undertaking the programme have been some of the most professionally rewarding of my career. My confidence in writing has increased and, although I still grapple with Foucault, I am beginning to see him now as a friend!

The subject of my research thesis reflects the struggle I have had to gain a doctorate.

It is entitled 'Student Teacher Retention. Why the passion dies'.

For the research methods, I not only interview those who have left initial teacher education courses but also those that are considered 'at risk' by their tutors, to give them an opportunity to talk through their concerns and maybe keep them on track. It may change the data but when students leave, not only a degree but a lifelong ambition such as teaching, it can have a devastating effect. Waiting for students to drop out, like waiting for heads to fall at the guillotine without attempting to find some way to support them through a difficult time seemed unethical. Hence the methodological choice to interview both 'quitters' and those 'at risk' seemed appropriate.

The positionality of the research mirrors my own experiences. I left my first doctorate course at the first attempt and it had a devastating effect, but the passion did not leave me. Some of the students I've interviewed who leave the course indicate that they still want to teach and, like me, they may return to their ambitions at a later date. Passion rarely dies if it is not consummated.

The long and winding road still has potholes ahead but I am wearing the right shoes and feel energised to overcome all barriers accompanied by stout colleagues and friends.

Cameo 2: How our experiences influence the research topics we choose

Alan Hearsum

I have changed the wording of my research title a few times over the last two years and have currently settled on 'Recognising non-traditional learners: education and the workplace'. When I completed my application form to read for a doctorate in the year 2001, I wrote that the scope of proposed research was, 'engaging non-traditional adult learners – what policies and procedures are required to increase take up in lifelong learning?'

If I compare these statements they are similar yet they have slightly different meanings and, therefore, outcomes. The words do, therefore, change the positionality of my research, but do they change the overall intent to help non-traditional learners by whatever means? The answer has to be that it is important to understand how my experience influences my research in terms of method or approach and certainly its value and outcomes and, therefore, its impact on my work as the chief executive of a national training organisation. My own lifelong education has been influenced by the way it has been achieved; its beauty has been in its utility.

So, for me, my research has to be relevant and useful. On reflection, my original title was more focused by the use of the words: engaging, adult, policies, procedures, and increase take up in lifelong learning. These additional words positioned my research to be of value to the government, firms I serve and the adult individual non-traditional learners. So why have I made the statement more general, perhaps less focused? I have purposefully repositioned my research through my experience of reading widely on informal and formal learning and the literature on the learning society. Also the concept of the 'unity of opposites', something I originally stumbled across in the work of Aristotle, has influenced me to rethink the value of both approaches to learning, formal and informal. Often it is not just one approach that is required, it is the unity of both approaches. Another example of unity of opposites would be qualitative and quantitative research. Often the most appropriate research approach may be a mixture of the two approaches, therefore a unity of opposites. Giddens would refer to this as a 'third way', perhaps slightly out of context, but different from thinking of approaches being one or the other, or simply a centre position. Of course many non-traditional learners I meet do not recognise their own informal learning and, in many cases, neither does the establishment.

Throughout my own schooling I excelled by learning from practical things, not just the task but the mathematics and science related to the task. I found my secondary modern education ideal for me as it gave me confidence and I did succeed in my academic subjects because of learning from the practical subjects, which were really interesting. I did not have any concern that I had been selected for this school and not the grammar school. I was later given the opportunity of day release to study for a higher national certificate and was proud when I won the second prize at college for the final year.

Eventually I became a chartered engineer. I have progressed my career in a number of line and staff management positions and I have always been particularly interested in getting people with low skills to reach their level of potential – not for altruistic reasons but because the workplace is much more efficient and effective if everyone has a range of skills, knowledge and experience to provide for job cover. Of course, we have to respect difference in industry as there are so many non-traditional learners coming out of schools. I have come up against the problem of non-traditional learners who have had a bad experience of learning at school. Many just do not enjoy being taught in a classroom and have excelled when they have started in employment particularly because they have learned by doing. Seeing what could be done outside traditional pedagogy makes one really passionate about the need for my research.

So, it can be seen from this vignette that my lifelong learning has influenced my experience in a macro sense and is being influenced by the current research process itself in order to include, in a micro sense, the voices of the non-traditional learners themselves to inform the development of future policy. Without this unity of opposites, those affected and those controlling, this research would not be correctly positioned to be of value to either. Non-traditional learners' lives are important and we need to know from them what they are going to do with our help and not to be overly concerned by the barriers ahead and from the past; they can all be overcome once they are recognised. Finally, undertaking a doctorate has given me another view on how I can perform my own job function differently and be better informed, wiser and, with a great deal more determination, make a difference in my corner of the field.

3 Learning on the Doctoral Journey

CHAPTER CONTENTS

The doctoral journey is a long and often arduous one. It leads not only through a particular field of research but sometimes enters a wilderness where nothing seems to make sense; or a desert where ideas simply dry up; or even places where relationships become difficult with 'significant others' who play a part in the journey. At the end of it, like anyone who has travelled for a long period, those who undertake this journey will have been affected and changed by it. The purpose of this chapter is to highlight the affective dimension of 'becoming a doctoral research student', and ways in which learning on and from a doctoral programme can be enhanced. It includes practical advice on keeping a learning journal, being critical, studying, and working with a supervisor.

> *my thesis research [involved] a conceptual journey and a journey of the self. (Walker, 2001, p. 422)*

> *both the meaning of our concepts and our understanding of ourselves may change and become something other than they once were. (Carr, 1995, p. 19)*

Introduction

In Chapter 2, we discussed how answering the question 'How did I get here?' can be helpful in clarifying the motivations, beliefs, values and assumptions that inevitably influence the kinds of research people choose to undertake, and how they go about it. We hope you now have a clearer understanding of your own starting point or 'positionality'. However, because we are aware that people embarking on the doctoral research journey have many different starting points and many different needs, we are mindful of the anecdote about the traveller who asks for directions and is told, 'If that's where you're going, I wouldn't start from here'.

As authors writing in a different time and place from where you are now as a reader of this text and a traveller on your own unique journey, we can neither come alongside you to share the journey, nor provide you with a detailed map or account of what you will encounter along the way. Nevertheless, we do have access to maps of territories that we and others have crossed, and to stories about the sloughs of despond and pinnacles of excitement and success that seem to be an integral part of all research journeys. In subsequent chapters we will focus on some of these maps and stories about 'doing' research – about ways and means of clarifying the research focus; undertaking a literature review; selecting an appropriate methodological approach; and writing it all up. In this chapter we shall be less concerned with where you are starting from, going to, or the possible routes you might take, and will focus instead on some of the implications of *becoming a doctoral research student*.

Identity and uncertainty

Alongside all those other considerations about doing the research itself, thinking about 'becoming a student' may sound trivial – no more than a straightforward matter of filling in the forms and making the necessary financial arrangements to become registered as a graduate student in your chosen institution. In practice, however, it can be much more complex than that because it involves coming to terms with a new identity.

Identity is itself a complex phenomenon. Rather like a kaleidoscope in which the patterns of coloured glass change and re-form as the wheel is turned, so the identity and associated patterns of behaviour and attitudes that we display tend to change and re-form according to social circumstances. To take a very simple example: people often adopt a different mode of behaviour when visiting parents or elderly relatives than when having a night out with friends; being with friends is likely to elicit different behaviours from those exhibited in a committee meeting. Confusion about the 'right' identity to display can occur in circumstances where two or more of the various groups in which individuals operate overlap unexpectedly. As Egan observes: 'Identity is a contested space; at different times our many affiliations, attributes and experiences – labels – jockey for prominence in how we describe who we are in the world, to the world … Sometimes I am a paradox of competing and seemingly incompatible identities' (2001, p. 101).

The identity and behaviour patterns we adopt generally involve ideas, habits, expectations and responses that have been learned and stored, often unquestioningly, over long periods of time. They are not just about what we *do*, or say, but how we *feel* about ourselves and our position in relation to others at a particular moment. Thus, although assuming the identity of 'doctoral research student' involves doing certain things, it also has a significant affective dimension that should not be neglected.

This is particularly important if you are embarking on your doctoral studies having already become established in a career. Egan's reference (above) to 'competing' and 'incompatible identities' is taken from a paper which draws attention to some of the challenges of being a 'grassroots activist' in his professional role as an adult educator and simultaneously attempting to undertake research associated with this work 'within the academy'. Many doctoral students, especially those studying on a part-time basis and maintaining a demanding full-time job, also find that balancing the expectations people have of them as an experienced professional against the expectations that a university has of them as a student can create unexpected tensions.

One problem is that the further up the career ladder you have moved, the greater the chances are that people turn to you for answers. Becoming a research student will almost certainly put you in a position where you are the one seeking answers – not only to significant research questions but also to basic everyday ones, like 'How do I get a library card?' or 'How often should I contact my supervisor?' This can trigger old and perhaps long-forgotten insecurities and fears of failure or 'looking silly'. As one doctoral student, an experienced Head of Department in a College of Further Education, told us:

> I was so used to being the person 'who knew' that it was really scary to find that, suddenly, I didn't. I didn't know where the rooms were or how to log on to the computer. I didn't even know what people were talking about in some of the first sessions – there was so much jargon and stuff I was unfamiliar with and everyone else seemed to understand it. It was only ages afterwards, when I'd got to know people better, that I discovered other people had felt the same way. I'd gone home feeling really stupid and thinking I'd made a huge mistake in convincing myself I could do a doctorate. Now, we've made a pact that if anyone, including 'outside experts', says something one of us doesn't follow, we'll ask for clarification. We've also got a group thing going where we'll say 'You're talking in code' if people start to use jargon.

Becoming comfortable with the uncomfortable nature of 'not knowing' is a crucial element of the doctoral research journey. Unfortunately, particularly in Western societies, uncertainty is generally viewed as problematic; something to be 'sorted out' as quickly as possible. The dominant image that has shaped such societies, and made them economically successful, is of machinery that works in a controlled 'clockwork' fashion: if X happens then Y will follow. This seems gradually to be changing to accommodate a more holistic world view and more complex understandings of psychological processes and social and environmental relationships (Hunt, 2000). Nevertheless, many of the key discourses in education, particularly at a policy level, remain embedded in clockwork imagery and suggest that learning is a linear, control-lable process and specific outcomes can be achieved by following certain procedures.

Even though this may not necessarily accord with their own personal experiences, the 'espoused theories' (Schön, 1983) that educators share with students often perpetuate these discourses. For example, Brockbank and McGill (1998) suggest that teachers in higher education unconsciously model 'absence of struggle' in coming to terms with complex ideas. Taking up this point, Haggis notes:

> *Faced with a student in a state of confusion, teachers in this situation are likely to empha-size the need for 'equilibrium' features of learning such as planning, organization and clar-ity. Whilst this advice may be helpful to the student, it is easy to gloss over the fact that confusion and disorientation are a common and often crucial part of the experience of learn-ing and writing. (2001, p. 154)*

Indeed, it is acknowledged that confusion and disorientation are triggers for what is generally referred to as 'transformative learning' (after Mezirow, 1981), through which adults come to challenge their own, often deeply held, assumptions and beliefs, including those about themselves and their world view.

Much of this book, including most of the rest of this chapter, is about the kinds of 'procedures' you may wish, or need, to undertake during your doctoral research in order to achieve that desirable outcome of donning your robes on graduation day. However, what we have tried to suggest in this chapter so far is that, as the opening quotations indicate, in 'becoming a student' you could well be embarking upon two journeys. The first is an 'academic' one which will take you through an ever-changing landscape of ideas, theories and concepts; the second may take you into the more personal territory of your own mind where understandings of yourself and your iden-tity may be challenged and changed. Part of this personal journey may also involve coming to terms with the consequences of juggling many roles besides that of 'student' or 'researcher' and managing the kinds of life-stage issues that mature students, in particular, often encounter, such as bereavement, divorce, job changes, child and/or elder care. This second journey is not irrelevant. It will inevitably leave its traces upon what you do as a researcher, and it will continue long after your thesis is finished.

Although much less attention tends to be paid to the personal and affective dimension of doctoral research, Miller and Brimicombe (2003) note that, in their work with PhD students trying to reach cross-disciplinary understandings of the research process, the students were 'most animated when talking about their hitherto private practices in and feelings about research'. For example:

> *a reading of a chapter on Becker's (1986) text on writing for social scientists* [see Chapter 8] *provoked a lively exchange about strategies for avoiding writing and some shameful confessions about personal rituals observed in relation to academic production. Becker's language clearly spoke across disciplinary divisions in capturing humorously as well as wisely the embarrassment, insecurity and fear of exposure experienced by many graduate students.*

> *Phillips and Pugh's (1987) text on how to get a PhD was another which gave rise to spirited debate. Some students found the authors' advice on how to manage supervisors instructive (particularly those who attributed superhuman status to their supervisors and in whom the notion of managing these beings involved a major paradigm shift). But there was consensus that the authors gave inadequate attention to the matter of how to handle emotional challenges and the stress induced by juggling too many identities and responsibilities ... Their diagram of a time-based programme of work, depicting the PhD process as 'the progressive reduction of uncertainty' (1987: 74) was seen by most students as bearing a very tangential relationship to their lived experience. A theme which ran through all the discussions about the research road map we were constructing together was the importance of representing affective as well as cognitive experience and development. (Miller and Brimicombe, 2003, p. 164)*

Miller and Brimicombe's students adopted a notion of 'the wilderness years' to refer to low points in their research experience when they felt they were 'wandering in confusion' and getting nowhere. Such points are almost inevitable; not easy to anticipate; and virtually impossible to provide ready-made solutions for, especially in a text of this kind. However, it will undoubtedly help you to survive and grow through such times if you can establish a personal support network with at least one or two fellow students with whom you can share frustrations and anxieties and, by looking at things from their perspective as well as your own, begin to find new ways of seeing and proceeding. In any case, never feel you have to struggle alone: make use of your supervisor and tutors and, if appropriate, of student counselling, welfare and support services.

Perhaps most importantly, we would urge you not to be afraid of a journey into uncertainty, self and the affective domain; and not to see it as an impediment to your 'real' research. It should be embraced in the knowledge that you are not just 'doing' research in a world 'out there' but that the process of research is also a process of learning and being. Especially for those who work in education and related professional settings, recognising and recording the twists, turns and implications of this process has provided valuable insights, through their own lived experiences, into the complexities of learning and of adopting and adapting to multiple roles and responsibilities. Such insights can make a significant contribution to personal development; inform professional practice; and, indeed, can often be incorporated into a reflective commentary in the final text of a thesis (see Hunt, 2001, pp. 357 – 60).

Keeping a learning journal

Keeping a learning journal is a useful way of recording and exploring your own learning, developing your thoughts and knowledge base, and capturing your insights. As we noted in Chapter 2, we strongly recommend it, and that you start one as soon as possible. Holly (1989) makes a distinction between logs, diaries and journals:

- *Log*: a record of performance, kept regularly. Facts are recorded systematically, unencumbered by interpretation.
- *Diary*: a record of personal experiences and observations over time. A personal document which includes interpretation, opinions, feelings and thoughts.
- *Journal*: a comprehensive, systematic attempt at writing, not only about events and personal thoughts and feelings but also to clarify ideas and experiences. Something written with the intention of returning to it in order to reflect and learn through interpretation of the writing

In our view, a 'research diary' is a combination of what Holly calls a 'log' and a 'diary'. What we mean by a 'learning journal' accords with Holly's description of a 'journal' but also contains elements of the 'diary'. It can be particularly useful during the 'taught' part of a doctoral programme, including the research methods training element of a PhD, as a means of identifying your own successful learning strategies and what creates blocks to your learning, as well as of sometimes 'letting off steam' at the inevitable frustrations of life and learning.

There is no 'right' way of keeping a learning journal. Some people prefer to use a small notebook that they can keep in a pocket or bag ready to use at a moment's notice in buses, trains or restaurants; others prefer a more substantial volume or a loose-leaf A4 folder. Some people have been known to use a shoebox into which they place random pieces of paper. Whatever you use, remember to date all your entries so that you can see the sequence of events when you look back at a later stage. Some people make entries every day; others only when there is something specific to report or reflect on. One of our students admitted to keeping a journal and torch by her bed so as not to miss, as she put it, 'thoughts that pass in the night' (this is not necessarily recommended – it might be better to get a good night's sleep and to focus on your journal when you are properly awake!). Journal entries can range from brief business-like notes, through an outpouring of thoughts and feelings, to 'mind-maps' and, sometimes, poetry. If words seem inadequate, try using sketches or diagrams to capture your thoughts. The use of metaphor can often be helpful too when you are trying to formulate ideas (see Chapter 7).

The processes of writing and reflection (see Chapter 8) can help to clarify some of the whirling and unfocused thoughts that sometimes get in the way of more productive thinking. This is encapsulated in the question (attributable, we think, to the novelist E.M. Forster): 'How do I know what I think until I see what I say?'. Holly puts it like this:

> Writing 'works' because it enables us to come to know ourselves through the multiple voices our experiences take, to describe our contexts and histories as they shape the many minds and selves who define us and others. Through writing we intentionally focus our attention and in so doing assert and affirm both our ideas and the mind itself. (1989, p. 78)

However, if all that sounds too 'airy-fairy' and/or the very idea of keeping any kind of journal fills you with horror, the following extract from what one student wrote about the process may help:

> I saw it as a 'learning dialogue' with myself. Keeping the journal was a powerful and therapeutic process in itself, enabling me to transfer thoughts from the fuzz and buzz of my head onto the cold and tangible neutrality of a sheet of paper where I could (sometimes anyway) begin to see some order in them.

> Occasionally I just wrote down a long moan about the way I was feeling about having to write an assignment when I would rather have been outdoors – it 'got it off my chest' and allowed me to move on. Sometimes I just wrote things like 'X says Y is a good book – must get it'.

Other times I was really systematic. I wrote down what I thought about a particular [group] session, left it for a day or two, then I went back to it and wrote down my reflections on what I had already written, asking questions like 'Why did I feel like that?'; 'Why did I let X annoy me so much?'; 'Why did I relate (or not) to that particular idea?'. After I'd done two or three of those, I went back and re-read all of them and thought about, for example, what was common to them, and what it was telling me about myself that I could take forward to the next sessions and perhaps do things differently. I jotted down some ideas, tried them out, then came back to the journal to record the consequences! I think it helped me to become more aware of what I was doing in the group sessions – as well as making me think more deeply than I'd done before about my assumptions and, dare I say it, prejudices. (Student Handbook, *Department of Educational Studies, University of Sheffield, 2002*)

A student who was a training manager kept a separate section in his learning journal to focus specifically on assignments. He said that jotting down answers to the following checklist of questions facilitated his reflection on what he had learned from the *process* of writing each assignment during the taught part of his programme and also provided a cumulative record of development, including a reminder of which ideas had excited him and which he felt most motivated to pursue in his thesis:

Before
Why have I chosen this assignment?
What use will this assignment be to me ... *and the organization?*
What are my learning priorities at the moment?
Have I understood the question?

During
Am I sticking to my plan?
Am I meeting my learning objectives?
(How) is doing this adding to my knowledge?
What new reading am I doing?

After
Am I satisfied with my efforts – is it the best I could have done in these circumstances?
(Taking into account all the other pressures of work and home.)
What were my strengths/weaknesses?
How would I *assess this?*
How could I improve my approach next time?

After the feedback
What is it telling me that I hadn't foreseen?
How can I apply this next time?
How can I consolidate my learning and learn from the success and mistakes?
Did I take enough risks?
Have I made any real progress? (Student Handbook, *Department of Educational Studies, University of Sheffield, 2002*)

Perhaps, as this checklist indicates, one of the most important aspects of keeping a learning journal is to provide a reminder that, although you may be required successfully to complete assessed pieces of work in order to obtain credits for various modules on your programme, the *learning* that can be derived from 'doing' each module, including the assessed work, is as important (and perhaps more so) than the final assessment itself.

C. Wright Mills, whose work has been highly influential in the development of the social sciences, was a strong advocate of journals, as the following extract from an essay entitled 'On intellectual craftsmanship' illustrates. Although he was writing primarily for sociologists and the sexist language of the 1950s is inescapable, Wright Mills's observations and advice remain invaluable for all researchers and writers.

To say that you can 'have experience', means, for one thing, that your past plays into and affects your present, and that it defines your capacity for future experience. As a social scientist, you have to control this rather elaborate interplay, to capture what you experience and sort it out; only in this way can you use it to guide and test your reflection, and in this process shape yourself as an intellectual craftsman. But how can you do this? One answer is: ... keep a journal. Many creative writers keep journals; the sociologist's need for systematic reflection demands it.

In such a [journal] as I am going to describe, there is joined personal experience and professional activities, studies under way and studies planned. [Here] you, as an intellectual craftsman, will try to get together what you are doing intellectually and what you are experiencing as a person. Here you will not be afraid to use your experience and relate it directly to various work in progress. By serving as a check on repetitive work, your [journal] also enables you to conserve your energy. It also encourages you to capture 'fringe thoughts': various ideas which may be by-products of everyday life, snatches of conversation overheard on the street, or, for that matter, dreams. Once noted, these may lead to more systematic thinking, as well as lend intellectual relevance to more directed experience. (Mills, 1959, p. 196)

It is very important that, as soon as you start to think about what it is you want to research for your thesis, you begin to capture your 'fringe thoughts', recollections and experiences on this topic on paper. At this stage, you may wish to begin a *research diary* as an adjunct to your more general learning journal. Burgess (1984) suggests that a research diary may contain several elements:

- a *substantive account* which involves records of events observed, conversations or interviews;
- a *methodological account* which describes the circumstances in which observations took place, the role taken by the 'observer' and how the situation and participants were chosen; and
- an *analytic account* which records how research questions are modified in response to emerging data, and thoughts on the ways in which the data may be analysed.

What such a diary does is to place the researcher very firmly in the research frame: it helps to demonstrate how 'factual' data and the developing ideas of the researcher interact to create new knowledge and understandings.

Once you have clarified your research question (see Chapter 4) you should continue to record your progress throughout your research. This will include, for example, recording what happened when you sought permission to interview individuals. Did you have any problems? Were some people more interested and enthusiastic than others? Did any appear anxious or unhappy about the prospect of being interviewed? These are all important clues which help you build up a picture of individuals and their situations (although, obviously, at this stage you cannot read too much into these reflections – you will need to check out carefully your personal interpretations and assumptions as the research develops). Similarly, once you begin your fieldwork and are visiting different institutions, places of work, or are present at a meeting, observe as much as possible and make notes about the location, the atmosphere, the people there and how they acted and interacted. This will help you to contextualise your research and enhance your understanding of, for instance, the conditions under which people work.

Your learning journal and research diary should be for your eyes only. Record what is important to you, and in a way that makes most sense for you. You should not be asked to show them to anyone else – although you may, of course, choose to do so, or to select extracts from them to share with your supervisor or fellow students. It is sometimes appropriate to include extracts from a research diary or learning journal in the final version of a thesis. If you do this you should provide references for the extracts as you would for any other text, including in the bibliography (for example, Smee, I.T. (2001) 'Personal research diary' [vol. 1: December] unpublished).

Learning and learning strategies
DOCTORAL RESEARCH AS AN ASPECT OF LIFELONG LEARNING

We noted earlier that undertaking research as a doctoral student is not simply about investigating something 'out there', in a world that is separate from oneself. Rather, it is a process of learning and being and involves issues of identity, of how one thinks of oneself and one's relationship with the world. Armstrong (2001) develops this theme, looking particularly at how the values and principles underpinning research in different contexts can impact upon the researcher. He argues that, because 'becoming and being a researcher' is inextricably linked with self-perception, research is actually 'a strategy and process for lifelong learning' (and, indeed, that the process of becoming a researcher is also lifelong) (2001, p. 33). If this is so, then it is important to focus on the *particular nature of learning on a doctoral research programme* in order to clarify how best to engage with it and to identify strategies for enhancing the opportunities it can provide.

As has been implicit in much that we have said so far, we believe that there are a number of values and principles associated with learning on a doctoral programme. These include:

● viewing yourself as a learner, even when you are also an experienced professional in your own field (taking such a view gives you 'permission not to know' – and therefore to ask naive questions. It also encourages you to examine the processes of your own learning, including habitual behaviour and response patterns);
● recognising the exciting but complex nature of the issues to be engaged with and of the processes of the engagement itself;
● engaging critically with issues, values and ideas; developing skills as critical readers and writers and as active contributors to emerging debates;
● understanding that the development of critical reflection can result in a conflict of ideas: this may be uncomfortable but it is an essential element of deep learning, and a prerequisite for change;

- recognising that moments of doubt, uncertainty and bewilderment within the learning process are inevitable and, rather than being avoided, should be regarded as creative spaces; and
- working collaboratively and providing respect and support for others' learning processes.

Especially for those undertaking a taught doctorate, the following may also be significant:

- being able to relate the micro-politics of personal and institutional life to the wider social political and economic context;
- appreciating the different ways in which policy creation, implementation and change can be understood and reflected upon; and
- making connections between such issues and your own values, practices and work contexts.

Untangling and becoming aware of these many aspects of learning on a doctoral programme illustrates the scale and multilayered nature of the whole endeavour. On those inevitable 'wilderness' days when you feel you have 'got nowhere', it can be salutary to stop for a moment to take stock of all the different ways in which your work on the programme is contributing to your development – and thereby creating a firm foundation for learning that will extend far beyond the completion of your thesis. Stay with it!

LEARNING TO BE CRITICAL

In the section above we have used the word 'critical' several times. We emphasise this because 'being critical' is often seen as a key marker of successful work at graduate level. However, while tutors may stress the need for it, what it actually means is not always clear to students. Let us think about this now because there is nothing more disheartening than having a piece of work returned to you suggesting that you should 'be more critical' when you have no idea what this entails.

Perhaps because some theatre critics have enjoyed a reputation for being so savage in their review of a new show that it can go out of business within weeks, 'being critical' is often equated with 'being negative' or even just 'being nasty'. In being critical, one *may* need to point out some shortcomings – but it involves much more than that. The term derives from the Greek *krisis*, meaning literally 'a sifting'; it indicates the need for discrimination – good judgement – in order to 'sift' the elements of a play, debate, book or whatever it may be, in order to determine which parts are good, poor or indifferent.

Thus, during a doctoral programme, you will be expected to 'be critical' in the sense of using and developing your powers of discrimination as you read, write and engage in discussion. There are, for example, various ways of thinking about a text as you read it, such as:

- *Text as information*: reading in this way assumes that the text is completely straightforward and contains no hidden agendas. It is perhaps a slightly naive way to think about text since it assumes that no one has made any decisions about what should be included or excluded from it, and that no values underpin what has been written. (For an example of how the written reports of a 'straightforward' news story are affected by such factors, of course, one only has to read two different newspapers.)
- *Text as argument*: thinking about what you are reading as if someone is presenting an argument to you gives rise to a number of questions about the text, like: 'what propositions are being advanced by the writer?' 'What assertions is the writer making?' 'What is the writer's evidence for these assertions?'
- *Text as a literary product*: in reading a text like this, the sorts of questions which may arise are: 'what feelings and emotions does it convey?' 'How does it try to appeal to people?'
- *Text as discourse*: 'discourse' is a term which you will encounter repeatedly during your studies to indicate the kind of framework and value-system within which a discussion is taking place. (For example, within a 'managerialist discourse', the issues raised and, often, the terminology used, would be framed by a management perspective and underpinned by an associated value-system; discussion might centre on competition, profit-margins, marketing and so on. Within a 'welfare discourse', the issues, terminology and values could be very different, perhaps involving discussion about personal development, state benefits, voluntary service, and so on (See Edwards et al., 2004, for a detailed analysis of discourse and rhetoric as used in education.) In reading text as discourse, the kinds of questions that might be asked are: 'what is the overall global view of this text?' 'Who is writing it and for whom?' 'What is the purpose of this text?' 'What is its relationship to other texts?' 'In what other ways could it have been written?'

You will also be expected to ask similar questions in relation to your own writing, and as you listen to, and take part in, debates. We strongly recommend that you try to work with your fellow students as 'critical friends'. This involves commenting on each other's work, using the kinds of questions indicated above – not with the intention of 'savaging' the work but of being supportive and positive in ways that will help you to develop your respective skills as reflective learners and writers.

PRACTICAL TIPS ON STUDYING

The benefits of working in a supportive way with fellow students cannot be over-emphasised. Apart from helping you to develop your skills, this can also boost your motivation, especially in 'wilderness' times of doubt, uncertainty and practical diffi-culties – or even in those moments when almost anything seems more inviting than turning on the computer or opening a book. Use the contact details of fellow students on your programme to set up your own support network, or just to give someone a surprise call to share thoughts on how your studies are going. (But bear in mind a basic 'ground rule' of support that anyone may choose *not* to provide or receive it at any particular time.) Within the constraints of your own time management, you will almost certainly help yourself by helping others.

The following study tips have been passed on by students who have journeyed ahead of you. If any of the ideas seem appropriate to your particular circumstances, you may like to try them out.

- *Negotiate support at work and at home.* 'Give to get.' People close to you will need to give you time and space to study. Is there anything you can offer in return? Doing so can make you feel a lot better about taking 'time out' from other things in order to study.
- *Find a 'comfort zone'.* You may not have a fully equipped study but somewhere quiet, and preferably airy and well lit, with a comfortable chair and plenty of table space is invaluable. If you can find somewhere where you do not have to pack all your books away at the end of every study session, so much the better. Can you isolate yourself by using an answerphone or finding a 'gatekeeper' to turn away unwanted visitors?
- *Establish a routine.* This can be very important both for you and those around you. As far as is possible, having certain evenings and/or parts of the weekend set aside every week as designated 'study time' is easier for everyone to remember and respect than odd hours here and there. Try to ensure that you can have at least two to three hours' study time whenever possible, especially when you are in the writing-up stage of an assignment or your thesis: it can sometimes take about half-an-hour to get your mind back to what you were thinking about when you left off and it can be very frustrating to have to

finish again without feeling as though you have moved forwards. Shorter periods of time are useful for reading – and, if you travel by public transport, you may find it useful to carry one of your slimmer texts to read on your journeys.

● *Capture 'fringe thoughts'.* Remember C. Wright Mills's advice! Always carry a notebook or mini-recorder. Brilliant ideas that occur on the bus or in the lunch queue have a nasty habit of evaporating before you reach your desk.

● *Identify your study-avoidance strategies and try to avoid them.* One student said that whenever she looked to the heavens for inspiration, she noticed that the windows needed cleaning! That may be true but, once you have set aside your designated study time, you may need to remind yourself firmly that you do *not* have to clean the windows, water the plants, rearrange the bookshelves or engage in whatever other 'task-avoidance strategy' you can think of *before* you start work.

● *Set yourself a 'cut-off time' for reading.* There will *always* be another book, journal or document that you feel you should read before you start to write. Life, never mind an assignment or thesis submission period, is not long enough to read them all. Decide how much time you are going to allocate to reading, and stick to it. Read wisely and as much as you can within that period – then start to pull it all together in your own writing.

● *Do not get it right, get it written.* Do not spend all your allotted study time perfecting the first few paragraphs and forget what you were going to write next (or have no time left to write it). Get your ideas down first, polish later – and if the finished product is not as perfect as you wanted it to be because you have also been dealing with other things in your life, maybe 'good enough' rather than 'excellent' is a trade-off that has to be accepted. Do the very best you can in the circumstances and the time available (and discuss the matter with your tutor if you think you really will not be able to complete satisfactorily on time).

● *Keep copies of EVERYTHING!* Computers can crash, dogs can eat assignments and briefcases can get stolen. Keep a copy of all your work. Especially when you embark on your thesis, keep *more* than one copy of work in progress in different places – but *date them* so that you do not get confused over which version is which. Also, *be systematic about recording the details of your references – and know where you have stored them.* Keep too many details rather than not enough. For every quotation or 'good idea' borrowed from an author, you need her or his name, initials, full title and date of the publication *and* the page number/s, name of the publisher and place of publication.

● *Quit while you are ahead.* Always leave your studies while you are wanting to continue with them. Carrying on until you are so tired that studying feels like a real chore can be counterproductive.

PRACTICAL TIPS ON WORKING WITH A SUPERVISOR

It almost goes without saying that your supervisor will be a 'significant other' on your research journey. A number of books are available which highlight different aspects of the supervisory relationship and how to get the most out of it. Phillips and Pugh (1987, pp. 82–95) include a whole chapter on 'How to manage your supervisor'. So, too, does Wisker (2001) who goes into considerable detail on how to set up a 'learning contract' as a key element in this process. Acker (1999, pp. 75–94) calls supervision 'the ambiguous relationship' and claims that its complexity is generally underestimated. She compares practices in Britain and Canada and examines the implications not only of different locations, but also of different models of supervision and students' registration status, gender and background.

We do not intend to replicate here the advice given by these and other authors. However, we cannot conclude a section on strategies without some reference to the advice we give to students who have to learn how to handle us as their supervisors!

Obviously, it is most important that you discuss your research question, approach and proposed methodology with your supervisor *before* starting out. Throughout the research, you should feel free to seek advice from her or him on any matter of importance associated with it (ethical, methodological or theoretical). You should also alert her or him to any personal or professional matters which may cause you difficulties in carrying out your research. It will usually be regarded as *your* responsibility to contact your supervisor and to keep her or him informed of your progress and/or concerns. In cases of difficulty, or even anticipated difficulty, it is always better to get in touch sooner rather than later! This also applies if you feel the relationship between you and your supervisor is not working out. Contact your programme director or another tutor if real problems start to develop that you feel are getting in the way of your work: do not try to 'sit it out' because you feel it is your fault or that you do not have the right to complain.

Although your institution will probably provide a booklet of guidelines about research supervision procedures, the responsibilities of supervisors are not always precisely defined and, in any case, each will have their own way of working. However, we would expect to give our students advice on:

- **relevant literature;**
- **formulating ideas;**
- **a proposed plan of work;**

- appropriate methods of data collection and analysis;
- problems encountered while the research is under way;
- discussion of analysis and conclusions; and
- the writing process, including commenting on the structure and detail of drafts of chapters.

When you first meet with your supervisor you should discuss how to make the most of the supervisory relationship and the time available. In particular, try to be clear from the outset about periods when you and your supervisor are especially likely to be 'out of action' because of other known commitments.

We have found the practices listed below to be helpful. You may like to discuss them with your supervisor, who will no doubt wish to add her or his own recommendations and preferences.

Keep written notes of meetings/telephone conversations

When you meet or speak on the phone to your supervisor make notes and, immediately after the conversation, write them up – summarising what was talked about and any conclusions reached. Some universities provide electronic forms for this purpose. Keep one copy of the summary in your own 'progress file' (which could be an extension of your learning journal) and send another copy to your supervisor. The essential point is that *you* should take responsibility for documenting the deliberations, decisions and actions taken jointly with your supervisor. This is not just to keep everything on record but it will help you to organise your own thoughts and feelings after each discussion. If you have any concerns at all about what has been suggested, implied or agreed, take this up with your supervisor immediately and try to clarify the situation.

Prepare progress reports

Most supervisors are busy with many duties in addition to supervision and so are unlikely to undertake day-to-day, or even weekly, checking of your progress. Receiving a short written 'progress report' from you at least once a month (even if you feel it has not been a very productive period and you have little to report) will help to keep the topic of your research fresh in your supervisor's mind. Additionally, copies of these reports kept in your own progress file/learning journal will form a useful record, acting as an adjunct to your research diary when you reach the writing-up stage of your work and refreshing your memory about how your research journey progressed.

Provide outlines

Rather than sending your supervisor a lengthy manuscript to read with no outline and no indication of what issues are important, it is extremely helpful if you also provide the following kinds of additional material (making sure that you keep a copy of everything yourself!):

- *a 'transmittal note'* listing what is being sent and a reminder of the date by which your supervisor has agreed to return comments (do try to agree mutually convenient send/return by dates as far in advance as you can to accommodate the many other known commitments that you and your supervisor will need to take into account);
- *a summary of key issues*, that is, a short statement on the contents of the batch of materials being sent and a brief description of each issue on which you would especially like to receive comments;
- *an outline of the chapter(s)/sections enclosed*, including a list of headings and subheadings. It may also be helpful, as your work builds up, to attach a list of all chapter headings so that your supervisor is reminded of where the current material fits into the context of the whole dissertation; and
- *the material to be read*. Try to break it up into sections with subheadings. Use double spacing and wide margins (to allow space for your supervisor to write comments for you). Try to ensure that your drafts are free from spelling errors, typographical errors (typos) and so on, and that all references contained in the draft are complete and accurate. This not only makes your supervisor's task easier but maintains a good standard of presentation throughout which should help to prevent any last-minute panics!

Your supervisor should be regarded as a 'critical friend', offering advice and support as requested. Although she or he will be able to advise you on the basis of past experience about what is expected of a 'good' thesis, do bear in mind that she or he *cannot* tell you whether or not your thesis will 'pass'. This is a decision made by examiners, at least one of whom is usually from outside the institution where you have studied, generally following an oral examination (the viva: see Chapter 10); it will probably also have to be given formal approval by a board of examiners. Your supervisor will almost certainly give you the best professional advice she or he can, but ultimately it has to be *your* decision as to whether or not this particular research journey is nearly at an end and your thesis ready for submission.

Cameo: Spiralling into control: a research journey

Tracy Marshall

A research journey is far from neat and linear: for me, the process has been more of a developmental spiral in which what I first thought I was going to research became caught up in new developments in my professional life and changed as a result. Alongside this, my personal life changed dramatically in ways I could not possibly have predicted.

Since commencing a doctorate, I have married, supported my husband through a serious life-threatening illness, discovered his infidelity, and divorced. Inevitably this impacted upon my research in terms of the time, energy and commitment I could give to it. At times I thought I would never see my finished thesis and seriously considered packing it all in. Conversely, though, my thesis gave me something to focus on – a distraction from personal issues – and my fellow students helped to support and guide me through a particularly rough personal journey. The mutually supportive environment of the doctorate has been, for me, its overriding strength; without it, I doubt I would have written my thesis – or this 'survivor's story'. I have certainly grown as an individual through engaging in the doctoral process. It has been a professional and personal development opportunity that I do not think I understood or acknowledged at the start of the process.

Professionally, I wanted to develop my understanding of 'Regionalisation': a new and exciting agenda being set by the government. My job was dominated by various initiatives that claimed the regionalisation title. I spent a lot of time thinking and writing about it, both as part of my job and in preparation for my thesis. All I really seemed to learn, however, was that higher education in England was changing and that much of the change was attributed to regionalisation. I had plenty of information and ideas but no clear research focus.

This period of confusion coincided with a decision by the university in which I worked to investigate merger with its neighbouring further education college. This was intended to help the two institutions address the regionalisation agenda and to widen participation. It fitted well with the reading and writing I had already undertaken and when the two institutions agreed to undertake a feasibility study to investigate different forms of collaboration, up to and including merger, I was appointed the Project Manager: a job I could not possibly have envisaged when I first registered as a doctoral student.

For the next year, I turned my attention to the feasibility study rather than my thesis. This was partly because it was easier to focus on the study than it was to overcome the stalemate I felt I had reached in research; and partly because my workload increased tremendously: it was difficult to find space for anything else, particularly as this period coincided with getting married. However, as the feasibility study drew to a close, I realised that it could provide an ideal focus for my thesis.

I re-conceptualised the thesis not so much as research into regionalisation per se but as research into my own professional practice as an active player in the regionalisation agenda. Getting to this point was not as straightforward as that sounds: it involved a lot of reading, writing and sleepless nights! I put down on paper everything that I had encountered in relation to regionalisation and gradually identified key themes to organise the mass of topics, issues and developments that claimed the regionalisation title. This provided the basis for a 'scene-setting' chapter when I finally wrote up my thesis.

Next, I began to write a review of everything we had done during the feasibility study. I knew the two institutions involved in the feasibility study were trying to respond to a range of government-led agendas, but this did not fully explain why events had unfolded as they had in that place, at that time. I realised that I now also needed to try to understand the two institutions from their history. I generated a mountain of notes – but found it really difficult to move beyond a descriptive level in pulling them together. This was possibly my darkest hour in terms of my research. I was professionally exhausted from the efforts of the past year. Personally, I was struggling to come to terms with the shock of my husband's unexpected illness while supporting him through a slow recovery. I decided to abandon my research. Thankfully this decision coincided with one of our study weekends and I was able to share it with the group. They persuaded me to hang on.

A breakthrough came unexpectedly as I read about the use of case studies. Bassey's (1999) concept of storytelling/picture-drawing case studies not only helped me to understand the process I had been through but to write a narrative that I later included in my thesis. It also helped me to identify my research questions and focus my thesis. Figure 3.1 illustrates this process.

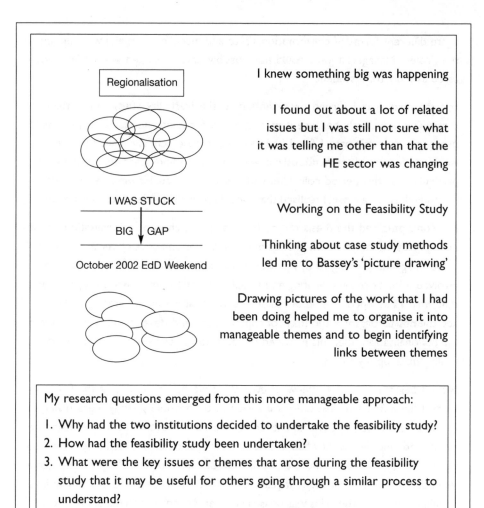

Regionalisation

I knew something big was happening

I found out about a lot of related issues but I was still not sure what it was telling me other than that the HE sector was changing

I WAS STUCK

BIG ↓ GAP

October 2002 EdD Weekend

Working on the Feasibility Study

Thinking about case study methods led me to Bassey's 'picture drawing'

Drawing pictures of the work that I had been doing helped me to organise it into manageable themes and to begin identifying links between themes

My research questions emerged from this more manageable approach:

1. Why had the two institutions decided to undertake the feasibility study?
2. How had the feasibility study been undertaken?
3. What were the key issues or themes that arose during the feasibility study that it may be useful for others going through a similar process to understand?

Figure 3.1   Illustration of how my research focus emerged

Since then there have been other rough times. I discovered my husband was being unfaithful and we have since divorced. I have also begun a new job and relocated to a new part of the county, on my own, where I have had to establish entirely new social and professional networks. In a way, my thesis gave me the strength to deal with this. I felt if I could write a doctoral thesis, despite all the odds, then I could do this as well. Additionally, the actual process of writing my narrative, and seeking to understand my professional journey, helped me to understand and come to terms with what had happened in my personal life: it was a cathartic exercise.

There are three messages I would like to pass on:

1. **Do not underestimate the personal commitment demanded by your research. It will impact on the people around you: they need to understand that and support you. It will also impact on you personally: you will be a different person at the end.**
2. **Your thesis will evolve. Do not be afraid of this, it is part of the process. No one I know is studying now exactly what they expected to when they began. Welcome new and changing ideas, engage with change and document it – other people will be able to learn from your journey, as you can from theirs.**
3. **The friends that you make on a research programme are precious. Help one another and enjoy your time together – after all, you are doing this by choice!**

Reference

Bassey, M. (1999) *Case Study Research in Educational Settings*. Buckingham: Open University Press

Part 2
Conceptualising and Focusing the Study

4 Framing the Research

CHAPTER CONTENTS

In this second part of the book we move from discussing the process of doctoral study as a whole to consider particular parts of that process. We start by looking at the development of a research focus in this chapter, and explore three key issues: theorising, focus and research design. Then, in Chapter 5, we consider how reviewing the literature forms an integral part of developing and conceptualising the research focus.

It has happened to all of us at some time or another, usually when we are off our guard or least expect it. You are at a conference when a colleague or acquaintance comes up and asks the fatal question, or perhaps just relaxing over a cup of coffee. The question may be perfectly innocent, asked in a spirit of genuine inquiry, or it may be mischievous and designed to tease. Or your supervisor may have been reading your latest efforts and is looking puzzled, and asks it with an air of what sounds suspiciously like frustration. And the question is: what is your research about, *exactly*? Or even more simply: what are you trying to get at, *really*? Naturally, there is no one answer to such a question. There may be a short version and a long version, and an even longer version. The answer you give may depend on the time of day, or on the most recent book or article that you have been reading, or on what you think the questioner is looking for. Sometimes you think your research is about everything, at other times about nothing, and quite often you are just confused and undecided about what it all means. Your response may be fluent but superficial, or tongue-tied but profound. If it happens to be both fluent and profound you have the urge to write it down before you forget it again.

In this chapter, then, we try a number of ways of addressing the question of understanding what you are 'getting at' in your research. This is about framing the research, which entails making sense of what you are doing and of what it means.

Conceptualising the research in this way implies having a clear idea of what it is about. Focusing the study suggests that it develops along a particular path, in a logical and sustained way. A well-framed study may well be sophisticated in its arguments, and intricate in its deployment of relevant data, but it should have a storyline that is straightforward for the informed reader to pick up and follow.

As aspects of cultivating this kind of approach, we single out here three key issues, which are not sequential and actually need to be wrestled with at the beginning, middle and end of your doctoral work. The first relates to 'theory' – what is it, how should you theorise, and what does it mean to develop a theoretical framework for your work? The second is about 'focus' – what is it, how do you clarify it, and how can you sustain it? Finally, we look at the 'design' of the study: what is a well designed thesis? This last issue is often addressed first, in terms of preparing a research proposal, but again this needs to be assessed and reassessed throughout the study as a whole.

Theorising theory

The idea of applying and even engaging with 'theory' can seem difficult, even intimidating, to many doctoral students, and they often do their best to avoid it altogether. To others it comes so easily that they prefer to concentrate on it, sometimes with very fruitful results, at other times rather wastefully, as though delaying the moment when they will need to talk about their data. Especially among mature, professional part-time doctoral students, there is often a reluctance to develop an avowedly theoretical or theorised approach. In some cases this can be ascribed to a fear of theory – a deep anxiety that it will be too difficult and show up the student's intellectual shortcomings. Even going into the viva examination, one such student talks of 'appearing more knowledgeable than I felt on modernism and post-modernism, structuralism and post-structuralism'. Here is a fear of being caught out that may well go back to bad memories of school examinations.

In other cases, the reluctance to engage in theory is based in the specific, often utilitarian motivations for embarking on the doctorate – to win promotion at work, or to develop in a particular professional context. One student remarks in relation to this: 'I feel embarrassed to admit that, initially, my intention to obtain a doctorate was of a rather "utilitarian" nature, a means to an end. I believed that becoming a "doctor" would strengthen my credibility as an academic in general and secure my position within the institution in which I worked.' However, in this case the doctoral experience served to encourage an interest in 'theoretical considerations', which helped her to develop a 'capacity for critical analysis and reflection in relation to my own values and beliefs and their bearing on my professional practice', and thence 'the critical capacity to perceive and interpret the world from a range of perspectives and thus gain a deeper understanding of the phenomena influencing our lives'.

So is there a role for theory which can support practice and policy, and be used to underpin research, to help conceptualise it, or provide a 'framework' for it? Our view is that theory does and must always play a part in one's thinking or writing, whether overtly or covertly, consciously or unconsciously. Therefore it must be made explicit for a thesis or in writing of a similar genre – otherwise, every piece of work or empirical study will stand in isolation, unconnected to all the other contributions to that area or field. The role of theory is to provide generalisation, to give us powerful abstractions and to create the links and frameworks that can connect and interlink studies that would otherwise remain stand-alone and disconnected.

There are a number of useful accounts of what we mean when we talk about 'theory'. One classic formulation, about theory in education, is by the French sociologist, Emile Durkheim, early in the twentieth century. He suggested that educational theory was 'nothing more than reflection applied as methodically as possible to educational matters'. According to Durkheim, there was an old French prejudice that looked with a kind of contempt on the idea of educational theory. He himself acknowledged that more than one educational theorist had put to 'scandalous use' their powers of reasoning. Indeed, he added, 'one may think that the systems are often very abstract, making very little contact with the world of reality', and he recommended proceeding very cautiously with speculations about education, given the prevailing state of the human sciences. Nevertheless, he insisted, 'simply from the fact that it has been distorted by the way in which it has been understood, it does not follow that the activity is impossible; from the fact that it has been deliberately modest and circumspect one cannot conclude that it is pointless'. Reflection was bound to be applied to educational problems as they came along; the question was not whether it was to be used but whether it was to be used haphazardly or methodically; to use reflection methodically was a do educational theory (Durkheim 1977, pp. 4–5).

Theory can be approached in terms of models, or representations of reality. These are invariably simplifications of a system, focusing on some aspects while usefully ignoring some of the complexity and 'messiness' of the situation being modelled. In this sense the world-famous 'map' of the London Underground train system is more a representation or a model than a map. It is this very simplification that gives models their value and in many cases their descriptive and predictive power. But models, like analogies, necessarily have both positive and negative aspects.

A good example is found in physics textbooks, which talk about the wave model and the particle model of light, often using the term 'model' as synonymous with theory, that is, wave theory and particle theory. Both models can help to explain things that we observe; they can help us to understand things such as reflection and refraction and why they happen; they can help us to predict future situations. In other words, they have explanatory and predictive power – and they aid our understanding and thinking.

Can the same be said of some of the models in social science? Again, let us take an example. Scott (2000, p. 21–2) writes about three models of the process of policy and policy-making:

1. **Centrally controlled, in which policy-makers develop and draw up a set of recommendations, consult on them, and then 'impose' them on practitioners who are obliged to implement the policy (essentially a one-way process).**
2. **Pluralist, in which a variety of interests are taken into account at every stage, that is, policy-making, presentation and implementation. It is democratic and two way.**
3. **Fragmented/multi-directed, which provides a far more 'messy' or muddled model of the process, involving unforeseen circumstances, flows in various directions and possibly undermines the original intentions.**

This summary does not do justice to Scott's explanation but hopefully it serves as a set of examples that might be useful in considering the policy process. Why are they useful? Rather like the models of light, they can aid our understanding or thinking. They can help in explaining specific examples or case studies of observed policy – the researcher can say of his or her case: 'That is an example that approximates to model X.' Thus they have some explanatory and descriptive value. If we are studying a case, then at the very least we are able to say 'this is a case of X'.

Do models have predictive power? This is perhaps more debatable – if we decide that a specific case is an example of model X, they may help to predict the future of that policy. This depends on the depth or sophistication of the model. Those who are sceptical or cynical of social science might dismiss this claim for predictive power. It could be said that models of this kind are little more than labels or classifications. Paul

Willis's (1977) well-known work, *Learning to Labour*, identified groups of school pupils, all boys, whom he called 'the lads'. This could be dismissed as just a label, and it is unlikely that anyone would call it a theory. Nevertheless, it is a useful label. If 'the lads' are said to have certain characteristics in common, for example certain attitudes to schooling, aspirations, shared humour, as a result of ethnographic research, then to identify a specific case as one example of the general label could be helpful. One would then expect that the case in point has certain important characteristics shared by the group labelled in this way. In some respects, all people in a certain group, or all policy processes in a certain model, are the same. It is important to remember also that in others they are all different.

Labelling and classification are valuable; whether we always call them theory is more debatable. An example worth considering comes from Hargreaves (1994) and his description of four forms of teacher culture: individualism, collaboration, contrived collegiality and Balkanisation. In the first form, the culture is one of independence and autonomy and, even, isolation. In the second, teachers are co-operative and collaborative, with good personal interaction, teamwork and open communication. This collegiality contrasts with the third culture in which norms for behaviour and collaboration are imposed from above ('management') and can be maintained only by external pressure. The final form of 'culture', labelled 'Balkanisation', occurs when groups and subgroups develop within a school or other organisation. There may be collaboration within these enclaves but not across them.

If a research project is looking at the climate or ethos of an organisation such as a school, then one of more elements of Hargreaves's four forms of culture may be identifiable. This can be an aid to understanding and possibly even predicting, if, as we have already stressed, the class or model is powerful enough. At the very least, the use of Hargreaves's forms in reflecting on new data can be a way of linking a study to previous work. In other words, the 'theory' again acts as a bridge or link between disparate studies, rather like a metaphor, which literally means 'to carry or transfer across'.

A metaphor that is widely used now in discussing learning is Vygotsky's notion of the 'zone of proximal development' (ZPD). The ZPD refers to the 'gap' between what a person can learn independently, without assistance or teaching, and what they are capable of learning if given appropriate support or 'scaffolding' for their learning process. Vygotsky's view was that learning through talking, interaction or teaching could take learners 'into' this zone of proximal development and actually enable them to construct knowledge for themselves (social constructivism). Now what exactly is the status of Vygotsky's ZPD? Is it a powerful model, a metaphor or just a useful way of thinking for teachers in deciding how to 'pitch' their lessons at the right level? It certainly aids our thinking about learning. It probably has descriptive power, for example it can describe how a lesson aimed well outside the zone will have little impact on learning. It may also have predictive power, in terms of using the model to predict how peer group interaction, scaffolding of learning or even direct instruction can be involved in developing learning, if targeted at the appropriate 'zone'.

Theory from one area or discipline can often usefully be transferred to another. Concepts can be borrowed and applied. For example, the ideas and theories of Ecology in the life sciences could sometimes be valuably applied to education. We can talk of the importance of the 'ecosystem' in considering where and how learning takes place. This will imply notions of a habitat in terms of where learning is located and the interactions between key inhabitants, such as learners, teachers and parents. The ecological ideas of interconnect-edness and interdependence could be transferred to educational habitats. These imply the more complex notions of causality which feature in ecology, that is, non-linear causal-ity, two-way causality (prey and predator), 'domino' causal models (causal chains), cycles, feedback loops, recirculation and webs. All of the ideas of an ecosystem and the ecological theory underpinning it could be applied to education and learning systems – a school, a college, learning at home, informal learning and university education.

The use of 'grand' theory, or theories about the social world as propounded by the major social theorists such as Karl Marx or Michel Foucault, raises further issues about engaging with theoretical issues for the purposes of a doctoral research project. It often seems apt to base the research on the understandings of a specific theorist or set of thinkers. Where this is done, it can be tempting to apply the theory in a more or less uncritical fashion in interpreting the evidence relating to a specific topic, rather than engaging critically with the theory itself, or engaging with the evidence in an effort to test or modify the theory. A critical approach to the theory as a way of approaching the evidence is much the more suitable way of proceeding at doctoral level, although we have seen many (successful) theses that take the line of least resistance to the chosen theory. At its worst, this can resemble the 'adulation of great thinkers' that was strongly criticised in the Tooley report of 1998 (Tooley and Darby 1998).

Another approach is to develop an eclectic mode of engaging with theoretical perspec-tives. This entails addressing a number of distinct bodies of theoretical literature with the objective of combining them for the purposes of the research, or of developing them further through their interaction. This can be a very fruitful and interesting approach.

The potential drawback is that this can lead to being 'bogged down in theory', to such an extent in some cases that several chapters may be devoted to a laborious trawl through a range of theoretical issues. We have come across a large number of doctoral theses where exactly this has happened. By the time one has read halfway through the work, one is longing for the writer to get on to an account of the fieldwork, which may never come. A useful way of avoiding this danger is to make sure that the theoretical discussion is targeted on the specific issues that the fieldwork will address, and sheds light on them in a direct way. A rule of thumb in this respect would be simply: do not raise questions that you do not intend to answer through your research.

These points take us into the relationship between the 'theory' and the 'data'. What kind of relationship should you be aiming for here? Quite often the data is seen as a means of 'proving' or of illustrating the theory, especially where the approach to theory is largely uncritical as noted earlier. This can be a highly problematic approach, as you need to be able to assess the extent to which the data raises awkward issues about the theory. It is vital to be honest and flexible enough to take account of this. A better way forward is to try to understand the data that you are generating through your research as a means of testing the theory, whether it validates or invalidates it or ends up modifying it in some modest way. When you reach your concluding chapter, you should feel in a position to return to the theoretical issues developed in the early chapters, and to address them rigorously with the help of the research data that you have amassed in your project. This is a hallmark of some of the strongest doctoral work that we have come across.

Focusing on focus

The second set of issues around framing the research study that we identified at the start of this chapter was that of focus. What do we mean by this term, and how definite and clear does the focus need to be? Can it change during the course of the study, or should you keep hold of it doggedly whatever happens? Finally, how should it be explained and sustained in your account of the research in the final thesis?

It can be helpful to make a distinction between the general area of the research project, the focus of the research, and the questions that you are seeking to address.

● **The general area is the field of study, to which you are hoping to make a contribution through your research. In identifying this you are seeking to relate your work to a coherent body of literature and theory.**

- The focus is the particular site of the research, which you will be concentrating your attention on. This provides you with a specific territory over which you need to demonstrate your mastery, so it is important not to make it too broad, and it should be as clear and distinctive as possible.
- The research questions are what you are trying to find out by means of your research. It is usually best not to have a large number of research questions, let us say more than five or so, as this tends to undermine the focus of the study. Generally one, two or three key research questions should be sufficient. Alternatively, it can be helpful to develop one major or primary research question with a number of minor or subsidiary questions that follow on from it.

An example of these differences applied to a research project might be as follows. Let us say that you are interested in teachers and how their private and family lives impinge on their professionalism. The general area of your study could therefore be described as being *teacher professionalism*. In order to get at this in your own way, you need to make a choice of one particular dimension. There are many studies of teachers in their schools and classrooms, and so you could decide to focus on their activities out of school. In this case, then, the focus of the study would be *teachers' out-of-school activities*. Carrying this forward to asking a key research question that you will seek to answer or address in your research, you might choose to find out about how teachers spend their holidays. Thus the research question would be, *what do teachers do in their holidays?*

There are a number of further aspects to the kinds of choices involved in deciding on the area, focus and research question. The first is that it is usually by no means easy or straightforward. The example we have developed here, although it may appear simple and logical, might well take a year of the research project to think through. Our view is that this would be a year well spent if you have used it to narrow down your options and made difficult decisions, rather than diving into your fieldwork without a clear sense of what you are aiming for and why.

A second point would be that the sequence in this example, from area to focus and, finally, to research question, is not the only kind of sequence that can be developed. In some cases the researcher might hit on an interesting research question first, and then try to relate it to a focus and an area of study. It is very common also to identify two different kinds of focus within an area of study, and then to have difficulty deciding between them. Such an issue needs to be confronted and resolved, or it will leave a basic tension underlying the study that makes it difficult to decide on how to proceed.

Thirdly, even if you have worked out the links between area, focus and question in a clear way, this is not enough in itself, because there are also further issues that need to be considered at the same time. One of these is the significance of the study – how will it add to our knowledge and understanding of the area being studied? This is an issue that must not be taken for granted, for technically it is this that will be most important in determining the award of the doctoral degree. In the case of our chosen example, this would mean thinking about exactly how focusing on teachers' out-of-school activities, and specifically finding out as much as possible about what they do on their holidays, would contribute to an understanding of teachers and their professionalism.

Another issue that you should not lose sight of in making these choices is how you will set about addressing your research question, that is, your method and methodology. Part 3 of this book focuses on issues of ethics and methodology, but here we would say briefly that the research question needs to be susceptible to being answered. There is no point in having an interesting research question if there is no way to answer it. In other words, the topic needs to be *researchable*, and not only in general terms but also in the particular circumstances that you are in as a researcher, with the time and resources that you have at your disposal. Again, then, looking at the example we have developed, you would need to decide on the best way of finding out what teachers do on their holidays, whether by survey or interview or following them around on the beach, or some suitable combination of these methods, or some other approach that you feel is appropriate.

It is also important to note that you may need to change or modify the focus or research question, or even the general area, as the research project develops. It may be that you are unable to find a suitable means of answering the question you have developed. Or you may find in reading around the topic that it relates not simply to the area that you have envisaged but to another closely related but distinct literature. Or, possibly, you may discover an earlier thesis that has taken a very similar approach to the one that you have envisaged for your own.

Sometimes in such circumstances a strategic revision of your project may be necessary. At other times, it may be possible to turn them to your advantage. For example, if you find an earlier study you may be able to compare your findings with that one, especially if you have developed a different method or if you are doing your research in a different context or another country. Also, what may be initially discouraging may actually help the study. In our chosen example about teachers' out-of-school activities, for instance, you might talk to a large number of teachers who tell you that they have no time to go on holiday, or they do not have enough money to do so or that they are too tired to go away. Rather than this being the end of the research, it is potentially a very important finding that might well tell you a great deal in terms of your chosen topic, and contributes to your area of study in a new and interesting way.

Having designs on research

Having explored the theory underlying the research and the focus of the study, we have also gone a long way towards thinking through the research design of the project. In many cases it is necessary to put together a research proposal before you get started properly on the research. Hopefully, we have already shown that this is very difficult as a front-loaded exercise and that it involves issues that you will continually need to contend with throughout the study. Nevertheless, it is understandable that supervisors, departments and often external agencies will wish to have some sense of 'where you are coming from' before they commit themselves to supporting or funding your work, and it is useful for you to try to get your head around the issues involved as early as possible.

The key points that normally need to be covered in a research proposal go something like this:

1. **Area of study.**
2. **Focus.**
3. **Research question.**
4. **Boundaries of the research.**
5. **Significance.**
6. **Theoretical basis/framework.**
7. **Method/s.**
8. **Ethics.**
9. **Problems.**
10. **Schedule of work.**

Many of these issues we have encountered earlier in this chapter, and indeed in a certain sense the research proposal is simply putting all of these together in a coherent design. We have already tackled the links between the area, focus and research question, and issues around the theoretical basis or framework were examined at the beginning of the chapter. This leaves the boundaries of the research, significance, method/s, ethics, problems and the schedule of work as matters for further discussion.

Defining the boundaries of the research is a further means of clarifying the focus. It entails explaining what is included in the scope of the research and no less important, what is excluded from it. There are always a number of interesting issues relating to the topic that could be useful for the project to address, and so it is useful for you to clarify which of these you intend to involve in the study and why. It may be that a particular matter, while potentially relevant, would be too large or too difficult to include; if you think this is the case, say so. In this way you have marked out your territory, and you have also signalled that there are significant issues still to be explored for future researchers to address. It might also be seen as a pre-emptive tactic to avoid the possibility that an examiner might criticise the thesis for failing to include a particular issue. If you have already taken care to explain the criteria by which you have developed your area of research, you will have reduced the scope for this kind of criticism.

Also within this category of defining your boundaries, take care not to overlook the obvious. If it is about England, explain why, and why you are not claiming to discuss the whole of Britain. If it is a historical thesis and is concerned with the period, say, 1925 to 1945, explain what is important and distinctive for your purposes about this 20-year period, and why you have decided to start in 1925 and end in 1945. In terms of our example of teachers' out-of-school activities, you might have a decision about whether to include their leisure activities in general, or their activities on bank holidays and during half-term holidays, or to confine your study to the longer holidays, or just to the summer holidays. Discuss these alternatives, explain the decision you have made and, if it might be helpful, adjust the title of the doctoral project to make clearer what you see as the kernel of the research.

A useful way of establishing the significance of the research is to show how it builds on what is already known and understood from previously published research. This gives you an opportunity to engage with the literature and to show its strengths and limitations in relation to your research. This may be achieved most easily by picking two or three key works that you have found relevant and useful, and showing the extent to which they have established the basis for your contribution. Thus, in relation to teachers' out-of-school activities, 'Smith and Brown (1996)' may have explored the importance of understanding teachers' professionalism with reference to their personal and family lives. 'Green (2000)' developed key issues about teachers' life histories but excluded consideration of their leisure and vacation activities. 'Brown (2003)', in a previous doctoral thesis, included an important chapter on teachers on holiday in the Canary Islands but kept to interviews, whereas you wish to pursue methods derived from anthropology. Explaining how such work has created a need and opportunity for your own study is an important part of the strategy of framing your research.

Explanation of the method or methods involves a discussion of how you propose to address or answer the research question that you have developed, for example through documentary methods, interviews or observation. This should include an explanation of why you have chosen one set of methods rather than another, and a sense of the expected strengths and limitations of your choice. You should also demonstrate how the chosen methods will help you to address the research question that you have defined. A surprising weakness of many research proposals is that the methods have no clear relevance to the question being addressed. Thus, for example, if you are wishing to find out about what teachers do on their holidays, it may not be very helpful to interview their pupils, or to send a questionnaire to all the parents of pupils at their school.

Consideration of ethical issues is now an important dimension of any research proposal. Even if you feel that there are no particular ethical issues involved in your research, you should demonstrate that you have considered this carefully. There are guidelines available for research projects which have been produced by a number of professional and academic associations, and many institutions of higher education have also produced their own, so you should at least show that you have consulted the ones most relevant to you and have taken them into account. In some cases, there may be significant ethical issues – for example involving participant observation, or insider research or interviewing children. These need to be clearly addressed. Often, there are issues that are not simply 'ethical' in the way that we tend to define this in relation to research, but legal or moral. Legal constraints and obligations, for example under the Data Protection Act, should be clearly acknowledged. The moral obligations of the researcher to their respondents, or perhaps to their colleagues, is a difficult but important theme, and it can be helpful to reflect on these here.

So far as teachers' out-of-school activities are concerned, there could be a number of possible ethical hurdles. If you have chosen an anthropological approach, will you follow them around without introducing yourself, or engage in participant observation? Either strategy could be fraught with ethical dilemmas. If the teachers engage in activities while on holiday that might be construed as embarrassing, have you guaranteed their anonymity? If they are involved in illegal activities, should you go to the police? What do you do if they invite you out for a meal? What use can you make of their bank statements, even if they have given them to you to peruse?

A section of the research proposal dealing with potential problems and pitfalls can also be very helpful. This might also be described in the current jargon as a risk analysis, and will serve to demonstrate that the project is not cut and dried, and that you understand that something may go wrong and probably will. One common theme for such a category is potential problems to do with access to data – what will you do if you are not granted access, or if the conditions stipulated for access make it difficult for you to use the data effectively? You may also feel that you require further research training in specific techniques that will be required for the research. It can often be useful to sketch out a 'Plan B' that you might follow if problems arise with your chosen strategy. Issues about cost and practicality may also be dealt with here. So, for example, with teachers' out-of-school activities, if you are hoping to follow teachers around while they are on holiday, you will need to consider how many cases you will be able to cope with on a limited budget. You may need to settle for semi-structured or life history interviews after all – but then what about that thesis by 'Brown (2003)'? Will you still be making a significant contribution through your research? And will you be able to believe what the respondents are telling you? You could ask the teachers to write diaries of their holiday experiences – but then will they leave out the most interesting bits, or else spice it up just for you?

Finally, you should try to suggest a realistic schedule for your research project. This should take account of both the nature of the project and your own personal and professional circumstances. Usually the research is not compartmentalised in a neat and straightforward fashion, and there will be overlaps. Background reading, for example, is likely to continue throughout the study rather than being confined to a single stage of it (see next chapter). However, this is an opportunity for you to point out some key phases of the research, especially of the fieldwork. You also need to take account of how long it is likely to take you to write up the research. Some researchers write more quickly than others, and it is important for you to acknowledge your own strengths and weaknesses in this regard. Personal considerations are highly relevant, such as considering whether the summer months will be suitable for fieldwork or for writing up. For some people the summer will be most convenient as there may be less pressure of work and you can make use of your holiday period; for others this would be the most difficult as they will have family commitments over this time. Also if you need to interview a particular group of people the summer months may be problematic as they may well be away. Sending out questionnaires in August may not be a good idea for the same reason.

Conclusion

We have used this chapter to explore a number of ways of framing your research. There is no single way of doing this, and you will need to select the most suitable depending on your purpose, your audience and the time at your disposal.

Nevertheless, we hope we have provided some useful strategies for helping you to clarify what you are trying to get at in your research. This will be helpful for those troublesome enquiries at conferences and over coffee, as well as for the formal require-ments of your research study. You should develop the confidence to be articulate and outgoing about what you are trying to do in your research, and to start to ask the same questions of your fellow students. This process can encourage collegiality and mutual support. The only risk is that your colleagues may start to avoid you at coffee time.

In the next chapter we focus on the importance of reviewing the literature in helping to conceptualise and contextualise your own study.

Cameo: How I theorised my thesis – My story

Carolyn Mason

The black student experience of undergraduate physiotherapy educa-tion: choice, identity and prejudice

Introduction and background
Probably like many other students before me I embarked upon my doctoral research with an agenda and a very naive understanding of educational research. From my experiences as a clinical physiotherapist and currently as a physiotherapy lecturer I had developed a theory that physiotherapy was a white middle-class profession. This research therefore grew out of my own gnawing concern that prejudicial practice might be partly to blame for the 'skew to the white' of physiotherapy students. I was determined to investigate and possibly to prove that institutional racism was a contributory factor to this phenomenon.

Initial review of the literature
Prior to going out into the field to collect data my literature review had consisted of an evaluation of the relevant political and sociocultural policies, and it considered the barriers that face students from ethnic minority groups as they confronted their choices of higher education programmes of study. Here I also constructed, decon-structed and generally opened up a debate on the notion of institutional racism ready to draw comparisons with the data that I anticipated I would gain.

The emergent data and re-evaluation of the research questions
The students that I interviewed provided narratives which both confused and intrigued me. On many occasions similar young people with analogous family backgrounds, dominated by the faiths which they had in common described very different experiences of their higher education courses. Whilst some depicted very negative experiences of their physiotherapy programmes, other students reported extremely positive experiences of their physiotherapy education. As the work progressed it became apparent that institutional racism may or may not be embedded in physiotherapy education and, therefore, I found that I was struggling to make any analysis of my data meaningful using the literature which I had up until that time reviewed. The reason for this was that whilst I had provided context to my study, as soon as I began to problematise my findings, ask why these students were acting the way that they did, I had no literature to refer to that would help me to analyse the data that I was now collecting. I had piles of transcribed data but had no idea what all the information was telling me. I had no pegs on which to hang my analysis. I had no theoretical framework. I had no grand theory.

Going back to the literature and constructing a theoretical framework
In an attempt to focus my thoughts I continually examined all the themes and sub-themes that my analysis conjured up and I constructed spider diagrams and mind-maps, lots of them. I scribbled 'physiotherapy education' in a box in the middle of a page and branched from this to the left and to the right boxes for positive experiences and for negative experiences. Referring to my data I then annotated my mind-map with examples of the students' experiences that had influenced them either way: Language difficulties, culture, citizenship – housing, education, class. As the mind-maps grew, enlightenment followed. It became obvious that the students' experiences of their physiotherapy education were dependant upon how their lives had been constructed thus far. Poor experiences of physiotherapy education were often synonymous with prejudicial treatment, language problems and the inability to form relationships in groups, whilst good experiences seemed linked with the student's ability to act white, that is, they had good command of the English language, they had good educational background and family support and so on. It sounds a bit of a cliché, but from my mind-maps, my data spoke to me. In a 'eureka' moment that I can almost pin to the day I found *that big issue* to define my theoretical framework, my platform of conditional understanding. Identity.

This eureka moment led me once again to the literature and specifically to explore some concepts of identity formation. From then on the literary flood gates opened to all kinds of theories that I had up until then never considered. The concept of the self, social, professional and ethnic identity, salience and so it went on. The problem now was that there were potentially too many theoretical frameworks. Was I going to interpret my work in this way, or would the other be better?

I had previously received lots of very good advice with regard to theorising research. One of the top tips was to find a philosopher or a theory that helps you to begin to interact with your data. For me this philosopher was Pierre Bourdieu. Bourdieu's concept of the *habitus* really helped me to consider my data from a different and theoretical perspective and to begin to explain how my interviewees' experiences could be framed within their individual social and cultural experiences. This said, I also remember being advised to be prepared to engage in critiques of the philosophers that I had read. The last thing that you want is to be labelled as a researcher who is guilty of uncritical adulation of a great thinker (Tooley and Darby, 1998). Further as I understand it, it is difficult to fully develop an analytical framework from one single theorist and commonly overarching techniques can be acceptably employed.

Once I had introduced Bourdieu as my main philosophical support, I also introduced the work of different philosophers to test out the analysis that I had made. This also served to complement the analysis that I had constructed. For me this was particularly valuable because whilst Bourdieu's theory provided a useful fit for my purpose the fit was not actually completely watertight. In truth, there were parts of my data that did not fit with Bourdieu's theories at all. Accordingly I found Giddens's theories of reflexivity useful. By combining Bourdieu's and Giddens's philosophies, I could provide a fuller analysis of the accounts that were given and therefore provide a deeper and more meaningful understanding of the students' experiences. If you can get a three-way discussion going between a couple of theorists and your own interpretation of events, it seems that you may receive even more approval for your efforts!

Summary and points to remember
In summary, remember that it is important to provide context to your study but that this is not your theoretical framework. The theoretical framework provides the pegs from which to hang your analysis.

You will find your framework through being curious, open-minded and reflective. Do not be tempted to simply describe your data. Problematise it all and, once you have done that, wrestle with problems. Question every assumption that is being made, and then do not be afraid to go back to the literature. Remember that the literature is supremely important. Read widely, refer back constantly and reference well.

Take care not to get too distracted by all the new literature and theories that you come across. Decide on which story *you* are telling and stick to it. Yes another researcher might interpret similar data in a different way but this is your research. It will always be your legacy and therefore it will have your thumbprints all over it. Do not be afraid to personalise it with your own eclectic use of theories and philosophies, and finally be sure, if you can, to interweave your own interpretations to complement those of the theorists you have used.

5 Reviewing the Literature

CHAPTER CONTENTS

Chapter 4 indicated the significant role that exploring the existing literature plays in developing and writing a doctoral thesis. In this chapter we focus on the process of reviewing the literature in more detail. The chapter begins with a note of caution. A traditional thesis (see Chapter 9) has an identifiable chapter or chapters which constitute a literature review. The purpose of such chapters includes: establishing what research has been done in the field of study; debating critically the issues arising in the literature in the context of the study being undertaken; and establishing the gap that the present study will aim to fill, or the further contribution the study will make to the field. However, such aims may be achieved in other ways than through a chapter or chapters devoted to the literature. Theses, dissertations and books do not all have specific chapters obviously dedicated to reviewing the literature. Searching and reviewing the literature form significant parts of the overall research process, and their purpose is not simply to write a chapter entitled 'Literature review'. Writing about the literature provides a means of working out a critical view of current thinking, ideas, policies and practice. As the thesis develops into a whole piece of work the overall research process may lead to an alternative way of presenting the literature to a dedicated 'literature review' chapter. In focusing on reviewing the literature in this chapter, we are aware that we may appear to encourage a separation of the literature from the wider research process, and we would caution against this.

The purpose of reviewing the literature

We want to emphasise that reviewing the literature is integral to thinking about the research that you yourself are undertaking. It relates to the formulating of research questions, the framing and design of your work, the methodology and methods; the data analysis; and the final conclusions and recommendations.

Undertaking a review of the literature allows you to:

- **define what the field of study is, by identifying the theories, research, and ideas with which the study connects;**
- **establish what research has been done which relates to the research question or field of study;**
- **consider what theories, concepts and models have been used and applied in the field of study;**
- **identify and discuss methods and approaches that have been used by other researchers; and**
- **identify the 'gaps' or further contribution that the present piece of research will make.**

All the above allow you to locate your intended study within a wider body of knowledge, and develop a theoretical rationale for your study.

The process of reviewing the literature encourages you to work out where your ideas have come from. For, as Murray (2002) points out, as researchers we are unlikely to have come up with something that is entirely new, it is just that we have not yet found out who is already working on this topic. Referring to and discussing existing literature will enable you to make substantiated claims about your area of study, and to avoid sweeping generalisations, by rooting the claims you make for your own research in the context of other studies and previous research.

As you undertake further reading for your study, one focus to help with your own review of literature, is to look at how other writers and researchers discuss, debate and use existing literature to contextualise the work they present.

One way of viewing the process of reviewing the literature is to see it as an 'inquiry trail'. An inquiry trail can explore how different types of literature, such as policy documents, historical documents, academic research literature, or literature aimed at practitioners, address a particular issue or focus, looking for themes, similarities and differences. It can seek out differences and similarities in definitions of particular concepts within a range of literature. It can compare the understandings that literature from different disciplines and different countries bring to a particular issue.

The list of references at the end of a thesis, book or article serves not only as a list of the sources used, but also tells a story about the sort of literature that has been used, the authors whose ideas have influenced the work, and often indicates or at least hints at the direction of the arguments that are put forward.

Getting started

The focus for a doctoral study may come out of reading about the work of other researchers, which provides a clear entry into the literature. However, the focus may also come from an area of personal or professional interest, or it may be an area in which research has been encouraged by a supervisor or sponsoring organisation, and is therefore at one step removed from the research literature. If you are undertaking research as an experienced professional in your chosen career, you may know 'what is hot', that is, what the burning or pressing issues are in your current professional practice. Exploring the literature allows you to relate these issues to research in the field and to create a depth and breadth of understanding drawn from wider reading. Reading widely in your area of study helps you to become immersed in your chosen field. Yet this can often feel like wallowing in a quagmire, or drowning in the ocean of literature that is available. You are confronted with questions such as: how do I know what is relevant? How do I know what is important? What counts as important in the eyes of others? What is important to my study? (Which may not be the same thing.)

While you therefore need to read widely, you also need to read with your study in mind, thinking about how the literature you read relates to your own research. This may sound straightforward, but it implies that the focus of your study is clear before starting to explore the literature. In reality, both the focus and the research questions are likely to be developed and refined as a result of wider reading, and the question of 'where to start?' can be a genuinely perplexing one. One way of visualising the range of literature you explore is to see it as comprising literature at three levels: firstly, background material which is of broad relevance to your study; secondly, literature and research studies which address issues that are closely related to your study, or a part of your study; finally, literature which is directly related to your study (Rudestam and Newton, 1992).

Questions to ask at this stage include:

● **What is known about the broad topic I am researching, and from what types of literature?**

- What are the most important 'landmark' works within the field, referred to regularly in other studies?
- What methods and methodologies are being used to research the area I am interested in?
- What theoretical and conceptual frameworks are being used to understand the field?

As these questions suggest, part of the task of broad reading at the first level includes identifying what literature is of closer relevance to your study and needs closer attention. Reading at this stage needs to be undertaken with an open mind, with a view to clarifying the focus of study, the methodological approach to be taken and the conceptual framework to be used. On the basis of wider reading, the following question can then be considered:

- Which areas of this work are centrally relevant to my topic and research questions?

Until you have undertaken initial wider reading, it is often difficult to address this question.

What are you looking for and how can you find it?

WHAT DOES 'LITERATURE' INCLUDE?

A first priority in reviewing the literature is to establish what research has been done which relates to the research question or field of study, and therefore the first source of literature is *significant research literature on the topic*.

You are looking for primary sources here, rather than secondary sources where the work of someone else is reported on by another writer. This literature may take a number of forms, including academic books, academic journal articles, theses and dissertations which have already been written or are being written, and reports of major funded research studies (funded by organisations such as the Economic and Social Research Council [ESRC], the Leverhulme Trust and the Nuffield Foundation amongst others). Further sources of literature depend on the nature and focus of the study being undertaken. *Historical documents and policy documents* may be of particular relevance in some studies. In addition, *scholarly and professional literature* on the topic, including practice-oriented books and articles may be included for the perspectives they offer, and *newspaper reports* may help to contextualise an issue.

SOURCES

Electronic bibliographical databases are many people's starting point for carrying out a literature search. There are a number of points to bear in mind here:

1. Some electronic bibliographical databases are devoted to journal articles rather than books.
2. Some of the databases are also available in print format.
3. Different databases hold different references, even though there may be over-laps. Check out what the database you are using covers, and search a number of databases to throw up a wider range of literature. We list some examples of social science and educational databases below.
4. Find out what search tools the database offers. This can make your search quicker and more effective.
5. Key word searches require some thought devoted to which key words will find the literature you are seeking. For example, the terms 'lifelong learning', 'lifelong education', 'adult education' and 'post-compulsory education', amongst others, may all lead to references which are relevant to 'lifelong learning'. Some journal articles list the key words they use as identifiers, and these provide a useful basis for further searches.
6. Using search strategies other than keyword searches may well identify new references.

Below are some examples of electronic databases for social sciences and education:

Bibliography of the Social Sciences (IBSS) http://www. lse.ac.uk/ collections /IBSS/ The IBSS is compiled at the London School of Economics. It covers the social science subjects Anthropology, Economics, Politics and Sociology. It can be accessed through BIDS at http://www.bids.ac.uk/

British Education Index (BEI) http://www.leeds.ac.uk/bei/ The BEI contains education articles and papers published in Britain.

ERIC: http://www.eric.ed.gov/ ERIC is an international database containing articles and papers on education.

ProQuest http://www.proquest.com/ ProQuest offer a number of different education products.

Web of Knowledge http://wok.mimas.ac.uk/ This database includes the Social
  Sciences Citation Index.

These databases provide references for journal articles, and may also have references
for conference papers and published reports, but they do not tend to give references
for books. The following databases do include books:

Books in print www.booksinprint.com This database contains American in
  print and out of print titles.
British Library Public Catalogue (BLPC) www.blpc.bl.uk This catalogue
  provides access to the main British Library catalogues, describing over 10
  million items, which are held by the British library.
COPAC http//www.copac.ac.uk/ COPAC allows you to carry out simultaneous
  searches of the catalogues of all members of the Consortium of University
  Research Libraries, including the British Library.
University library catalogues. These catalogue all books held by the library
  concerned. To search several university catalogues at once, see COPAC.

Research funding organisations usually have websites, including databases, which
contain details of the research they have funded and reports and publications arising
from such research. These sites not only provide a source of references, but they indicate
areas of work which have attracted national and international funding. Thus they offer
an insight into what is currently being prioritised by research funding organisations.
Examples of research funding organisation websites include:

Arts and Humanities Research Board (AHRB): www.ahrb.ac.uk
Economic and Social Research Council (ESRC): www.esrc.ac.uk
Leverhulme Trust: www.leverhulme.org.uk
Nuffield Foundation: www.nuffieldfoundation.org
Joseph Rowntree Foundation: www.jrf.org.uk

Other people's references are an obvious but sometimes overlooked source. Not only
do references in books and journal papers direct you to further references, but they
help you to develop a picture of what work is being cited regularly, and what work is
informing the field – who is reading whom. This involves an iterative process of
discovering regular reference to particular writers, reports and studies.

Government and organizations' websites are now an increasingly important source of policy documents, reports, statistical data and links to other resources.

Libraries and subject librarians are not just the place where literature is located, but are an important source of ideas and help with searching for literature.

Opportunistic searching, such as browsing library shelves, looking through the contents list of edited collections, looking at contents lists in journals, asking other people, and noting references to other work made at conferences and seminars, makes connections and provides openings into relevant literature that no amount of detailed database searching will uncover.

Many of the above approaches take full advantage of the resources available through the World Wide Web. It is worth remembering that material not only needs to be carefully referenced, but the sources need to be considered critically for their quality and origins.

What to collect, what to read and how to store it

SYSTEMATIC REVIEWS AND BEING SYSTEMATIC

A 'systematic review' is a term used for a particular type of literature review, which aims to give an overview of primary studies that have used explicit and reproducible methods (Greenhalgh, 1997). The term is commonly used to refer to reviews which debate and synthesise the findings of a number of research trials, often of a statistical nature. Although such reviews have tended to be more typical of medical and scientific research, they are now occurring more frequently in educational research. You can find out more about systematic reviews from a book on the subject by Carole Torgerson (2003) and from the EPPI Centre website and database (http://eppi.ioe.ac.uk/EPPIWeb).

In our experience, reviews of literature in doctoral theses rarely follow this approach. Nevertheless, however you go about reviewing the literature, you should be systematic in collecting, recording and organising the literature. It is helpful to work out a strategy that works for you when collecting and organising literature. Start with references and abstracts, then decide which work you need to read in full.

We recommend that you spend as much money as you can afford on books and journal articles. You are likely to want to revisit reading that you do early on and you may well have a different interpretation of your reading once you have read more widely. Read enough of a book, but do not feel that you have to read it from cover to cover with the same attention to detail throughout.

Do not spend hours copying out of books and articles. To avoid this temptation, we have used various strategies. These include marking important parts with a highlighter or underlining or sticky labels, which can be revisited after reading to decide whether they need to be incorporated into any form of notes or writing that you do. In addition, making a short summary of key points after reading is often more helpful than making detailed notes while reading. Allocating what you have read to a category relevant to a particular theme or chapter of your work is also a useful way of storing your reading for future use.

STORING INFORMATION, NOTES AND REFERENCES

We strongly encourage you to start saving your references right from the start, keeping all necessary details by following a recognised referencing system such as Harvard. There are now computer software programs specifically for this purpose such as Endnote (http://www.adeptscience.co.uk/products/refman/endnote/). Endnote also allows you to make and store notes on your reading, which are attached to the relevant reference. However, a word-processing programme also works for this purpose. A document containing all references encountered, which is regularly updated, can act as a source document for referencing all your writing. It is easier to select from references you have stored, than to hunt out full references at a later stage.

You also want a system for storing papers, documents and notes. This needs to be a system that works for you, and allows you to find and use your reading in an effective way. You might therefore store material according to relevant themes in your work, or as you work on your doctorate, according to chapters in your thesis. These suggestions mean that you may want to reorganise your collection of material as your work progresses. This can provide a hands-on way of making connections between different literature and connecting, for example, policy and source documents with theoretical debates and concepts.

When to stop

Rather than seeing the literature review as a linear process, which has a start and an end, it can be more helpful to view collecting, reading, reviewing and writing about the literature as a cyclical process. Reading widely helps to clarify the research focus and research questions, and is a stage in the literature reviewing process, rather than the end of it. Revisiting and clarifying your research focus and questions allow you to refine your literature search and collection, to identify what literature you need to explore in more depth, and what gaps there are in the literature you have explored to date. Repeating this process of returning to your research focus and clarifying it as a result of wider reading also helps to answer the question many doctoral students ask: 'how much literature is enough?' If your overall aim is to consider the theories, research and ideas with which your study connects, then by returning to the aims and purposes of your study regularly, you should be able to clarify whether you have considered the range of literature which is relevant to your focus, and whether all the literature you have gathered is still relevant to your focus. It is how the literature relates to and informs your study that enables you to decide what you should bracket in, and what you should bracket out.

WRITING WHILE YOU COLLECT AND COLLECTING WHILE YOU WRITE

This cyclical process also applies to writing about the literature. Writing as you go along offers a way of creating a dialogue, which can be between you and your reading, between you and your supervisor, and between you and other researchers. Not only can this help to clarify your thinking, but waiting to write about the literature until you have read 'everything' can easily turn the task into something unwieldy and unmanageable. As Murray (2002) points out, writing about the literature acts as a way of learning about the literature. First attempts at writing will be a way of beginning to understand the literature, which can subsequently be refined as more reading allows for deeper and wider understanding and knowledge. However, this also means that the writing you do along the way will rarely be the end product that goes into your final piece of work, and it is helpful to establish a purpose and focus for such writing, so that it helps you to move forward. Often it may be that you focus on a part of the wider picture, bringing together some of the literature and rehearsing your arguments.

TALKING ABOUT IT

Reviewing the literature does not only mean going away, gathering literature, reading and writing in isolation. It involves talking about it, presenting it, and generating ideas and arguments through working with others. Sharing your ideas and learning from others in these ways can help to make sense of what you are doing, and give you an opportunity to develop your ideas and arguments in preparation for writing about them.

'Build an argument, not a library': writing about the literature (Rudestam and Newton, 1992, p. 49)

Writing about the literature does not mean reporting on everything that has ever been written about your research focus that you have managed to find. The wide reading that you undertake gives you the expertise to build an argument, but this does not mean that all the reading you have done will be cited in what you write (Rudestam and Newton, 1992). The discussion of literature should link in with your research aims or questions, and identify key themes that are relevant to your work, and then engage with and debate the issues raised. The aim is to debate critically the issues which arise in the literature in the context of the study you are undertaking. It can be useful to see writing about the literature as a 'dialogue between you and the reader', at the end of which the reader should be convinced that this is the study that needs to be done at this moment in time to move knowledge in the field forward, and that you are in a position to do it.

The literature can be treated in varying detail. Rudestam and Newton (1992, p. 51) talk of using 'long shots, medium shots and close-ups', suggesting that some work can be considered in a broad overview, while other research is examined in detail. Background material may be acknowledged and referenced as part of a broad overview. Studies that bear on a relevant issue need to be summarised clearly enough to indicate the status of the research in relation to the present study. Studies with most direct relevance to the research question or focus need to be examined carefully and with a critical examination of the detail of the study.

You need to guide the reader through, by making your purpose clear from the start, and by not only organising and structuring your writing, but explaining the structure to the reader. This might be done by clarifying guiding questions or issues from the outset, and keeping to this focus (Wallace and Poulson, 2004). In particular, you need to explain how the literature that you are reviewing links to your own work. In addition, it can be helpful to explain what literature you have *not* reviewed, as well as what you have included, and why you have made this selection.

Some people find it helpful to use diagrams to clarify the literature that has been used, and to show the links that have been made between the literature and the study being undertaken. Figure 5.1 shows some different ways of 'picturing' a review of the literature. Some people like to see it as 'zooming in' on a topic, starting from a wide angle view and eventually focusing on the key area (Figure 5.1(a)). Others may prefer to picture it as three or four areas of literature intersecting, with some areas overlapping and the central focus being the intersection of all the sets of reading. This is shown as the dark shaded area in Figure 5.1(b). Others envision reviewing the literature as a funnelling process (Figure 5.1(d)), which is similar to zooming in; we have also seen the process described as piecing together a patchwork (Figure 5.1(c)), suggesting that it involves weaving together a wide range of areas of reading, perhaps in a creative way. One of these pictorial representations might work for you, or not. Whatever image you hold, or story you have to tell in your own review of literature, you should be able to explain it as part of the written account and also orally in the viva.

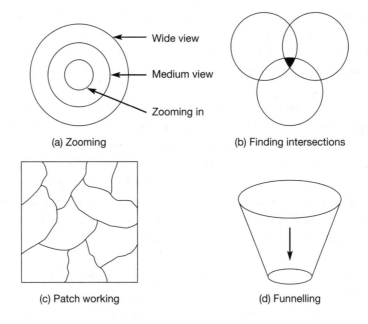

(a) Zooming   (b) Finding intersections

Wide view

Medium view

Zooming in

(c) Patch working   (d) Funnelling

Figure 5.1 Possible ways of picturing the literature review

If your review takes the form of a literature review chapter, then it is helpful to include a summary at the end showing how the chapter sets up or leads to your own study and research questions, which should come out of the review you have undertaken.

You might like to think of the review as a story, which has key threads that are drawn from the literature, but where you are in control of the plot and the unfolding of the arguments that you wish to put forward. Jackson et al. (2000) say that drawing the literature together benefits from intuition, inspiration and insight, and suggest six ways which can help with constructing the 'story':

- **Portray by painting a picture, indicating similarities and differences, and relationship, as well as identifying gaps.**
- **Trace the history by discussing changes over time, identifying the lineage of a field of research, and situating the research in a larger historical context. Also identify the causes and consequences of the evolution.**
- **Categorise, that is, sort into a taxonomy based on similarities and differences of underlying characteristics.**
- **Summarise by identifying main commonalities and central tendencies.**
- **Problematise or undermine by identifying chaos in apparent order, and showing the variation and complexity of the situation.**
- **Synthesise by pulling together into a new whole. Explain and reconcile apparent contradictions, redefine, identify order in apparent chaos.**

In writing about the literature, you are adding to it, by creating links, drawing attention to particular issues and contributing your construction of the 'story' to be found in existing research.

Being critical

The aim in reviewing the literature is to provide a critique rather than a report. But what is meant by 'critique' and 'being critical'? In the cultural context of a Western university tradition, it is both accepted and expected that academic enquiry will involve questioning the work and ideas of others, and students are often advised to be critical or at least to be 'more critical' by supervisors. Anyone's work may be challenged and exposed to criticism. As Wallace and Poulson (2004, p. 4) observe: '[I]t is quite acceptable for students to question the ideas of leading academic figures in their area of study, as long as they can give convincing reasons for their view.'

But what exactly does this advice mean? The term 'critical' is widely used but rarely defined. The *Oxford English Dictionary* (*OED*) often provides a good starting point for a discussion. The *Shorter OED* uses terms such as 'involving or exercising careful judgement or observation'. It also includes the phrase 'given to judging', and the terms 'fault finding' and 'censorious'. The latter terms connect with the more pejorative aspects of being critical and its occasional use in everyday contexts when it relates to words such as 'judgemental', 'scathing' or the more vernacular 'nit-picking' – in these contexts to be critical can be seen as verging on being hostile, rude or confrontational.

Our interpretation is more akin to the first aspect of the above *OED* definition, that is, the notion that being critical involves the exercise of careful, deliberate and well-informed judgement. It is important to be sure that your critique is based on what is in the literature, and does not represent a misinterpretation or an ignorance of the literature. We can present all this in terms of opposite poles, some of which relate to our actions and some to our dispositions or attitudes. Thus criticality involves:

- healthy scepticism ... but not cynicism;
- confidence ... but not 'cockiness' or arrogance;
- judgement which is critical ... but not dismissive;
- opinions ... without being opinionated;
- having a voice ... without 'sounding off';
- being respectful ... without being too humble or obsequious;
- careful evaluation of published work ... not serial shooting at random targets;
- being 'fair': assessing fairly the strengths and weaknesses of other people's ideas and writing ... without prejudice;
- having your own standpoint and values with respect to an argument, research project or publication ... without getting up on a soap box;
- making judgements on the basis of considerable thought and all the available evidence ... as opposed to assertions without reasons; and
- putting forward recommendations and conclusions, whilst recognising their limitations ... without being too apologetic.

Thus, being critical is about having the confidence to make informed judgements whilst still retaining and displaying a degree of humility and modesty. It is about finding your own voice, your own values and building your own standpoint in the face of numerous other, often apparently stronger voices (from the literature and elsewhere) and many other viewpoints. To use a boating metaphor, we can be buffeted about by reading and listening but it helps if we do not capsize.

OTHER VIEWS ON CRITICALITY

Ronald Barnett, who has considered in some depth what it means to be critical, offers a helpful definition, albeit somewhat circular, of the 'critical mind' and 'critical thought': 'The critical mind is, in essence, an evaluative mind. Critical thought is the application of critical standards or values – sustained by a peer community – to an object or theory or practice.' (Barnett, 1997, p. 19).

Yet elsewhere in this book, Barnett argues that we should do away with critical thinking as 'a core concept of higher education and replace it with the wider concept of critical being' (Barnett, 1997, p. 7). He goes on to explain this notion. Critical thinking skills are constraining in that they 'confine the thinker to given standards of reasoning' in a field, whilst his broader notion 'opens the possibility of entirely different and even contrasting modes of understanding' (p. 7).

Barnett suggests that criticality should be seen as occurring in three domains: knowledge, the self and the world. Consequently, three forms of *critical being* are possible, which he calls 'critical reason, critical self-reflection and critical action'.

In the three domains of critical thinking, Barnett argues that a person can be critical of:

- **'Propositions, ideas and knowledge' as they are presented in 'the world of systemic knowledge';**
- **'The internal world' that is, yourself, and this form is 'demonstrated in self-reflection'; and**
- **The 'external world' and this form leads to and is shown by critical action.**

Barnett uses in several places the image of the Chinese student confronting tanks in Tiananmen Square, Beijing, as a classic case of critical action. We would not advocate here that research students should stand in front of tanks, either before or after their viva examination. However, criticality in Barnett's first domain is certainly an attribute or disposition that would seem to be an essential part of doctoral work. The second domain also seems to be indispensable to a doctoral thesis or any critical research and writing, that is, the ability to reflect on yourself. This imperative to be reflective and indeed reflexive (see Wellington, 2000, for a discussion of these two terms and their difference) is an essential part of any thesis.

A helpful definition of critical thinking by Bickenbach and Davies (1997, p. 10) resonates with this idea of reflecting on our own thinking and our thought processes:

'Critical thinking, then, is the art of evaluating the judgements and the decisions we make by looking closely at the process that leads to these judgements and decisions.'

This need for metacognition (thinking about thinking) and then, of course, the need to display it, is reminiscent of school mathematics when pupils are urged to 'show your working'. This is a useful adage for a doctoral thesis too. Similarly, Halpern (1996, p. 29) talks of 'becoming mindful' by directing attention to 'the processes and products of your own thought' and becoming consciously aware of the way we think (a version of metacognition again perhaps).

In summary, we would argue that critical thinking has several facets, many of which are essential in producing a strong thesis or indeed any publication. These facets include dispositions and attitudes as well as skills and abilities. The necessity to be self-aware, reflective and reflexive, and to display this self-awareness, forms a key element. But there are other dispositions and other skills. Being critical involves adopting a position of healthy scepticism, respect for others without undue deference, confidence without arrogance, caution without timidity and, most of all, fairness. It requires the ability to engage with texts and scrutinise them, to evaluate evidence, to critique methodologies, and to examine the steps by which others move from data to discussions and conclusions.

These are lofty aims and require practice and reflection, with guidance and supervision. But a useful starting point in becoming critical is to have a vision of what we are aiming for and that has been the purpose of this section.

All packaged up and nowhere to go

WHERE DOES A REVIEW OF LITERATURE GO?

We suggested at the beginning of this chapter that you may have a specific chapter or chapters dedicated to reviewing the literature. Alternatively, you may choose to interweave your literature into broader chapters which debate and contextualise your thesis. A part of your thesis dedicated to reviewing the literature has the advantage of focusing your attention on debating and critiquing what you have read. A disadvantage is that your literature can become separated from the rest of the thesis. So it is worth remembering that the 'place' of the literature is connected to its role. Early on in the thesis, the literature helps you to establish and contextualise your study, and the values and concepts informing your approach. As you progress, what you have found in previous literature will interact with the original work you are conducting and form part of the discussion you engage in about the material you have gathered. Towards the end of the thesis, referring to the literature will help you to identify your particular contribution to the field. Thus, while reviewing the literature appears to be a specific and bounded task early on, by the end of your thesis, your aim is to undo the boundaries between your work and the wider field.

Summary

Reviewing the literature involves searching, collecting, prioritising, reading with a purpose and seeking out key issues and themes, and then presenting and discussing these critically. The aims in writing about the literature are:

● **to give the reader of your work a clear idea of your study;**
● **to provide a context for your study;**
● **to convince the reader of your knowledge of the field; and**
● **to build a case for your study.**

This chapter has considered a number of key questions which students ask when they are working on reviewing the literature, including practical issues of where to start, when to stop, what to collect and how to store it. The chapter has also discussed writing about the literature, and considered the important issue of 'being critical'. The two chapters in the next part of the book consider the business of writing, alternative writing styles and the production of your final thesis. We end this chapter by giving a short list of points on how, and how not, to review the literature.

How should you do it?

● **It should be framed by your research questions.**
● **It must relate to your study.**
● **It must be clear to the reader where it is going: keep signposting along the way.**
● **Wherever possible, use original source material rather than summaries or reviews by others.**
● **Be in control, not totally deferent to or 'tossed about by' previous literature.**
● **Be selective. Ask 'why am I including this?'.**
● **It is probably best to treat it as a research project in its own right.**
● **Engage in a dialogue with the literature, you are not just providing a summary.**

How not to do it

- Do not become overly-preoccupied with the literature so that your own study loses centre place.
- Avoid catalogues and lists: Smith said this ... Gurney concluded that ... Brewer stated ... Uncle Tom Cobley asserted that ... .
- Do not stop reading before you have submitted your thesis (keep reading until the last minute).

Cameo: Reviewing the literature

John O'Neill

When I started out on my doctoral research, the required amount of words for the thesis appeared somewhat daunting. By the time I had gathered a vast amount of literature, I found that I had suddenly ended up with enough written material for two theses even before reporting on the fieldwork data. All of this material was very precious as I had searched frantically for the literature and spent long hours reading and tapping away on the computer to construct what I now felt was a good piece of critical writing. Here I reflect on how I went about collecting and reviewing the literature that formed part of my thesis.

Initially I faced a practical issue of how I was going to access the resources I needed. I live in Ireland, more than two hours away from the nearest university library, and all major bookstores are located in the main cities. However, a local institute of technology and a college of education are affiliated to one of the main universities closer to home and I arranged to make use of both their libraries via the directors of each institute. I also set up Internet access to journals and databases through the university at which I was registered. This meant that I could conduct searches, download electronic articles and compile lists of relevant articles to obtain through a library at a later stage and maximise time visiting libraries to best effect. No journey was ever made throughout the period of my research that did not involve a visit to local bookstores, or the university library in the city that I was visiting.

The next stage was to answer the question, what am I going to include in my review of literature? At the beginning it all appeared extremely daunting and an almost impossible task when placed against the backdrop of both my professional and personal life. I did not embark on this endeavour entirely devoid of expertise. With over 20 years as a practitioner I had considerable knowledge in the area that I was researching. However, while I was aware of the major problems and, indeed, questions surrounding the research issue, I needed to inform myself of the findings of previous research and the views of other researchers in the field. This knowledge in turn was used to fine-tune my research questions and to allow me to make decisions concerning research methodology, strategy, methods and so on.

How did I keep track of all the literature, particularly in the early days when my initial searches were not very well refined? Conducting a literature review is a bit like climbing your way up a pyramid, where the total area at any particular point in the climb represents the search area for the review at that particular moment in time. You start in the largest area at the bottom and slowly move upwards, all the time refining and narrowing your searches. This process generates a tremendous amount of paper, all of which has to be filed or catalogued in such a way that you can find it when you need it.

The system I used was essentially based on a standard system of box filing. A box would be established to store journal articles, for example on Lifelong Learning (LLL); this would be further subdivided into LLL and Social Exclusion, LLL and long-term unemployment and so on. An index card system filed under topic areas was used to track the contents of the box files as well as books, reports and policy documentation. Each card held full details regarding the publication on one side and either a short synopsis of a relevant chapter or quotation on the other. Any one publication could have a series of index cards holding relevant information for my work.

My bibliography was constructed on an ongoing basis. For every publication I read, the appropriate reference details were immediately entered on my computer in the correct format. It was only on completion of my first draft of the thesis that I revisited this bibliography to compile one that only contained the references that I eventually used in my thesis.

What greatly assisted the whole task were meetings with my supervisor where we set out what I would do, in terms of reading and writing up. I have deliberately linked the literature review with the writing up process as, for me, they went hand in hand. I started by writing chapters on economic development and education and training development in Ireland. The rationale behind this was that the literature required was readily accessible and would facilitate productive output while I continued my search for literature on the substantive issue. It was also agreed that I would not attempt to write the perfect chapter, but a rough first draft that would assist in the development of both my thinking and knowledge in these areas.

I addressed the task of editing by asking the question that was continuously posed by my research supervisor, namely, what is the story? From the research a number of different stories had emerged, that provided differing but valid insights. I had to decide what story to focus on in the thesis. Other, and indeed equally valid, stories would have to wait for another day. Once I had worked out what the story was, the process of editing down the voluminous amounts of written material became somewhat easier. It involved three initial drafts before I completed what I called the first draft of my final thesis.

Meetings with my supervisor were a key component of my passage through the doctorate. These meetings would follow a format that required me to present my findings, discuss and, indeed, debate them with my supervisor, and finally agree areas for further exploration as well as agreeing deadlines for future meetings. This format was very effective in both keeping me focused and challenging my thinking as it developed.

In addition, I cannot emphasise strongly enough the importance of fellow students as a resource, not only in terms of knowledge regarding the area under investigation, but also as a sounding board for developing ideas. Engagement with fellow students in this way challenged my thinking while at the same time demanding a clear presentation of my findings and arguments at any particular point in my research.

I do not want to give the impression that doing a literature review is an orderly endeavour that involves following a set sequence or recipe. It was, in my case, a messy process, not least because I was rarely in a position where I could allocate a sufficient chunk of time, dedicated entirely to the task. It was at times frustrating because I could not afford the time to read something because it was interesting. 'Interesting' had to wait and give way to 'relevance'.

In summary I would advise that prior to commencing the process of reviewing the literature, careful consideration is afforded to the key task of planning. During this planning phase all of the what, when, where, who and how questions must be explored, even if they cannot be answered conclusively. Work on reviewing the literature may be the first thing that you start work on, but the completion of an effective and insightful literature review may not occur until nearly the end of your doctoral studies. Finally, manage the engagement with your supervisor in a manner that will contribute to the development of an insightful literature review, by ensuring that he or she is fully aware of your thinking as it develops and invite him or her to challenge and guide you throughout the whole process.

Part 3
Thinking about Methodologies

6 Doing Research: Reflecting on Methods, Methodology and Ethics

CHAPTER CONTENTS

One of the challenges for social science researchers is to get to grips with the plethora of methodologies and methods which may be used in conducting research. This involves not just choosing appropriate methods for answering specific research questions, but working out the values, beliefs about the world, and understandings of the positioning of the researcher, that contribute to using a particular methodology. This and the following chapter explore these issues and are aimed at helping you to consider what lies behind the decisions you will make on methods and methodologies.

Introduction

Contrary to the impression given in many research texts, be they research reports or 'how to' guides, the research process is rarely neat, linear, coherent or straightforward. In the conventional format for doctoral dissertations, the chapter/s dealing with methodology and method usually come after chapters entitled 'Introduction' and 'Literature Review', implying that this is their proper place in the process (see Chapter 9). Similarly, research guides often advocate that decisions concerning how to actually go about doing the research should follow the definition of the focus and aims of the project and the development and drafting of research questions (or hypotheses). This sequential, logical procedure follows the traditional scientific, technicist and positivistic model and may best fit research conceived and approached from within that paradigm. Research framed in other perspectives, however, may develop and evolve differently. Our view is that there is no one 'proper' way of doing research and that issues arising in the course of planning and enacting any particular project may be pertinent at different stages and may need to be interpreted differently, for different styles of research.

Regardless of the nature, theoretical orientation and focus of a research project, researchers do need to make decisions about how they are actually going to do the research: about what methodological approach they are going to adopt and which method/s they will use. Justifying methodology and methods is an extremely important part of any research account since it is on the match between methodology and methods and research focus/topic/questions that the credibility of any findings, conclusions and claims depends. In this chapter we shall be considering some of the general issues around selecting methodologies and methods. We shall not be looking in detail at, or giving guidance on how to use, specific methodologies and methods since there is already a vast literature dealing with these topics and readers should have no trouble finding appropriate texts. What we will be doing, however, is emphasising that selection of methodologies and methods is very much a reflective, philosophical endeavour, rather than the technical business that it is sometimes presented as being.

Defining methodologies and methods

The fundamental purpose of research design is to decide and define what can be found out to answer, or provide information that contributes to answering, the research questions being asked, whatever form these take and however they are framed. It is up to the researcher to decide what is going to constitute 'valid' data, or evidence, for their project, and which methods are going to be used to collect and interpret it. They then have to justify their choices and decisions. Sometimes this is a relatively straightforward business, particularly perhaps when you are asking unequivocal questions about how many or how much (quantities and measurements). However, once it becomes possible to interpret and make sense of questions and their answers in different ways, it becomes considerably more complicated. Any research that involves people in social settings inevitably implicates a range of potential contributory causal factors and multiple perspectives and interpretations (even if the researcher does not take a postmodern stance) and this needs to be borne in mind when selecting methodologies and methods. A good rule is never to think that anything is simple or 'obvious', never to take anything for granted and always to question all one's fundamental assumptions about how things work and what makes sense. In a limited way, this questioning is our main concern throughout this book. In this chapter particularly, we are encouraging you to take a reflective and reflexive approach to thinking about methodologies and methods, suggesting that you go beyond what is sometimes presented as a simple choice between the quantitative, positivistic, nomothetic, objective and the qualitative, interpretivist, idiographic and subjective. This is, perhaps, easier said than done, for despite so many writers on research (for example, Inglis, 2003; Pring, 2000) suggesting that the qualitative/quantitative dichotomy is artificial, unhelpful and even anachronistic, the polarisation persists, perpetuating a situation by which certain methodologies are seen as superior regardless of their relative appropriateness for investigating specific areas, issues and questions. Such debates aside, what is essential is that researchers are aware of the epistemological implications of opting for particular methodologies and methods. In other words, they need to have thought about how the ways in which they conceive of, approach, and go about, doing their research influence the type and nature of the knowledge they claim their research produces.

At this point it is worth making clear what we mean when we refer to methodology and methods. They are not the same thing, although we have seen the terms used interchangeably, and treating them as such can only add to confusion and inadequate research design. Grandiose though it sounds, the purpose of research is to generate knowledge. *Methodology* refers to the theory of acquiring knowledge and the activity of considering, reflecting upon and justifying the best *methods*. Methods are the specific techniques for obtaining the data that will provide the evidence base for the construction of that knowledge. Thus methodology is concerned with the theoretical and overall approach to a research project rather than with the characteristics and practical application of particular methods. So, for example, ethnography (methodology) may involve observation of various kinds, interviews, documentary analysis, and sometimes even questionnaires (methods). Similarly action research (methodology) will use methods such as tests, questionnaires and interviews to collect information in order to evaluate the intervention that was its focus.

Methodological work involves philosophical thinking and reflection. In research concerned with human beings it is far from straightforward because, as Mo Griffiths notes, 'Unlike the physical sciences, (*social science*) is always on/for/with other people – and getting knowledge on/for/with other people is a complex matter. It is complex for three main reasons: human agency; social relations, especially the effects of power; and ethics' (1998, pp. 35–6). People taking part in research situations, whether as researchers or research 'subjects', make their own interpretations of those situations and this affects how they behave in them. That human beings do this has implications for what it is possible to know about them and for how anyone (that is, other human beings) might be able to come to know it. This is the fundamental difference between research in the physical and natural sciences and social science research, and should sound a caution against the uncritical use, in research that involves people, of methodologies and methods which do not take human agency and social relationships into account. It is also important to recognise that different types of data are more appropriate than others when developing different kinds and theories of knowledge. One size does not fit all.

Selecting methodologies and methods

Even when a relatively eclectic, multi-method approach is taken, selection of particular methodologies and methods usually involves the rejection of types of data that would have been obtained had others been chosen. It is simply not possible to do everything, either on grounds of pragmatism and feasibility or from the point of view of maintaining philosophical, theoretical, ontological and epistemological coherence. It is the case that methodology and methods determine the nature of the findings of research and it is essential that this is acknowledged if the research is to have integrity. For example, life history work with one individual can yield detailed, thick description that tells us a great deal about one person's experiences in, and perceptions of, the world. We can consider and interpret those perceptions and experiences in the light of how the person is socially positioned, with regard to how their gender, ethnicity, social class, faith background, sexuality and so on might have influenced their life. Consequently, we can learn a great deal about how the social world works. However, life history does not provide a basis for making generalisations. We cannot use one or even half a dozen life histories to say that this is how it is for everyone else who has the same social characteristics as our informant/s. Similarly, we should not make claims to represent people's beliefs and values following an investigation which had used only observational methods and had not directly sought the views of the people concerned through methods such as interview or questionnaire. Such a study could tell us things about behaviours which might indicate values and beliefs but, until we actually asked, we could not have any degree of confidence that these were indeed held. For various reasons people sometimes do things that contradict their deeply espoused beliefs. For instance, a mother who is morally and theoretically opposed to physical punishment may smack her child in a moment of acute frustration. To say that she believed in it because she was seen to do it would be to make an erroneous interpretation and analysis of the data.

Research design and the selection of methodologies and methods is sometimes presented as a rational, logical and objective decision of the 'horses for courses' kind (for example, Denscombe, 2001, p. 3). Whilst acknowledging the attraction of this view, we would suggest that it is simplistic and naive at best, and misleading or dishonest at worst. Rarely is there only one way to go about things and most research topics could be approached from a range of different theoretical and philosophical positions, and could be investigated by using most of the available methodologies and methods. To admit this is not to say 'relativism rules OK', but rather places the responsibility for justifying and constructing a rationale for their chosen methodology and methods, and for demonstrating rigour in their theorising and practice, firmly on the shoulders of the researcher themselves.

The methodologies and methods selected will be influenced by a variety of factors, including: the personal predilections, interests and disciplinary background of the researcher; why the research is being done and the desired outcomes; the sorts of questions being asked; situational and contextual factors; ethical and moral issues relevant at different stages of the research process; the resources and time available; and the nature of the research population and the ability of 'subjects' to give particular types of responses. Even though the five authors writing this book have a great deal in common, we are well aware that we would approach the same research topic in different ways, and would be likely to come up with differently emphasised findings, partly as a result of our different disciplinary backgrounds in history, science, sociology, psychology and social-psychology but also, simply, because we are different people. In Chapter 2, where we were thinking about researcher positionality, we noted the importance of interrogating one's philosophical position and fundamental assumptions concerning ontology, epistemology and human nature and agency. These sets of assumptions probably have the most significant influence upon choice and use of methodology and method, and we now want to spend some time looking briefly at each of these. We should point out that, for reasons of clarity and in order to provide a framework for comprehension, we will be describing extremes of opinion – that is, saying people either see things in this way or they see them in that way – 'this' and 'that' being diametrically opposed. However, views and positions are rarely as clear-cut as this and we do not mean to imply that they are. People hold views at different points on any continuum and may, indeed, sometimes contradict themselves. Nor do we want to suggest that we believe views to be fixed and immutable. Indeed, as we have said before, the sorts of experiences you are likely to have as a student working towards a doctorate should be leading you constantly to question, and maybe alter, your views.

So, selection of methodology and methods has a great deal to do with where researchers 'are coming from' in terms of three sets of assumptions that we now will consider in turn.

ONTOLOGICAL ASSUMPTIONS CONCERNING THE NATURE OF SOCIAL REALITY

Ontology is a term that comes, originally, from theology, and is concerned with the nature or essence of things, with the principle of pure being. Thus ontological assumptions about social reality will focus on issues around being human within the world and on whether a person sees social reality, or aspects of the social world, as external, independent, given and objectively real or, instead, as socially constructed, subjectively experienced and the result of human thought as expressed through language. How, in an ontological sense, you perceive the social world has implications for the sorts of research questions you are likely to be interested in and the methodologies and methods you are likely to consider 'valid' means of collecting 'valid' data that can be used to make a 'valid' interpretation, thus creating 'valid' knowledge.

Basically, if you see the social world as given, you will believe that it can be observed and accounted for through 'objective', quantifiable data. You will adopt positivist, scientific, experimental methodologies and use methods such as tests and structured observation schedules. However, if you take a social constructivist position, it will be necessary to collect subjective accounts and perceptions that explain how the world is experienced and constructed by the people who live in it. Your methodologies will be naturalistic, phenomenological, ethnographic, auto/biographical and you are likely to use methods like participant observation and unstructured interviews.

Given the theological origins of the concept of ontology it seems appropriate here to quote a verse from the Victorian hymn, 'All things bright and beautiful', which nicely sums up the objective reality end of the spectrum. This verse is seldom sung in these secular and politically correct days and it is not included in up-to-date hymnals:

> *The rich man in his castle,*
> *The poor man by his gate,*
> *God made them high or lowly*
> *He ordered their estate.*

For researchers concerned with social justice issues, taking the ontological position that social reality is given and independent has very significant consequences. Believing that people are rich or poor because God has ordained it so, means that little can be done, by humans, to change matters. Similarly, with regard to research focusing on differences arising from social characteristics such as gender, ethnicity social class and sexuality, which are believed to influence achievement, attainment and experiences in the world generally, there is less room for improvement if the differences are believed to be natural and immutable rather than the outcome of social organisation and socialisation.

Nowadays, many people take the view that both nature and nurture have a contribution to make in the business of difference but even so it is likely that they will see one or the other having the edge and dominating. This will, inevitably, influence their views on what constitutes valid data, and the methods they use to collect, analyse and interpret it. It may also affect any action arising from their research. Clearly, therefore, researchers' ontological assumptions can have ethical consequences and everybody doing research that involves other people, in whatever way, needs to carefully think through what these might be.

Also important is the question of consistency and coherence, which means that researchers need to be sure that the methodologies and methods they use are in line with their ontological position. They also have to be able to argue that the methods they use collect the sort of data that legitimately and validly answers the questions they have posed. It is equally important to make their position clear in any account they produce – be that a dissertation or a journal article. To fail to do so would be to lay themselves open to criticisms of unacknowledged bias.

EPISTEMOLOGICAL ASSUMPTIONS CONCERNING THE BASES OF KNOWLEDGE

Many of the bitter arguments about the significance of research findings are founded in fundamental disagreements about knowledge and how to get it: these are precisely disagreements about methodology and epistemology. (Griffiths, 1998, p. 33)

Epistemology is the theory of knowledge, thus epistemological assumptions are concerned with how we know, with the nature of knowledge, with what constitutes knowledge, with where knowledge comes from and whose knowledge it is, and with what it is possible to know and understand and re-present. The reason for doing research is to acquire knowledge and to communicate that knowledge, often with the ultimate view of informing practice and/or policy and, thereby, improving things in some way. Consequently, it is impossible to engage in research and not be concerned with epistemology and with epistemological questions and issues. Central to such concern is the notion of 'truth': truth in terms of how the data/evidence that research methods obtain is believed to correspond to and support the knowledge it is claimed that it does; and truth in terms of how the researcher communicates and re-presents the knowledge they get from their research.

Then there is also the crucial political issue of whose truth is being re-presented through the knowledge that is generated. Around this concern, feminist (and more recently, queer) scholars and researchers have raised some important questions about: how we know what we think we know; who can know and who decides what knowledge is; what are the criteria for deciding what constitutes acceptable and appropriate knowledge; and whose experiences are informing knowledge production (see, for example, Gamson, 2000; Olesen, 2000; Ramazanoglu, 1990). In other words they have highlighted the ways in which, to use a populist phase, knowledge is power. Being in a position to impose particular knowledges in such a way that they are presented as taken for granted, 'normal' and even 'natural' is to exert tremendous control over people's lives. To a greater or lesser extent, this is what researchers do. Take, for example, the ways in which male knowledge, based on male experiences has been presented as the norm in the physical, natural and social sciences. (It is only relatively recently that the hegemony of androcentricity has been challenged: a key instance of this being Carol Gilligan's [1982] critique of Freud, and other 'founding fathers' of psychology, *In a Different Voice: Psychological Theory and Women's Development*.) Researchers do have to think very carefully about their epistemological assumptions and what they mean for the methods they use. Clearly, therefore, and as Mo Griffiths (1998) quoted previously suggests, epistemology, and particularly the relationship between methodology and methods and knowledge and truth, is a contentious and controversial area for researchers and consumers of research.

Basically the main focus for disagreement centres on whether,

> *it is possible to identify and communicate the nature of knowledge as being hard, real and capable of being transmitted in a tangible form, or whether knowledge is of a softer, more subjective, spiritual or even transcendental kind, based on experience and insight of a unique and essentially personal nature. (Burrell and Morgan, 1979, cited in Cohen et al., 2000, p. 6)*

If it is assumed that knowledge is real, objective and out there in the world to be obtained, researchers can use methods that observe, measure and quantify it. However, if knowledge is believed to be experiential, personal and subjective and socially constructed, they will have to use methods that engage with, talk to and question and explore the experiences of the people involved. These differences are much the same as those identified with regard to ontological assumptions.

Finally, regardless of their epistemological assumptions it is essential that researchers are clear in their own minds as to the implications of their stance, that they state their position explicitly, and that they are either able to substantiate any claims to knowledge on the basis of their research or are tentative and cautious in presenting their conclusions.

ASSUMPTIONS CONCERNING HUMAN NATURE AND AGENCY

These assumptions are essentially concerned with the ways in which human beings are believed to be able to act within the world. Do people initiate action and make choices or do they respond in a mechanistic way to their environment and the things that happen to them? Do they act voluntarily and of their own free will, or is their behaviour determined by innate instinctual forces or by external conditions and forces? For researchers, who are themselves, human beings, this is an interesting area because whatever they decide inevitably applies to them as well as to their research populations.

Once again we have described two extreme positions and most people would probably put themselves somewhere in the middle. We do some things voluntarily and others because, for various reasons, we have little or no choice. Of course, this is a complex area that highlights issues of social power and agency as well as raising questions about natural behaviours. Basically, the more social power you have, the more you can choose what to do. The scenario is further complicated by the way in which people may have power in certain social settings but not in others. Consider, for instance, a woman in a high status position within an organisation, for example, a female headteacher. She will have considerable organisational power which may be carried out of the work environment and into certain social settings. However, and at the same time, as a woman she may, in certain circumstances, be 'subordinate' and lacking in social power relative to most men.

Assumptions about human nature and agency have obvious implications for choices of methodology and methods. If people are believed to behave in a predetermined or reactive way, then observation and experiments will be appropriate techniques, if, however, they are felt to make decisions about what to do, methods which seek explanations and understanding from their perspective will be needed.

Our aim in this chapter has been to encourage you to think about the implications of choosing particular methodologies and methods for your research. We hope that we have demonstrated that such choices go far beyond the simple 'what's the best way of finding that out' variety, having consequences for all aspects of the research process and for all of those involved, or touched, in any way by the project. We also believe that researchers who have taken time to reflect on their assumptions, who continue to do so, and who are prepared to make their positionality explicit within the research accounts that they write, provide themselves with a strong basis on which to design and conduct rigorous work that they can justify and which will stand up to scrutiny. Good research is research that starts from a sound philosophical basis. Good researchers acknowledge that they are engaged in a social and political activity and, as such, they accept that their work carries a heavy ethical load. With specific reference to this last point, in the final section of the chapter we raise, albeit briefly, a number of ethical considerations that researchers need to have thought about.

Ethical considerations

According to Sieber, 'ethics has to do with the application of moral principles to prevent harming or wronging others, to promote the good, to be respectful and to be fair' (1993, p. 14). On this definition it is clear that ethical considerations, issues, concerns and questions apply to each stage and aspect of the research process, regardless of the methodologies adopted and the specific methods used. Nowadays researchers are often required to have their research proposals approved by ethics committees before they can proceed or are, at least, exhorted to ensure that they adhere to ethical guidelines or codes of practice devised by professional or discipline based organisations (for example, and in Britain, the British Psychological Society [BPS], the British Sociological Association [BSA], the British Educational Research Association [BERA]). Useful though such guidelines are, we agree with Richard Pring (2000) that it is necessary to distinguish between 'considerations which relate to general principles of action and those which relate to the dispositions and character of the researcher' (p. 141) and that, with regard to what constitutes ethical practice, each research situation has to be considered in its own right. A researcher's assumptions regarding ontology, epistemology and human nature and agency also come into play. As one of us has written elsewhere:

> *It is certainly the case that researchers from different traditions and with different theoretical and political positions have different conceptions of what constitutes moral practice ... In Pring's terms, they have different characters and dispositions and much depends upon whether the emphasis is placed on outcomes or processes. This emphasis has implications for the sorts of methodologies and methods that researchers choose. (Sikes and Goodson, 2003, p. 38)*

Obviously, as ethical researchers, we need to have thought through the implications so that we can justify our decisions. At the most basic level though, when choosing methodologies and methods, perhaps the best test is to ask yourself how you would personally feel if you, your family or your friends were 'researched' by means of them. If you have any qualms whatsoever, you need to think very carefully about applying them to anyone else.

Even though we have said that each research project is unique, the following list of questions can, we believe, act as a valuable prompt towards ethical practice.

QUESTIONS FOR ETHICAL RESEARCH

- What exactly do you want to know and why do you want to know it? Can you justify your interest? How will your research make things better? In what ways will your work make a positive contribution to knowledge?
- How do your chosen methodologies and methods relate to the knowledge claims you are hoping to make?
- If you are intending to do anything that is in anyway 'experimental' what are the implications for the people who will be involved? If you are using a 'control' group, will people assigned to it miss out on anything that you suspect will be beneficial? If so, can this be justified?
- In so far as you are able, have you thought about potential unintended or unexpected consequences either to the people directly involved in the research or as a result of what you might find out?
- If you are intending to do covert research of some kind, how can you justify it?
- How do you regard the people you are going to be 'researching'? Do the words you use to describe them acknowledge their humanity?
- How are you going to access your research population? If you choose to do your research with people who do not possess much social power (for example, working class, children, captive populations, your own students) can you justify why? And are you exploiting their 'weakness'?
- Are you asking people questions that you would not want to be asked? Should you be?
- Are you asking people to do things you would not want to be asked to do? Why should they?
- You have a basic human moral responsibility towards the people you are working with. Are you sure that you are doing as you would be done by?
- Could you be accused of 'rape research' (Lather, 1986)? That is, getting what you want then clearing off.
- Are you manipulating people and relationships in order to get 'good' data?

● Are you sensitive to the implications of any differences in terms of social power between researcher and 'researched'?
● Do you explicitly acknowledge any theoretical frameworks or value systems that may influence your interpretations and analysis?
● Have you been honest in telling the story of your research as it was? Or have you presented a tidied up version? If the latter, how can you justify your actions?

Maurice Punch writes, 'Without adequate training and supervision, the neophyte researcher can unwittingly become an unguarded projectile bringing turbulence to the field, fostering personal trauma (for researcher and researched), and even causing damage to the discipline'. (Punch, 1994, p. 93). To people starting out on a small-scale doctoral research project such words might sound alarmist and extreme and unlikely to apply to them. Nevertheless, it is the case that any research that involves people has the potential to cause (usually unintentional) damage. This damage is usually the consequence of how the researcher's assumptions have shaped the ways in which the research situation has been conceptualised, and have influenced decisions about methodologies and methods. Throughout this chapter, our aim has been to alert you to the significance of, and responsibility involved in, making these decisions.

In the cameo account that follows, a successful ex-doctoral student, Bernard Longden, reflects on how he came to write his thesis in a way that minimised or downplayed the messiness of his research journey. The account also shows how decisions about methodology and method influenced the nature of the data obtained. It also demonstrates how practical concerns can intrude and can have a major influence on what it is actually possible for a researcher to do.

Cameo: Methodology and methods

Bernard Longden

The research process is a messy business yet when researchers communicate with each other through journals, or experts attempt to explore the nature of the research process, little of this 'messiness' emerges. This short reflexive account focuses on the methodology and methods I used to explore the research question of why students leave higher education before gaining the qualification they enrolled for. I have drawn on my memory of the time, the field notes I kept and the final product – the thesis.

In preparation for writing this piece, for the first time since the evening before my viva, I read the thesis to remind myself what I had written and what I had made explicit of the research process. Two profound questions emerged. The first question was: 'Did I actually write this?' It is interesting because in one sense time separated me from the text, from the ideas, proposition and arguments. The text seemed to have ownership elsewhere as if someone else had written it. However, it did not take long for me to remember the many hours of 'crafting the text', of editing and re-writing.

The second question was: 'Was the research process as smooth, logical and as organised as the text implied?' In my chapter on methodology and methods I had written about the research process in such a way that it implied there were no false starts, no compromises and no mistakes. It was presented in such a way that the text suggested a logical, seamless progression from the identification and articulation of the research question through to the final conclusions and recommendations.

In reflexive accounts of doing research Walford (1991) attempts to provide a similar insider account of the research process, all the failed starts, compromises in the research design because of external and internal factors, and serendipitous occurrences that in retrospect saved the research design from certain failure.

Many years earlier Medawar had challenged the scientific community about the way the research process was reported. In the seminal paper 'Is the scientific paper a fraud?' (Medawar, 1963), he suggested that the research paper was an important way in which scientists communicate and share ideas with each other, but that it may be fraudulent because: 'it misrepresents the process of thought that accompanied or gave rise to the work that is described in the paper' (Medawar, 1963, p. 377). Medawar subsequently developed his thinking around the research process and suggested that to understand the research process it was advisable to ignore most verbal and written accounts of research as they are infused with vanity.

The moral dilemma for this piece is whether a thesis writer should continue with the illusion or provide a commentary on what was behind the text. In my thesis I implied that what was written in the methodology and methods chapter was a shorthand version of the actual events. I had accepted that progress would not be linear and that it would not necessarily progress from hunch to test to conclusion, and that it would more likely reflect the picture painted by Walford rather than the idealised model projected in social science research texts. Walford captured aspects of a particular research strategy through a backstage account by: 'unveil[ing] some of the idiosyncrasies of person and circumstances which are seen as being at the heart of the research process' (Walford, 1991, p. 3). Throughout my doctoral programme there were numerous occasions when the research process was the main focus of the discussion, reading and thinking. There were many opportunities to reduce the risk of false starts, misunderstandings of appropriate methodological approaches and understanding of consequences of adopting certain methodological stances. Despite being aware of the pitfalls, I still managed to fall into some.

Methodology refers to the choice that needs to be made on the focus of the study; the methods of collecting data; the forms of data analysis necessary and finally the planning and conducting of the research. It defines how the researcher proposes to: 'go about studying a phenomenon' (Silverman, 2001, p. 4).

It has been interesting to return to my field notebook to see how I journeyed towards my choice and to be reminded of the issues and concerns that I had at different stages. I have used some extracts from the field notebook where appropriate and where I feel it illuminates the point being made.

1. Introduction
- why this, why now?
- justification for the inquiry
- overview
- contextualisation
- limitations and boundaries
- research question

2. Literature Review.
1) set out
2) summary

3. Methodology.
what I did
why I did
how I did

what happened

Figure 6.1   Extract 1: Moving towards a working definition of methodology

At this early stage in the field notes (Figure 6.1) it is clear that I was attempting to clarify the meaning of methodology and attempting to make a distinction against method – where method could be defined as the application of a particular technique within a specified methodology. I had settled on an unrefined working definition that helped focus my writing on issues associated with 'doing'. In the second extract (Figure 6.2) I was struggling with the location of the work within the case study tradition. I had at this stage decided to jettison 'grounded theory' as an acceptable methodology – a wise decision much influenced and encouraged by my supervisor.

It is important to note that in retrospect there were considerable gains to be made from having a clear research question.

> Methodology – confusion exists between the different 'tribes' of methodology.
> I think that my study is rooted in the case study tradition but could be
> considered ethnographic. Crosswell pp. 59–64 sets the two traditions out but
> I remain confused; either this will be a case study of students who actually do
> leave early (a smaller number) or it will be a study of students who might
> want to leave early.

Figure 6.2 Extract 2: Teasing out a decision on methodology

The research question defined the parameters for the research. It was clear that I needed to design the research within the constraints of an individual needing to collect data within a two-year data cycle.

False starts and serendipity

Early in the field notes there is clear commitment to grounded theory. Several pages of notes set out the main points of Strauss and Corbin's (1998) methodological approach. While this did not become the approach adopted it did provide a serendipitous opportunity to be introduced to a method of managing data – NUD*IST.[1] While I invested considerable time and effort into the software it was eventually to pay dividends in the ease and confidence that I had in extracting transcribed text of student experience of early departure from higher education.

Disappointments

The timescale for the research design required collection of permissions from students who had decided to leave higher education within the first year of study. My ethical protocol required me to write to each student at their last known home address saying that I would contact them by phone to seek their agreement to become part of the interview sample. I had set a target of 20 plus students to form the basis of the analysis. Many refused to talk to me; many had changed their address and so were excluded or had provided inaccurate contact details. The sample size was starting to reduce.

The next disappointment related to the number of students who, having agreed to take part in the study, changed their minds and decided they did not wish to continue with the interview.[2]

The diverse location of students who had departed early and who were potentially part of my sample prevented me from meeting each one. It was therefore necessary to explore alternative ways of gathering the necessary data.

Questionnaires were an obvious option – an option I rejected on the grounds that a questionnaire is often a closed questioning process. I was interested in the unexpected responses and needed a means of following them up.

By accident I came across a paper by Conklin (1997) that provided an answer to the problem – use the telephone. There were some disadvantages, but many more advantages, to this. The main benefit was the ability to speak to interviewees in their own surroundings, thus changing the style of the interview more to a conversation where the interviewee had control over the interview and where my focus was on the conversation rather than extraneous visual signals that can influence interpretations.

The biggest disappointment was on those occasions when time and date had been agreed and equipment set up to record the interview – but interviewees forgot, rethought or simply decided they were not in the mood to talk.

Final thoughts

It may not be possible to fully record all the factors and issues arising that influence decisions to adopt a particular methodology rather than another. It should not be a surprise therefore, when the section of a thesis that describes methodology and method avoids all the compromises and makes no mention of all the false starts and the disappointments experienced along the way. But the researcher approaching the work for the first time and experiencing all these real issues is left with a feeling that they alone encounter such problems. Maybe next time I would do it differently!

Notes

1 NUD*IST is a software program that provides a means of managing textual data – qualitative data – such as transcripts.
2 The interview was scheduled to last 45 minutes and an hour.

References

Conklin, K. (1997) 'Telephone survey research: an overview'. paper presented at the AIR Forum 97, 7 May, Orlando.

Medawar, P. (1963) 'Is the scientific paper a fraud?' 'Listener', 12 September: 377–8.

Silverman, D. (2001) Interpreting Qualitative Data: Methods for Analysing Talk, Text and Interactions. (2nd edn). London: Sage.

Strauss, A., and Corbin, J. (1998) Basics of Qualitative Research. 2nd edn. Thousand Oaks, CA: Sage.

Walford, G. (1991) 'Reflexive accounts of doing educational research', in G. Walford (ed.), Doing Educational Research. London: Routledge.

Approaching Research as Lived Experience

CHAPTER CONTENTS

One of the founders of modern psychology, William James, once noted that we are born into a world of 'bloomin' buzzin' confusion' and we spend our entire lives trying to make sense of it. The sense we do make is influenced by our physical circumstances, including the body we have, and the ideas, images and behaviours of the time and culture in which we live. Within the social sciences, research is often also underpinned by the need to make sense of the human condition, especially how and why people's 'lived experiences' cause them to respond to, and talk about, apparently similar things in different ways. This chapter considers the impact of 'lived experience' in and on the research process. It looks first at methodological approaches in which accounts of the lived experiences of both researcher and research participants become part of the research data (which may also incorporate details of the shared experience of the research encounter itself). The central part of the chapter draws on the autobiographical writing of one of the authors to illustrate how the conduct and writing-up of a doctoral thesis may be affected by the lived experience of research supervision. It concludes by demonstrating how such experience can be articulated in terms of 'ways of knowing' that extend beyond the 'thinking and theories' with which research is most often associated.

> *We are what we write, we are what we read and we are what we make of what we read. Researching and theorizing, like other forms of learning, are historically, socially and personally positioned and constructed. (Bloomer et al, 2004, p. 41)*

Introduction

In Chapter 2, we suggested that 'reflexivity should be an inherent and ubiquitous part of the research endeavour (see Hertz, 1997) regardless of which methodologies and paradigms are employed'; then, in Chapter 3, we drew attention to the affective dimension of 'becoming a doctoral research student'. In Chapter 6, we argued that the selection of research methodologies and methods is much more of a philosophical endeavour than a technical procedure. Thus, underpinning much of what we have written is a particular view of doctoral research. We acknowledge that such research will almost certainly be prompted by, and will centre around, a theoretical and/or practical investigation, but we also see it, perhaps even more significantly, as a process of personal and professional development. This process, in turn, feeds back into the ways in which doctoral students conduct their research, how and what they write about it, and the kinds of researchers/professionals they subsequently become.

In the article from which the keynote quotation for this chapter is taken, Bloomer et al. (2004, p. 19) argue that 'we need to understand academic research and theorizing as partly personalized social practice, in ways that pose challenges for those who view research as an inherently rational and logical process'. The aim of this chapter is to illustrate that to present research and knowledge simply as 'rational and logical' is to ignore other ways in which, as human beings, we understand, interpret and re-present the world to ourselves and others. Our intention is to draw attention to ways of knowing and researching that have not always been approved within the academy – where 'thinking' and 'theories' continue to maintain a privileged position. Implicit in this are challenges to 'traditional' approaches to research, and the form in which research, including the doctoral thesis, has normally been presented.

Chapter 9 discusses how a thesis is conventionally approached, structured and presented. Here, we are more mindful of the point made by Usher and Bryant (1989, p. 193) that 'the hunches, assumptions, false starts, informal theories and inner reflections' of researchers are generally either buried or become sanitised in presentation. Our purpose in the present chapter is therefore to acknowledge the struggle that can be involved in making the transition from grappling with the chaotic mixture of intuition, first ideas and personal and professional interests that often give rise to a research project – to capturing and expressing these in an acceptable written form. Our concern, in other words, is with how a coherent research story emerges from what may initially be sensed in non-verbal forms, experienced in a non-linear fashion, and processed through the emotions and gut feelings of 'lived experience'.[1] Through analysis of a critical incident, we also want to illustrate, as a cautionary tale, how other people, especially a supervisor, can influence how, or, indeed, whether, a research story eventually gets told.

In the next section we will draw on insights provided by feminist and auto/biographical research and storytelling to provide a rationale for acknowledging openly, rather than 'burying or sanitising', the messy, developmental and sometimes intensely personal elements of research. We hope it will give you the confidence, if needed, both to ride out these processes as they affect your own research – and, if appropriate, to articulate and take ownership of a research design, methodology and/or a form of presentation that may not necessarily fit established conventions.

Rationale

INFLUENCES OF FEMINIST RESEARCH

There is now considerable acceptance within the social sciences of 'lived' approaches to research and its presentation. As we indicated in Chapter 6, numerous challenges to 'those who view research as an inherently rational and logical process' have been made during a quarter-century of feminist research which has constantly questioned whose story is presented in research and policy narratives, on whose terms, and how certain kinds of knowledge become subordinated to others. A particular feature of much feminist research has been the involvement of the researcher *as a person* in one or more of the following:

- *Identifying the research questions,* **that is, the study may stem from, or be part of, the researcher's own life.**
- *Describing the process of research as a lived experience* **– this often leads to a merging of what some define as 'public' and 'private' domains.**
- *Using one's own voice in writing* **– this requires writing in the first-person and, possibly, including accounts of the angst, passion and emotion of both doing the research and documenting the process.**

Reinharz says of this approach:

> *Feminists found that their troubling or puzzling experiences became a 'need to know'. Being an insider of the experience enabled them to understand what (some) women have to 'say in a way no outsider could'. Researchers who adopt this view draw on a new 'epistemology of insiderness' that sees life and work as intertwined. (1992, p. 260)*

The 'cameo' included in this chapter highlights the issue of 'insiderness' in research from the perspective of a gay man.

There are many strengths to being an insider, such as the ability to draw on one's own everyday experiences to understand what may be going on within the research study (including, for example, the subtleties of power relationships allied to sexism, homophobia or race or disability issues). However, it is also important to recognise the inherent weakness of becoming oblivious to one's own assumptions: an apparent commonality of experience between researcher and participants as women, say, or gay men, or of disability, may mask important differences associated with social class or ethnicity. Commonality of experience needs to be subjected to scrutiny just as much as that which emerges from the research as new and different. For some feminist researchers, the key issue of locating themselves within the research and staying true to their own voice and understandings – whilst also 'giving full voice' to their participants *and* meeting the expectations of academia – remains a real dilemma to which there are no formulaic answers; each study needs to be shaped within its own framework of competing demands and ethics, including how/where to draw boundaries between 'private' and 'public' domains (see Ribbens and Edwards, 1998).

In the early days of feminist research there was an almost universal rejection of quantitative research methods and a predilection for unstructured or semi-structured interviews as the 'principal means by which feminists have sought to achieve the active involvement of their respondents in the construction of data about their lives' (Graham, 1994, p. 115). These particular methods were felt to encourage:

- free interaction between the researcher/interviewee;
- clarification and discussion of ideas and issues;
- maximisation of discovery and description;
- exploration of people's views of reality;
- people to speak for themselves;
- an inductive approach to the analysis of data;
- theory that is grounded in the data collected;
- production of non-standard information; and
- recognition of differences among people.

This was originally seen as an antidote to research in which women's voices were ignored or which allowed men to speak for women. It was also felt to be consistent with a non-hierarchical and empowering approach to research 'with' rather than 'on' people. Arguments against using quantitative methods included:

- Statistics as 'hard facts' conform to patriarchal definitions of research.

- Surveys assume neutrality can be achieved: that is, they ignore (or play down) the asymmetrical research relationship (researcher–researched) and the role of gender.
- Conceptual frameworks in much statistical data collection render women invisible.
- Many data sets in both official statistics and social research surveys have ignored women.
- Some data are invisible or mis-recorded when using survey data collection (for example, intimate information on violence).
- Surveys focus on social facts not on social definitions (that is, they ignore processes and the existence of different accounts).
- Statistics are not always trusted and therefore they do not always have the power to persuade.
- Feminist research is always challenging, therefore the use of a statistics convention will not protect it from criticism.

Maynard (1994, p. 13) has since argued that a number of feminists have confused quantification with positivism. She questions the version of positivism which feminists have rejected and notes that, in any case, what counts as positivism has been contested over time. There has certainly been a softening of attitudes since the early days of the Women's Movement when a deliberately provocative stance was necessary in order to challenge the status quo. Many feminist researchers are now willing to employ a wide range of methods because, as Kelly et al. (1995, p. 246) note, if one assumes a feminist epistemology 'it is possible to bring a feminist standpoint to a range of methods; we do not have to accept the 'scientific' model of surveys or reject surveys as necessarily non-feminist'. (See S. Webb (2000) for further discussion of feminist methodologies in social research.)

AUTO/BIOGRAPHICAL RESEARCH AND STORYTELLING

Understandings derived from feminist research have had a considerable impact upon the nature of research in the social sciences generally. In particular, the use of biographical methods has become widespread in researching social and psychological processes and in theorising learning, especially adult learning. As Chamberlain et al. (2000) point out, the 'biographical imperative' focuses attention on the dialectic of the sociocultural and personal and affects the orientations of many disciplines as well as their interrelations with each other. It also challenges overly abstract, experience-distant approaches to sociological writing and the notion of a world 'out there' that is separated from personal experience and an 'inner life'.

Drawing explicitly on feminist writing, West speaks of what he calls the 'auto/biographical' imperative in these terms:

> *Doing biographical research with adult learners made me realise how much, in asking questions of others and their learning, I was asking questions of myself. In hearing their stories of the psychosocial complexity of lifelong learning, I was struggling to understand mine. I became aware of the importance of surfacing and interrogating my experience of and assumptions about learning, and how these shaped, for better or worse, my interaction with the 'research other' and their narratives. Auto/biographical perspectives challenge the idea of a detached, objective biographer of others' histories ... Michelle Fine (1992) insists that: '... we are human inventors of some questions and repressors of others, shapers of the very contexts we study, co-participants in our interviews, interpreters of others' stories and narrators of our own' ... Auto/biographical approaches require constant, inclusive and shared interrogation of what is known, and how we come to know it. The objectivist, scientistic myth of the detached, dispassionate researcher has gravely damaged and constrained the stories we tell. (West, 2001, pp. 427–8)*

The notion of 'telling stories', and especially of making meaning through this process, has a long history, pre-dating the written word: the travelling storytellers of old were not merely entertainers but valued members of dispersed communities who were entrusted with passing on the cumulative wisdom of their culture from one generation to the next. Despite modern methods of information storage and retrieval which might seem to render the practice of story telling obsolete, the importance of this practice is increasingly being recognised as both an educational and a research tool.

Didion (1979, p. 11) goes so far as to suggest that: 'We tell ourselves stories in order to live. We live ... by the imposition of a narrative line on disparate images, by the "ideas" with which we have learned to freeze the shifting phantasmagoria which is our actual experience.' Drawing on work in narrative therapy, Freedman and Combs make a similar point:

> *The narratives we are talking about are the stories that people live. They are not 'about' life; they are life as we know it, life as we experience it. Since, as far as meaning, hope, fear, understanding, motivation, plans and the like are concerned, our life narratives are our lives, it makes all the difference in the world what sort of narrative is available to a person. (1996, p. 77)*

McDrury and Alterio (2003) put forward a strong case, which draws on a wide range of literature (including the two texts just cited), for using storytelling to enhance learning in higher education. Working with stories in group settings, they also use the concept of the dialectic – in moving from differing realities to new realities – to under-pin their work 'with different ways of knowing such as cognitive and affect, thought and action, individual and group' (p. 142), noting that:

> *When this dialectic is purposefully engaged, there is a shift in focus from the self as the axis of all action and centre of all development, to recognition of multiple players that impinge on change. The action is seen to be embedded not only in personal knowing but also in the collective knowledge of professions, communities and cultures. It involves recognition that others have awareness, insight and different knowledge and can therefore provide alternative approaches and solutions to situations and problems. (2003, p. 143)*

Research using an auto/biographical approach draws on similar ideas; it recognises, too, how a new synthesis, a new way of understanding and interpreting individual stories, can emerge from what West (2001, p. 428) referred to as the 'shared interrogation' by interviewer and interviewee of the narratives they generate in dialogue with each other. Research informed by a belief that it should be conducted 'with' not 'on' other people would also pick up on the point made by Freedman and Combs (1996, p. 77) that 'it makes all the difference in the world what sort of narrative is available to a person'. An important element of the research process might then become to try to ensure that research participants were enabled to have access to alternative narratives – a process in which ethical considerations about what impact such access might have on participants' lives, both during and after the research, would be significant.

Embedded in these approaches is tacit acknowledgement that education and research can (should?) be 'whole-person' processes. (However, as we noted in Chapter 6, ideas of this kind stem from ontological and epistemological assumptions which you may not share and/or may wish to challenge.)

In the context of 'authentic educator/student relationships', G. Webb suggests that: 'we communicate with others at a (total) emotional level. We do so in order not simply to develop or teach others, but also in search for ourselves. We extend our understanding and humanity in our development and teaching relationships' (1996, p. 101).

We believe that this can also occur in the research relationship – not just in that with research participants, though some of the authors of this text would argue that there is great merit in constructing that overtly as an authentic educational relationship, but in the relationship between supervisor and student. It is in this context that the transition from first thoughts to final, written product is mediated; it is a place where confidence can ebb and flow, and from which a student is expected to emerge as an independent scholar ready for admission to full membership of the academic community.

The next section highlights some aspects of the supervisory relationship. We want to stress that, while your supervisor will bring a wealth of experience and expertise to the relationship for you to draw on, you should also listen to, and work with, *your own* 'hunches, assumptions, false starts, informal theories and inner reflections'. It is by living with, and through, these, and ultimately being able to give voice to them, that a thesis both takes shape and shapes the researcher.

Speaking what we know

ENCHANTMENT

Given, as we have suggested, that there are several well-established traditions within the social sciences to 'legitimise' research that is embedded in personal experience and the co-construction of knowledge, the task of 'speaking with one's own voice' in presenting a thesis may sound relatively straightforward. However, as Willis (2004) illustrates, the doctoral journey from 'novice to expert' can be far from straightforward for either student or supervisor. Writing from the perspective of a supervisor attempting to provide 'person-centred supervision', he describes his 'attempts to respond to three interwoven challenges which varied in strength at different times of different students' candidature' (p. 319). The challenges involved 'mentorship', 'encouraging various forms of transformative learning' and 'offering tactful nurturance'.

Willis argues that the suggestions made by a supervisor as mentor 'carry a tacit message of enchantment': they say 'you, the learner, have potential enough for the project you have in mind. You can do it, and do it well!' (p. 323). Reinforcing points that we have already made, and which are also a feature of the personal narrative in the next section, he adds:

> *Enchantment speaks to the imagination and the heart – faculties not usually in great demand in the rational, scientific arena – but in the field of PhD research a lot more than rational knowledge production, which is itself so important and demanding, is going on. ... PhD learning tends to be about deeper changes in the inner self of the learner/researcher. It is, to a greater or lesser extent, a road of transformation ... (Willis, 2004, p. 323)*

Willis goes on to discuss learning transformation in three forms: 'organic', 'unitary' and 'critical'. The first refers to the student's transformation from novice to expert where 'finding her or his "voice" in which there is an authenticity and energy' is crucial (p. 324). The second involves working with image-making to integrate what are often deeply embedded and largely unarticulated personal understandings and beliefs with new insights and options. The third, based on Mezirow's (1991) seminal notion of 'perspective transformation', is generated by contradictions experienced between roles and relationships in different parts of a research student's life and the need to reconcile these, usually by adopting a stance not previously envisaged.

We shall return to these points in the conclusion. First, we include a 'cautionary tale' drawn from the experience of one of the authors. It concerns the problem of what happens if the 'tacit message of enchantment' from a supervisor sounds as though it is saying 'You *can't* do it'. If nothing else, this tale highlights the importance of main-taining a dialogue with your supervisor even in difficult circumstances – and of doing something proactive about it if the relationship does appear to break down. We hope it will also illustrate something of the processes of transformation to which Willis refers, as well as how the telling of a coherent doctoral research story can often have its roots in, and/or be filtered through, the lived experience of the researcher.

A CAUTIONARY TALE OF DISENCHANTMENT[2]

Unlike the main text of the rest of the book, this section is written in the first person singular. It is essentially a personal cameo by one of the authors. We decided to pres-ent it in what is almost its original form for two reasons: first, because the question of 'whose voice?' is an important part of the story; second, because it provides an exam-ple of how critical reflection can help to 're-story' an earlier experience with the poten-tial for a different conclusion.

> *I became an 'academic' quite late in my professional life, having been involved for many years in adult and community education. I embarked on a PhD not with any great desire to do so but to 'legitimise' a new role as a full-time lecturer. I intended to build on a number of action research projects associated with the policy, management and practice of community education that I had already completed. I could (should?) have presented a relatively straightforward piece of work within a conceptual framework shaped by existing theories of community educa-tion and tempered by emerging ideas about the 'new managerialism' that helped to charac-terise Thatcherite policy in the UK during the 1980s and early 1990s. Had I done so, I might have obtained my PhD much sooner and less painfully – but I got 'sidetracked'.*

(The moral here is to decide the extent to which you wish to use your doctoral research as a vehicle in which to explore fascinating topics and newly developing interests – or whether it might be better stay within a more limited framework and revisit them *after* you have submitted your thesis.)

The more I read, the more I became convinced that the traditional ways of modelling and analysing the history, practices, principles and contexts of community education had parallels in the ancient Sufi story of the blind men who tried to describe an elephant: the person holding the trunk thought the elephant resembled a snake; the one touching the tail thought it more like a rope; the leg was likened to a tree – and so on. In description, the elephant's 'wholeness' was lost. Within community activities there is also an intangible quality (I have 'felt' it as a participant in many different groups) which, like the life in the elephant, is almost impossible to 'get hold of' in description. I decided to work with the premise that the wholeness of community – and hence the identification of what community education is, and what a professional role within it might be – was also greater than the sum of the models through which it had so far been articulated. I had no clear idea how I was going to do this – but I felt certain that I needed to tap into a spiritual discourse to complement those which usually set the parameters of such debate.

When I first began to consider how the thesis should be structured, I rather naively envisaged it as the telling of a 'community education story' which, drawing on my action research work, would begin with analysis of particular events at a local level, extend into a broader examination of social and political issues and academic model-making; and culminate in a general discussion, in the context of ideas about spirituality, of the story thus told. It was not that simple!

The story quickly lost its 'from here to there' shape. I found myself increasingly using phrases like 'as I shall note later' or 'this is to anticipate the final chapter'. I realised that, if the concept of spirituality was to be incorporated in the thesis, it had to be named up front. Thus, what I had thought would be a final chapter had to be written first, even though I was still fighting to make proper sense of the concept and exactly how it related to my ideas about 'community'.

Even now, my understanding of spirituality is embedded in a 'felt-experience' that is difficult to express in word form. While I was struggling with such expression as I tried to write the thesis, Wittgenstein's (1955) injunction frequently came to mind: 'Whereof one cannot speak, thereof one must be silent'. (Needleman, 1983, p. 20) I cannot tell you how often I wished I had heeded it! Nevertheless, I battled for several months to write what I privately called my 'world-view chapter'.

The sense of being in a void was always present. It was a dark place, fluid and formless, where half-glimpsed images and ill-defined thoughts 'told' me there were links between concepts and experiences of community and spirituality, and between these and the holistic principles represented by the concept of Gaia *in which I had also become increasingly interested. Tantalisingly, though, they mostly appeared too far away to be grasped completely, or my mind too slow to hold them together for long enough to see order in their shapes. Gradually, as I struggled to make meaning out of this cognitive chaos by drawing extensively on metaphors, my own lived experience and a wide range of literature from several disciplines, I began to feel a 'solidifying' of ideas. Just as randomly scattered pins can be brought together in one heap by the presence of a magnet, so the ideas began to cluster in a way that then gave me something more solid on which to build new models. As a result of their construction, I was eventually able to climb out of the void onto a new platform of understanding – but not without incident or pause!*

It took me several months to write the 17,000 words that constituted my world-view chapter. Initially, I was quite pleased with it but it subsequently became the focus of what can only be described as a 'critical incident' with my supervisor. At a much later date, I wrote about the incident within the thesis itself,[3] in these terms:

> I think I must have imbibed at an early age what Bernstein (1977: 120) calls the 'underlying rule' of an 'invisible pedagogy': 'Things must be put together'. I find it quite hard to live with things that are kept apart.

> Indeed, in quoting the 'rule', I recognize it as a personal imperative which has pushed and shaped my approach to this thesis as well as my interest in community education and reflective practice ... It is, perhaps, what Brookfield (1995: 2) would term my deepest 'paradigmatic assumption'. Using Bernstein's model of different pedagogies, I can now also recognize how circumstances in which that assumption was challenged effectively blocked me from writing much more on the subject for well over a year. The circumstances were as follows:

> My supervisor, a senior and respected colleague who had always been very supportive, read the first draft of my 'world-view chapter', pointed out a few minor typographical errors, and gave me the following fairly encouraging feedback (written in red ink at the top of the front page):

> *Well argued at a good philosophical level. My only comment would be to suggest some recognition that not everyone shares even the underlying premise. This will*

pre-empt the examiner's first line of questioning! A little more of 'I' rather than 'us'
or 'we' might indicate your recognition of contrary views. None of which is an argu-
ment against the strong presentation of your thesis. There is, in my view, always an
avoidance of power in your approach which might also need attention somewhere.

I accepted the criticism of the 'inclusive' language, duly adapted the style,
corrected a few typos, and made several substantial additions and alterations to the chapter before moving on to the next. In order to keep my
supervisor up-to-date with my progress, I passed on a copy of the amended
chapter. It was later returned with nine points written on both sides of the
used brown A4 envelope containing it: each effectively demolished some
aspect of what I had written. Two short examples may help to illustrate the
nature of this feedback:

3. *Page 8 – Why should we assume that there is any more meaning in human lives*
   than in the life of an ant?
9. *...I would not endanger my mind or mental health with such practices [medi-*
   tation] any more than I would use LSD or other drugs for such purposes.

They are undoubtedly legitimate observations, as were most of the other
remarks – but even as I look at them again I can feel a stirring of the sickness
in my stomach that so strongly accompanied my first reading. Since the 'nine
points' still clearly wield such emotional power over me, I probably need to
question why I have not only returned to them but included an extract here.
I certainly had no intention of doing so when I began to add this section to
the present chapter. Moreover, I can hear a voice at the back of my mind
asking anxiously whether it is OK to make this inclusion: not, interestingly
now I listen more carefully, in terms of how this might help or hinder my
own reflection and development, but in relation to the power/status of, and
ownership of the words by, the person who wrote them. (Perhaps I can justify
their use by assuming that they will have been long-forgotten by their author
but have evidently not yet fully played out their impact on me!)

I have no idea what prompted the apparent change in the nature of my
supervisor's feedback. Maybe it is a manifestation of the internalization of
the rules of Bernstein's 'visible pedagogy' where 'Things must be kept
apart'. That was certainly the message transmitted to me, though that
interpretation and the following comments on it have only just presented

themselves. At the time, I was incapable of rationalizing what felt like an enormous side-swipe which knocked me off balance and convinced me that I did not have the intellectual ability to undertake a PhD. Within the framework of Bernstein's model, I can conjecture now that the sense of disorientation and powerlessness came from a sudden contextual shift.

In his more recent work, Bernstein (1990) has indicated that his earlier analysis of pedagogy, in which the acquirer is referred to as 'the child', is to be understood as encompassing all types of educational transmissions. With this in mind, a key to my state of disorientation can perhaps be found in one of his defining characteristics of an 'invisible pedagogy':

> ... Where within this arranged [by the teacher] context, the child apparently has wide powers over what he [sic] selects, over how he structures, and over the time-scale of his activities (Bernstein, 1977: p. 116).

After many years in adult education settings I find such a context comfortable, and mostly take it for granted. However, my belief that this was the context in which I was operating in writing a PhD thesis under the aegis of an adult education department was abruptly challenged by the sudden and unexpected total demolition of what I had written. The implicit message (only now decoded in these terms) was that my writing 'activities', though hitherto seemingly encouraged, were not acceptable within the visible pedagogy of the University and its requirements for a PhD. Even more significantly, it was not just my 'selection and structure' of material that was apparently deemed unacceptable but the very ground from which it sprang: the articulation of a personal belief system.

In entering my present reflecting-through-writing state, I am mindful of ... two other works which seem to have some significance in the context of the 'decoding' in which I have just engaged.

The work of Boud et al. (1985) in modifying Kolb's (1984) 'experiential learning model' to include a more detailed process at the reflection stage stresses the importance of returning to experience, *attending to feelings*, and re-evaluating experience. This return to the feelings which helped to create and sustain not just a writing block but a sense of intellectual inadequacy, and the re-framing of the experience in which these arose, seems to have bestowed at least some legitimacy on my 'world-view material'. I can now accept that, perhaps like a dandelion that appears in a carefully-tended lawn, the material was not intrinsically 'inferior' but merely presented in the wrong place at the wrong time. If the experience had not had quite such a debilitating effect, maybe I could simply have redefined it in the vernacular as my supervisor 'having a bad hair day'.

However, as Miller (1993: p. 132) puts it in summarizing one of her own early assumptions about research:

> ... Debate between researchers, at least as it surfaced in print, was like a gladiatorial struggle, a fight to the death to defend one's own definition of 'truth'; another vivid metaphor for this process is to be found in Bernstein's statement that, 'It is very rare to have an intellectual dialogue which is not at some point transformed into symbolic cannibalism; my formulation can eat up yours' (1977: 7).

Symbolically speaking, and to mix a number of metaphors, my erstwhile supervisor's 'nine points' not only created a contextual shift which knocked me off the gladiatorial platform but I felt that the 'formulation' of my world-view, acquired over many years, and much heart-searching, but only tentatively presented on this new platform, had been eaten up and spat out. In order to preserve something of it, I gathered up the remains, took it away from the gladiatorial/academic stage and retired hurt. The person who had earlier noted mildly that *'there is, in my view, always an avoidance of power in your approach which might also need attention somewhere'* was absolutely right: when that same person later wielded it right over my approach, I avoided it, rolled over ... and played dead on the academic stage.

... other players have since encouraged me to stand upon that stage again and to speak of what I 'know', of a world-view which has a tested legitimacy for me in my own lived- experience, using my own voice.

... what began as a fairly simple report on other people's policy and practice in community education has prompted a voyage of discovery into my personal meanings and values. As a result, I think I have become more tolerant of ambiguities. I no longer assume that a choice has to be made between either 'my' world-view or 'yours', but that they both have their own internal validities, constructions, comparisons and contradictions ... (Hunt, 1999: 18–20)

You may find it hard to believe that such apparently trivial circumstances could have caused me to abandon what I had been trying to write. With the benefit of hindsight, I can certainly see all sorts of ways in which I could, and no doubt should, have responded. In the event, however, I responded from what I would now identify as a very gendered position. My (male) supervisor had already had a significant impact on my thinking and, indeed, was the person who first encouraged me to submit work for publication. Because I remained some-what in awe of him and not very confident of my own intellectual abilities, I tacitly permit-ted him to define not only what it was 'allowable' for me to write but, in the process, to cut across a new identity that I was attempting to forge as a full-time academic after many years of part-time work and childcare. I followed an habitual behaviour pattern of non-confrontation and quietly decided that, at this comparatively late stage in my working life, I did not need this sort of hassle, or a PhD. The empirical part (about 50,000 words) of my potential thesis had already been written. Large sections had been published in various reports and a couple of journals but, rather than taking this as a cue to continue, I inter-preted it as 'being good at the practical work' – and a sign that I should concentrate my ener-gies on the teaching elements of my job which had, in any case, always been my first love.

(The moral here relates to what was said in Chapter 6 about people taking part in research situations making their own interpretations of those situations and this affecting how they behave in them. Because the same applies to the research *supervision* situation, *always* try to check out your interpretation of any events or discussions which seem to be having an adverse effect on your work – either with your supervisor or a third person with an 'outside view'. As indicated below, this could be a 'transformative moment' when a new approach will present itself.)

My thesis would have remained unfinished had it not been for an event which took place more than a year later. Attending a workshop as part of what became known as the 'Schön Inquiry,'[4] I mentioned some of the ideas I had included in my 'world-view chapter' and my reasons, which by then I believed to be perfectly valid and rational, for deciding not to complete the thesis. Although I was not aware of it as I was speaking, it was subsequently brought to my attention that my voice had become much huskier than usual. I was asked whether, despite all my 'rationalizing', I had not simply been 'silenced' from speaking of my own knowledge in my own voice.

It was a 'transformative moment' in which I suddenly saw myself and 'my' knowledge differently – and realized that I had allowed both to be devalued. To cut a much longer story short, I was encouraged to return to what I had already written and to recontextu-alize it within a reflective format that would enable me to present my emerging knowledge and understanding as exactly that, and thus to take proper ownership of it. I am pleased to say that it worked, though it remains difficult to explain exactly what difference this new approach made to what and how I was subsequently able to write.

Essentially, I suppose, instead of simply telling the comparatively objective 'community education story' that I had originally envisaged, I became a part of the 'plot'. As a result, in presenting what I understood of the theory and practice of community education whilst at the same time deliberately exploring, in the text of the thesis itself, my own meanings and values and how I was grappling with ideas about spirituality and Gaia, I could begin to make explicit how syntheses seemed to occur, often in the very process of writing, which produced insights and ideas that had not hitherto been available to me. (The reframing of the critical incident, above, provides a minor example of such reflection-through-writing.)

In writing the final chapter I spotted some interesting parallels between this process and the content of the thesis. There is not the space to elaborate on these here (Hunt, 2001, does so) but they are linked to models of 'ways of knowing' developed by Wilber (1998), Heron (1996) and Belenky et al. (1986).

Reference is made to these models in the next section in order both to set aspects of this 'cautionary tale' into a broader theoretical framework and to highlight that approaching research as lived experience involves more than the 'thinking and theories' with which research is often associated.

Ways of knowing

MODELS

Both Wilber (1998) and Heron (1996) refer to the existence of different kinds of knowing and how these seem to relate to one another. Wilber notes:

The core idea of epistemological pluralism is that each person has available the eye of flesh, the eye of mind and the eye of contemplation [spirit] … the crucial point about each of those eyes is that they are experiential. You can have sensory experiences, mental experiences and spiritual experiences. These can be investigated with direct empirical and phenomenological techniques, in a very grounded and this-worldly fashion. (1998, p. 12)

Heron suggests that there are four 'levels' of belief and knowing and describes in great detail how these can be explored through the processes of co-operative enquiry. Figure 7.1 maps these levels against Wilber's. It also illustrates how both can be mapped against the model of 'women's ways of knowing' developed by Belenky et al. (1986) and the lived experience of the author in writing up the thesis to which the 'cautionary tale' above refers.

To experience what both Wilber and Heron regard as the 'deepest level' of knowing, where all connections exist (where, as Capra puts it, there is a sense of 'connectedness to the cosmos as a whole' 1997, p. 7]), is, in Wilber's terms, to open the 'eye of spirit': to be receptive to universal principles and interconnections within and beyond the

Wilber (1998) Heron (1996)		Belenky et al. (1986)	Personal experience of writing the thesis referred to in previous section
Eye of:	**Dimension of knowledge:**	**Way of knowing:** (*ostensibly associated with 'Mind'*)	**Stages:**
Flesh	Practical (*knowing how to exercise a skill*)		Taking this knowledge into professional practice
		Constructed	Experiencing 'creation of knowledge'
	Propositional (*intellectual*)	Procedural	Own ideas developing from 'obtaining/ communicating knowledge'
		Received	Needing to find justification in other people's writing
Mind	Presentational (*intuitive grasp of the significance of imaginal patterns*)	(Subjective)	Conceptualising spirituality using *Gaia* and other metaphors
Spirit	Experiential (*feeling the presence of an energy, entity, etc.*)	(Silence)	Sensing connection between spirit and community

Figure 7.1 A comparison of the 'ways of knowing' proposed by Wilber (1998), Heron (1996), and Belenky et al. (1986), and as experienced in writing the thesis to which the 'cautionary tale' above refers.

individual. For Heron, this is to have *experiential knowledge* which is 'evident only in actually meeting and feeling the presence of some energy, entity, person, place, process or thing' (1996, p. 33) – it is the very essence of lived experience.

Wilber's 'eye of mind' broadly corresponds to Heron's next two 'levels': *presentational knowledge*, where 'feeling' is translated into images which can be expressed and shared (through, for example, art, music, movement and metaphor), and *propositional knowledge*, where, as the name implies, feelings and imagery are translated into the formality of words, propositions and theories. *Practical knowledge* takes all of this into the arena of practice, where Wilber's 'eye of flesh' operates.

The work of Belenky et al., undertaken in the relatively early days of feminist research, is primarily concerned with knowledge associated with mind – and how women experience(d) this. In their terms, *received knowledge* is in operation when women feel capable of receiving, and perhaps reproducing, 'knowledge from the all-knowing external authorities but not capable of creating knowledge on their own'; *procedural knowledge* defines a position where 'women are invested in learning and applying objective procedures for obtaining and communicating knowledge'; *constructed knowledge* involves a view of all knowledge as contextual where women 'experience themselves as creators of knowledge' (1986, p. 15).

These three forms relate closely to Heron's 'propositional' knowledge. The reference of Belenky et al. to *subjective knowledge* where 'truth and knowledge are conceived of as personal, private and subjectively known or intuited' is close to his 'presentational' level where outward expressions of what is known occur primarily in non-verbal forms. What Belenky et al. call *silence*, however, would seem to represent a much more deadening and externally created experience than Heron's 'experiential knowledge'. The author of the critical incident described above believes she was caught during that time somewhere between the two representations: the beginning of her attempt to capture her own experiential knowledge of community/spirituality in the 'presentational' form of the imagery of *Gaia* and other metaphors was effectively 'silenced' by 'external authority'.

Subsequently seeing herself through someone else's eyes, and thus recognising the stifling power of a silence created by an unacknowledged mixture of gender, power and self-confidence issues, constituted a transformative moment which eventually enabled her to find her own authentic voice and move forward on the road from novice to expert: in Willis's terms, this might be defined as 'organic transformation'. She experienced a form of 'unitary transformation' after reading Wilber's, Heron's and Belenky's work: it enabled her to see that her struggles with feelings, images and metaphors were valid 'ways of knowing' which, though not as commonly presented in a research arena as 'propositional knowledge', nevertheless have a direct relationship with it. She now firmly advocates the use of metaphor and imagery, including picture-drawing, as a way both of beginning to express ideas that are not yet at a propositional level and of engaging in reflective practice which seeks to identify unarticulated beliefs and assumptions. Several moments of 'critical transformation' occurred at different times as she tried to reconcile 'doing a PhD' with her status as an 'academic', a lack of self-belief in her intellectual abilities, and a family life.

SO WHAT?

We began by discussing a now well-established rationale for engaging in research as a 'whole person' with your own 'ways of knowing'. We have also pointed to the importance of articulating what this means for your relationships with research participants, with your research supervisor – and for the way in which you choose to write up your research. We have tried to illustrate with our 'cautionary tale' that there may well be times when it seems impossible to put what you want to say about your research into words, or when it seems possible to say it only in unconventional ways, including through the use of 'submerged' discourses. At such times, drawing on the models presented above, we hope you will now be able to ascertain the extent to which you may be being 'silenced' by messages from 'external authorities' that you are not yet capable of 'creating knowledge on your own' (these can be internalised over many years and may not actually exist in the present moment); and/or whether you need to try to 'translate' what you 'sense' into word form by consciously working with the 'levels' of your knowing.

The message of this chapter has been that research is not something simply to be 'done'; rather, it is a process to be lived. This applies, as we have attempted to illustrate, not only to the data-gathering stage of research but also to that of writing up. The next chapter examines further the part that writing plays in research as well as in the lives of a number of researchers.

Notes

1 A term popularised by Max Van Manen, 1997 (first published in 1987), in a book with that title: the book examines the methodological function of anecdotal narrative in research. A later text (Van Manen, 2002) provides further examples of how human experience may be explored and how the methods used for investigating phenomena may, in themselves, contribute to the processes of human understanding.

2 Acknowledgement: this section draws on an article in *Teaching in Higher Education*, 6(3): 351–67, published by Carfax Publishing, Taylor and Francis Ltd.

3 See Walford (1998), cited in Chapter 9, for discussion about the desirability of reflexivity within the doctoral thesis.

4 A national collaborative inquiry in organisational learning and reflective practice, facilitated by Susan Weil through the SOLAR Centre, Nene University College, November 1996–May 1997.

Cameo: Queer matters in methodology

Mark Vicars

My own research is into finding out how responses to literature are used to embed/resist sociocultural understandings of sexuality and how the production of a socio-sexual self becomes inculcated through the process of reading. This requires a new perspective on methodology and I am increasingly drawn to the idea that it is possible to do methodology that challenges traditional epistemologies and destabilises conceptions of what are considered appropriate models of educational research. This means taking control of the tools available and reworking them so that they become infused with traces of the social and cultural dynamics that have shaped my identity as a gay/queer man. Harnessing researcher positionality as both a mode of knowing and being has meant resisting the structural frameworks that operate with a pinioning force to legitimise a mode of telling within educational discourse. Drawing on concepts provided by queer theory such as fugitive knowledge and performativity has meant rethinking what it is I do when I come to do methodology.

Never quite sure out of which voice I should speak has meant at times becoming a ventriloquist to tell stories of sexual otherness. My approach to methodology attempts to articulate my social sexual positioning as a white, middle-class gay/queer man and draws on my being part of the queer communities in which my research happens. The extent to which my methodological approach is informed by and performed through these social and cultural identities means that my stance as researcher constantly shifts as I enact hybridity. My methodology is interested to explore the problematic relationship that comes with inhabiting and speaking from a normative centre or a queer periphery.

Threaded through my methodology is a performance of a preferred identity, familiar terrain within the practice of everyday life. Researching the lives of gay men in education as a gay man in education has meant I have had to enlist my sexual identity as a category of belonging to find informants who would agree to participate in my research. I have been fortunate in that I could turn to an ex-colleague who from a network of ex-lovers and friends was able to recruit informants. Without this insider access it would have proved difficult to find gay men in education who would be willing and prepared to talk openly about their experiences.

In conversations with my informants, questions have been asked about my identity and I am conscious of the insider/outsider polarity that characterises my relationships with the men involved. What exactly is it that I am doing when I sit and ask them to tell me intimate details of their lives? Why is it that they are willing to share with me their sexual stories and are explicitly candid about subterranean desires? The ethical responsibilities I have to these men is I feel located from a shared sense of belonging and one that has emerged out of the telling of my stories of self. Enunciating a vulnerable self as a researcher, engaging in acts of collaborative storytelling has enabled me to enter the group in a way that has disintegrated the boundaries between the knower and the known. The stories I have chosen to tell these men of myself has helped form an interpersonal bridge along which flows the two way traffic of our lives. In actively disrupting allegiances of belonging, in crossing over and becoming part of the stories that are told, I am inhabiting the borderlands that Rosaldo (1989) considers as 'sites of creative cultural production' pp. 207–8). I regard this as part of a continuum of problematising how research can be conducted and extend what can count as being substantial representations of experience.

In reconceptualising the act of writing as a performative act, I am attempting to make available representations of experience that are informed by and emerge out of my methodological approach. The stories that are told to me by my informants will be co-crafted to lay bare the multiplicity of perspectives embedded within the collaboratively told accounts of experience. In considering how writing operates as an enactment of freedoms and a way of resisting systems of domination, a central concern of my methodological approach is to address the problem of trying to make queer voices visible within the largely heteronormative framework of hegemonic educational discourse. By experimenting with different modes of composition such as pictures, multiple typefaces, dialogues and monologues the possibility of producing a queer, performative text becomes part of my method-ological approach and in doing so goes some way to disrupt orthodox notions of reader, narrator and participant.

Thinking how the concept of the performative operates within my methodology is to consider and reflect on how far it is is possible to critically break with the notion of the researcher as having authority and mastery over the research process and the written artefacts produced. By tracing the influence of the performative within my methodological approach I am suggesting that it is possible for the researcher to attend to the social/cultural habits of being that shape and influence the practice of identity. With regard to my research into literacy and sexuality I consider analysis of the performative as doing valuable work in making visible queer subjectivities that exist within the largely heteronormative spaces of schools.

References

Rosaldo, R. (1989) *Culture and Truth: The Remaking of Social Analysis*, Boston: Beacon Press.

Part 4
Writing the Thesis

8 Writing and the Writing Process in a Doctoral Programme

CHAPTER CONTENTS

One of the activities common to every doctoral programme is the business of writing. Producing the thesis for submission is the ultimate goal and this is examined in Chapter 9; this chapter argues that writing is also a key part of the thinking and development process. We also look at different styles, genres and approaches to writing that can be included in doctoral work. The chapter selectively considers some of the published research and guidance on writing and attempts to distil the main points. We include comments from our own interviews with writers, who have varying levels of experience, to show that all writers are different. There can be no set of handy hints or infallible guidelines which apply to all writers and genres of writing. Perhaps the main messages of this chapter are: writing is part of the thinking process; there is no one right way to write; start writing from day one; draft and redraft; and 'don't get it right, get it written'.

Classical models of writing and their dangers

The traditional, popular model of writing was based on the idea that 'what you want to say and how you say it in words are two quite separate matters' (Thomas, 1987). Others have called it the 'think and then write paradigm' (Moxley, 1997, p. 6), that is, we do all of our thinking before we start writing. Writers first decide what they want to say and then choose the words to express their thoughts and their meaning, that is, you decide what you want to say, and then you write it down. Elbow (1973, p. 3) is, like Moxley and Thomas, a critic of the so-called classic model, and he sums up the view as follows: 'In order to form a good style, the primary rule and condition is not to attempt to express ourselves in language before we thoroughly know our meaning. When a man [*sic*] perfectly understands himself, appropriate diction will generally be at his command either in writing or speaking.'

Thomas (1987, pp. 95–8) analyses several ways in which a belief in this classical model can be harmful, or 'lead to trouble' as he puts it. First, belief in the model creates the expectation that writing should be easy if 'you know your stuff'. Then, when people find it difficult (as we all do), feelings of inadequacy and frustration set in. Second, the model leads to the implicit and incorrect belief that thorough knowledge will lead to clear, high-quality writing. This is not always true and can again lead to negative feelings. Third, the expectation that writing is a linear process can lead to feelings of inadequacy and frustration as soon as the writer realises that it is in fact recursive or cyclical. Finally, the classic model goes something like: do all your reading, grasp all your material, think it through, plan it out, then write. Writers who follow this would never get started.

In reality, thinking and writing interact. Thinking occurs during writing, *as* we write, not before it. Elbow (1973) described this model, the generative model, as involving two processes: growing and cooking. Writing various drafts and getting them on paper is growing; rereading them, asking for comments from others and revising is part of the cooking process. Adopting and believing in this 'generative model' (Thomas, 1987) will lead to several important attitudes and strategies:

- greater willingness to revise one's writing (drafting and redrafting);
- a willingness to postpone the sequencing and planning of one's writing until one is into the writing process (it is easier to arrange and structure ideas and words once they are out there on paper, than in our heads);
- a habit of 'write first, edit later' (although this will not suit the working style of every writer, in our view);
- the attitude that extensive revisions to a piece of writing are a strength not a weakness;
- more willingness to ask for comment and feedback, and to take this on board; and
- greater sensitivity to readers and their needs, prior experience and knowledge and their reasons for reading it.

In fact, writing is a form of thinking – it is not something that follows thought but goes along in tandem with it (Wolcott, 1990). Laurel Richardson (1990; 1998) often describes writing as a way of 'knowing', a method of *discovery* and analysis. Becker (1986, p. 17) puts it beautifully by saying: 'The first draft is for discovery, not for presentation.' This process of learning, discovery and analysis does not precede the writing process – it is part of it. Richardson tells of how she was taught, as many of us were, not to write until she knew what she wanted to say and she had organised and outlined her points. This model of writing has 'serious problems': it represents the social world as static and it 'ignores the role of writing as a dynamic, creative process' (Richardson, 1998, p. 34). Most harmful, for new writers, is that the model undermines their confidence and acts as a block or obstacle in getting started on a piece of writing. If we feel that we cannot start until we know exactly what we think, intend to write and how we are going to organise it, then we will never get started. This is one of the reasons why Richardson objects to the term 'writing up' of research, as if it comes afterwards. Like the linear model of writing, this is based on a similarly linear model of the research process, which puts 'writing up' as the last task (discussed fully in Wellington, 2000, pp. 46–9). Over 40 years ago, the Nobel prize winning scientist Sir Peter Medawar (1963; 1979) argued that virtually all scientists write up their research as if it were a clean, linear, non-messy, carefully planned process. In reality the process is far more messy and cyclical, hence Medawar's accusation that the typical 'scientific paper is a fraud'.

Planning, thinking and writing

The view that writing is a form of thinking does not rule out the need for planning. Plans are a starting point for writers. Although a few writers follow them meticulously, most treat the plan as something to deviate from.

Here are some of the points made by experienced authors whom we interviewed (extracts taken from Wellington, 2003, ch. 3):

I like to write to a plan. I produce section headings and fairly detailed jottings about what these will contain and then follow them through. Sometimes I find that the plan isn't working so I revise it – I never write without an outline to my side though. (Female author)

I do plan my writing but I usually find that in the process of writing the plan might take a new direction. I will then 'go with the flow'. (Female)

I have ideas in the back of my mind but I only really know what I want to say as I begin to write things down. I rarely write the proper introduction until I have finished. (Female)

I usually pre-plan it, though on the occasions when I've just let it 'flow' it seems to have worked quite well. The more sure I am of the theme the more natural it would be to let it flow, at least on first draft. I think I do a lot of thinking beforehand but invariably the act of writing is creative for me – some new links and strands pop up. I think I do structure my writing though the structure often gets revised. (Male)

I put a lot of emphasis on pre-planning and particularly on structure, because the nature of what I write is argumentative. So I need the structure of the argument mapped out – and I work to this map. But quite often I don't actually, myself, understand fully what the argument is until I've done the first draft. So the first draft is a learning curve. (Male)

And finally, from a female writer:

I plan things visually, with a spidergram. I brainstorm ideas then try to connect them with a spidergram or a mind map. I find that as I'm writing the plan changes. If I write under sub-headings it's easier to move things. I can cut and paste, or move things to the bottom of the page if I don't know where to put them.

These comments show that different people adopt different approaches to planning and even that the same writers sometimes use different approaches. Planning is an important activity for all writers. The extent and style of the planning seems to vary from one to another but all plan in some way. Some writers plan in a very visual way by using mind-mapping or spidergrams and use metaphors such as sketching the landscape, taking a route or forming a map. Others seem to plan in a more verbal way.

Writing is seen as a learning process by most authors. They talk of learning through their writing, as opposed to writing activity occurring as a result of their learning. Learning and thinking come from writing rather than preceding it. This ties in with several studies reporting that writers see the act of writing as an aid to thinking (for example, Hartley, 1992 and Wason, 1980).

Writing is difficult

Perhaps the main thing to remember about writing is that it is hard, even painful, work. It is a struggle. It is difficult. Writing clearly and succinctly is even more difficult. Having extensive experience of writing does not make it easier, it simply makes the writer more confident. In discussing the question of 'what people need to know about writing in order to write in their jobs', Davies and Birbili (2000, p. 444) sum up by saying: 'We would suggest that the most important kind of conceptual knowledge about writing should be, in fact, that in order to be good it must be difficult.'

Our own interviews with different writers, many of them experienced and widely published, is that they all face barriers to writing – and the 'aids' they use to overcome so-called writers' block can be quite creative! (Again, these comments are taken from Wellington, 2003, ch. 3):

> I get it all the time and I don't deal with it. I just stay there and plug away. I have to have total silence else I can't think. I do sometimes go and stand in the shower for 15 minutes or so and I find that can make me feel better.

> If I get stuck I re-read what I have already produced and often spend a bit of time re-phrasing things or clarifying. This usually helps me get in the frame of mind for writing and I can then continue by building on the writing already there. If that is no help I might read for a while and this may give me a few ideas on how to get going or I might draw diagrams. I use the diagrams to set out my ideas in a different way than words and this might then help to clarify what I am trying to do.

> I don't know where to go next. Sometimes I just give up and do something else. Other times I go back to another chapter or a different sub-heading, or even my spidergram. Other times I just try to write my way through it, knowing that I'll probably delete most of it.

Different writers like to work at different times of the day, under different conditions and have different routines and avoidance strategies:

> I find procrastination to be a useless but common avoidance strategy. I write (and do most things) best in the morning and would regard 9–1 as being optimum writing time. I tend to leave routine chores (referencing, etc.) for late afternoon.

> I need silence, no noise at all. I write at the desk in my study, with the desk cleared of clutter. I write best in the morning between 8 and 1. A round the block or to-the-newsagents walk for 10 minutes helps enormously.

> I had a colleague once who said: 'If I don't write in the morning, I can't write all day'… and I really relate to that. There can be days on end where I just sort of go back and only move forward a sentence at a time. I find it's best just to leave it and do something else. Often if you do leave it, you find that something happens, out of the blue, that suddenly gives a different perspective on what you were writing about … and you can come back and start again. I suppose it's the sub-conscious working on things – it leaves the mind open.

We suggest that many people, during writing feel the need for incubation, for lying fallow, or for mulling things over during the business of writing something – especially during a long piece of work such as a doctoral thesis or a chapter in a thesis.

Getting started: when to stop reading and start writing

Starting a piece of writing is the hardest thing to do, except perhaps for finishing it (or at least knowing when to stop). Getting started on a piece of writing usually involves a kind of build-up to it: various authors have called this cranking-up, psyching up, mulling, organising and so on (see Wolcott, 1990, p. 13; Woods, 1999). One of the ways of building up is to read widely (making notes on it, distilling thoughts, and jotting down your own ideas and viewpoints). The problem, of course, lies in knowing when to stop reading and to start writing. Initial reading is needed to help in the build-up process (cranking and psyching up) but one has to start writing before finishing reading – mainly because, in a sense, the reading can never stop. Reading should be done in parallel with writing ('in tandem' as Wolcott, 1990, p. 21, puts it). The two activities need to be balanced, with reading being on the heavier side of the see-saw initially and writing gradually taking over. Wolcott's view is that writing is a form of thinking and therefore 'you cannot begin writing early enough'.

There is a problematic connection between *reading* and *writing*:

> *The move from doing your reading to doing your writing can be a difficult one. I sometimes start by doing just a piece of 'stream of consciousness' writing, to say 'what do I feel about the issues?' Just to break that fear of going from 'all these people have written all these things', where do I start? Reading can be inhibiting, it can take away your confidence to write. Reading different things can toss you around like a cork.*

> *Reading is a good way of filling in time and not starting to write. When should we stop? When things start to repeat themselves. Reading gives you a feel for what the 'hooks' are, and at least gives you some key headings for what you're writing. Sometimes I read until I find the hook really.*

Ideally, the writer reaches a point where his or her own writing is just waiting to get out there, onto the page. A kind of saturation point is reached. It starts to ooze out.

This is the time when we should spend more time writing than we do reading – the balance shifts to the other side. At that stage, ideally, one is impatient to get back to writing. But even then, most of us engage in all sorts of displacement activities: vaccuming the hall carpet or walking the dog. Tidying up the hard disk on the computer or checking the e-mails as they come in can also be excellent distractions.

Managing time – or creating it

Dorothea Brande (1983) in her classic book, first published in 1934, suggests that a beginning writer should start off by writing for a set period at the same time every day. Once this discipline becomes a habit she suggests that you can write at a different time each day, provided you always set yourself an exact time and keep to it. This advice may be too rigid and impossible to adhere to if one has a busy and unpredictable working day or a complicated home life (as most people now have, even if they did not in 1934). Brande tends to use a physical education (PE) analogy for writing, talking of exercise, training oneself to write, using unused muscles and the value of early morning writing. The PE analogy can be useful to a point (it can be helpful to think of keeping in trim, exercising our writing muscles and taking regular practice) but perhaps should not be overstretched.

One of the great dangers preventing us from finding or creating time to write is the tendency to wait for a big chunk of time to come along when we can 'really get down to it'. People convince themselves that productive writing will happen when they have a large block of uninterrupted time. This is one of the most common forms of procrastination: 'I'll just wait for that day, that weekend, that holiday or that period of study leave and then I can really get some writing done'. Boice (1997, p. 21) calls this the 'elusive search for large blocks of time. First colleagues wait for intersession breaks. Then sabbaticals. Then retirements.'

Haynes (2001, p. 12) suggests adopting simple routines for the beginning and end of each session. For example, one could begin with a 'freewriting' session of four or five minutes, just bashing out some words and sentences without pausing for correction, revision and certainly not editing. Haynes recounts that he likes to start a new writing session by making revisions to the text that he produced in the last one – a kind of warming up exercise. He also suggests the ploy of finishing a writing session before you have written everything you want to write, with the aim of making you look forward to the next session. Some writers, he claims, even end a session in the middle of a paragraph or even a sentence.

Abby Day (1996, pp. 114–15) suggests that one should limit any writing session to a maximum of two hours. After that, one should take a break, perhaps have a walk or a coffee and come back to it another time feeling refreshed. This is also good health advice if working in front of a screen – most safety guidance suggests short breaks at frequent intervals away from the screen, standing up and looking at distant objects to rest the eyes and neck.

Different ploys, different times of day, different starting strategies will work for different people. The main general advice is to carve out some time to write when it suits your working and domestic day best, and your own preference for your 'best time'; and then try to write little and often, not hope for an entire day when you can work uninterrupted. This may never come and anyway, who can write productively for an entire day? Two or three hours, if you can find them, can yield as much good writing as a solid day that you look forward to with great expectations and then you force yourself to write. However, as we keep saying, everyone differs and if you are really one of those people who cannot write unless you have a substantial time in which to do it, you will have to find ways of clearing the decks and making it possible.

What are the distinguishing features of skilled, productive writers?

'PRODUCTIVE' WRITERS

Hartley (1997) produced a useful summary based on his own research into what makes a productive writer in the discipline of psychology. His eight points can be transferred to writing in other areas, although point three looks a little dated now. His view was that 'productive writers' exhibit the following strategies. They:

1. Make a rough plan (which they do not necessarily stick to).
2. Complete sections one at a time (however, they do not always do them in order).
3. Use a word processor.
4. Find quiet conditions in which to write and if possible write in the same place or places.
5. Set goals and targets for themselves to achieve.

6. Write frequently, doing small sections at a time, rather than in long 'binge sessions'.

7. Get colleagues and friends to comment on their early drafts.

8. Often collaborate with long-standing colleagues and trusted friends.

Haynes (2001, p. 11) offers an even shorter list of the 'qualities of productive writers'. From his experience as a commissioning editor, the productive writer:

- seeks advice;
- shares drafts; and
- writes regularly (little and often).

SKILLED WRITERS COMPARED WITH UNSKILLED WRITERS

A large body of research has been published on the differences between 'good' and 'poor' writers. The most commonly cited authors are Flower and Hayes. Their 1981 work, for example, concluded that good writers engage in 'global planning' that incorporates rhetorical concerns such as audience, purpose and intention. So-called 'poor writers' engage in local planning, focusing on surface features of their writing. Hayes and Flower (1986), and other researchers since, have done extensive work on the differences between people in terms of how much revising they do. They suggest that 'experts' revise more than novices. They also revise at a higher level.

More generally, they and other authors have tried to identify the key differences between experienced, skilled writers and those who are less skilled or perhaps novices. The key points from this literature can be summarised (see Hartley, 1992) as follows:

- Skilled writers revise more than novices. 'Expert' writers (as Hayes and Flower, 1986, call them) attend more to global problems (for example, re-sequencing, moving and rewriting large chunks of text) when revising than do novices.
- Skilled writers are better at detecting problems in their text, diagnosing the problems and putting them right. (Generally, however, writers find it harder to see problems in their own writing than they do in others' – hence the importance of a critical friend as we saw in the interview data.)

Grabe and Kaplan (1996, p. 240) give their own summary of the behaviours of good writers. Some characteristics of 'good writers' are that they:

- plan for a longer time and more elaborately;
- review and reassess their plans on a regular basis;
- consider the reader's point of view when planning and composing; and
- revise in line with global goals and plans rather than merely editing small, local segments.

Grabe and Kaplan (1996, p. 118) also, rather cruelly, identify behaviours of 'less skilled writers'. Mainly, they begin to write 'much sooner' with less time taken for initial planning, producing less elaborate 'pre-writing notes'. They do not or cannot make major revisions or major reorganisations of their content and they do not make use of major ideas in their writing which could act as overarching guides for planning, composing and making the piece more coherent (Scardamalia and Bereiter, 1987).

SUCCESSFUL WRITING

Woods (1999) provides an excellent discussion of what he calls successful writing. One of his criteria for good writing is what he calls 'attention to detail'. He quotes the novelist David Lodge who describes how he learnt to 'use a few selected details, heightened by metaphor and simile, to evoke character or the sense of place' (quoted in ibid., p. 13). This art, or craft, applies equally well to writing for a thesis, especially in the social sciences or humanities. Woods also talks of the importance of being able to express these in writing. The ability to connect or synthesise ideas is actually an aspect of creativity which some-times shows itself in academic writing and research. It might be the ability to connect and interrelate one's own findings with existing research or theory, it might be a synthesis of ideas from two completely different domains of knowledge, for example using literature from a seemingly unrelated area, or it might be the application of a theory or model from one field to a totally new area. Syntheses or connections of this kind can be risky, and require a degree of self-confidence, but done well they can be illuminating and original.

In discussing the writing up of qualitative research, Woods (1999, pp. 54–6) also talks of the importance of including 'other voices' in the text, besides that of the author. One of the objectives of social science research is to give people a voice or a platform, and this must be reflected in the written medium through which the research is made public. Giving people a voice, however, leads to some difficult choices. Every write-up is finite. Do you include lengthy statements or transcripts from one or two people, or many shorter points from a larger variety? (See Woods, 1999, p. 56 for discussion.)

A final point made by Woods concerns the importance, when writing, of not missing the humorous side of research, for example by including an ironic comment from an interviewee.

Structuring writing

Sprent (1995, p. 3) puts forward the terms 'macrostyle' and 'microstyle'. The latter is concerned with style and structure at the level of words, sentences and paragraphs; while macrostyle is concerned with larger blocks and structures such as sections, chapters and the use of tables and figures. This distinction can be useful in thinking about writing and this section examines elements of both.

There is considerable debate about how much structure authors should include in writing a report, thesis, book or article. Here we consider structure at four levels: overall contents structure; within chapters; paragraphing and sentence level.

HEADINGS, SUB-HEADING, SUB-SUB-HEADINGS ...

Headings are valuable signposts in guiding a reader through a text and maintaining their interest or concentration. But it is always difficult to decide how many *levels* of heading to use. It is essential to use some headings, even if it is just chapter titles.

Students need to be clear, when writing, about the level of heading they are using at any given time. Headings are then given a level (level A, level B and level C) and each level uses a different font or typeface.

For example:

Level A: **CHAPTER HEADINGS** (upper case, bold)
Level B: **Sub-headings** (lower case, bold)
Level C: *Sub-sub-headings* (lower case, italics)

Writers then need to be (or at least try to be) clear and consistent about which headings they are using and why. If a writer goes 'below' level C this can be difficult. Writers, and readers, begin to flounder when they get past the sub-sub-level.

CHAPTER STRUCTURE

Headings and sub-headings can help to structure a chapter and break it down into digestible chunks. But there is also a useful rule, followed by many writers, which can help to give a chapter a feeling of coherence or tightness. This rule suggests that a chapter should have three (unequal in size) parts:

- **a short introduction, explaining what the author is going to write about;**
- **the main body, presenting the substance of the chapter; and**
- **a concluding section, rounding off the chapter.**

This overall pattern works well for many writers, and readers, especially in a thesis. It is rather like the old adage associated with preaching: 'Tell them what you're going to say, then say it, and then tell them what you've just said.' For many types or genres of writing it works well and assists coherence. However, if overdone it can become tedious.

One other way of improving coherence is to write link sentences joining one paragraph to the next or linking chapters. For example, the last sentence (or paragraph) of a chapter could be a signal or an appetiser leading into the next.

CONNECTING PHRASES AND SENTENCES

One of the important devices in writing is the logical connective. Connectives are simply linking words and can be used to link ideas within a sentence, to link sentences or to link one paragraph to the next. Examples include: 'First', 'Secondly', 'Thirdly', 'Finally'; also 'However', 'Nevertheless', 'Moreover', 'Interestingly', 'Furthermore', 'In addition', 'In conclusion', 'Thus', and so on.

Connectives can be valuable in maintaining a flow or a logical sequence in writing; but be warned – readers can suffer from an overdose if they are used too liberally, especially if the same one is used repeatedly. Ten 'howevers' on the same page can become wearing.

All the tactics and strategies summarised above have the same general aim: to improve clarity and communication. Table 8.1 gives a summary of four useful strategies which can be used in writing, whether it be an article, a book, a thesis or a conference paper.

Table 8.1 Four useful strategies in structuring writing

Strategy	Meaning	Examples
Signposting	Giving a map to the reader; outlining the structure and content of an article, book or chapter, that is, structure statements	This chapter describes … The first section discusses … This paper is structured as follows …
Framing	Indicating beginnings and endings of sections, topics, chapters	First, … Finally, … To begin with … This chapter ends with … To conclude …
Linking	Joining sentence to sentence, section to section, chapter to chapter …	It follows that … The next section goes on to … As we saw in the last chapter … Therefore …
Focusing	Highlighting, emphasising, reinforcing, key points	As mentioned earlier … The central issue is … Remember that … It must be stressed that …

Signposting is particularly important in a long thesis. Signposts should refer back to the previous chapter or section; they tell the reader what to expect and they often pose a question or introduce a theme that the forthcoming section, paragraph or chapter is going to explore.

PARAGRAPHING

Different writers and different readers see paragraphs in different ways. If you give different readers a page of un-paragraphed prose and ask them to divide it into paragraphs, they are unlikely to break it down or categorise it in exactly the same way. A paragraph should ideally contain just one main theme or concept or category – but concepts come from people, and people vary (Henson, 1999, p. 64). It is really up to the writer to make these partly arbitrary decisions on paragraphing. The main criterion is that each paragraph should centre on one idea: 'when the author progresses to a new idea, a new paragraph should be used' (Henson, 1999, p. 66). As authors move from one clear idea to another, Henson suggests, a new paragraph should be used. But this is easier said than done, especially in the heat of the writing process. It takes practice, it is an art (Henson, 1999, p. 66) and personal preferences will vary from one writer to another (and between editor and author sometimes).

Henson gives some useful tips on paragraphing (pp. 37–8). He suggests that short paragraphs help the reader – the reader should be able to remember in one 'chunk' all the ideas contained in a paragraph. His rule of thumb is that half a side of double-spaced typed text is enough for most readers to retain. Henson also suggests that whilst reading through what you have written, you should see if each paragraph follows from and advances upon the ideas in previous paragraphs. If not they should be re-ordered. This process, of course, is greatly helped by the cut-and-paste facility in word-processing programs.

Getting it off your desk and gradually exposing your writing

Reading your own work is important but is no substitute for having another eye on it, first perhaps from a critical friend, then your supervisor and later (if possible) from an 'outsider'. The writer's own tacit, implicit knowledge of what one wishes to say makes it hard to identify the missing elements or steps in one's own writing that are somewhere in 'the head' but have not made it out onto the paper. These may be missing episodes in an account, or missing steps in an argument, so that the writer seems to jump to a conclusion without adequate premises. The Greek word 'ellipsis' (meaning 'cutting short') seems neatly to sum up these omissions. Readers can spot a writer's ellipses more readily than writers can spot their own. Readers can also identify sentences that are clumsy or simply do not read well or 'sound right'. It is also easier to spot long-windedness or repetition in someone else's writing than in your own.

It is worth leaving your writing 'to stand' for a few weeks before rereading it yourself, but the outside reader is essential too. Richardson (1990) talks of the value of 'getting early feedback' on your writing. This can be achieved by giving an 'in-progress' seminar or paper to fellow students, or in a departmental seminar, or using some other public forum such as a conference. Wolcott (1990, p. 46) suggests that reading your own words aloud to yourself can help but, even better, a friend or colleague (it would need to be a good one) could read them to you so that you can listen and concentrate on 'what has actually reached paper – the experience you are creating for others, out of your own experience'. When the oral reader stumbles or 'gasps for air' (as Wolcott puts it) then it is time to 'get busy with the editing pencil'.

Editing, drafting and redrafting

I spent all morning putting a comma in, and the afternoon taking it out again. (Attributed to Lord Byron, in Woodwark, 1992, p. 30)

Most writers on writing seem to agree on one thing: do not try to edit and write at the same time (Becker, 1986; Henson, 1999; Smedley, 1993). Haynes (2001, p. 111) identifies two parts to the writing process: the compositional and the secretarial. In the first stage, writers should concentrate on getting words onto paper, generating text, trying to get the subject matter clear in their own minds and covering the ground. The secretarial stage involves sorting out the structure and layout, correcting things like spelling and punctuation, and tinkering around with words and sentences. Haynes describes the first stage as 'writing for the writer', the second as 'writing for the reader'. This second stage is perhaps where the writer really needs to be aware of the intended audience; in the first stage, the writer can care far less about what anyone will think about it, and this slightly carefree attitude can encourage freer writing.

The act of editing can interfere with the activity of writing. Smedley (1993, p. 29) observes that 'when people first sit down to write, they begin a sentence and immediately take a dislike to the way it is worded and start again'. This is the editor interfering with the writer. Both are essential, but both should be kept in their places. 'The writer writes, the editor edits.' She suggests leaving the first draft for a day or a week and coming back to it with your editor's hat on this time. Editing involves seeing if it makes sense, feeling for how well it reads, asking if things could be put more neatly and succinctly and cutting unnecessary words. She argues for a number of drafts: 'Write without editing, then edit, then re-write without editing, then edit once again. When you exhaust your own critical eye as an editor, enlist the assistance of your spouse, your colleagues, your students, your trusted friends … and ask them to be brutal' (Smedley, 1993, p. 30).

Becker (1986, p. 20) believes that writers can 'start by writing almost anything, any kind of a rough draft, no matter how crude and confused, and make something good out of it'.

This could be called the pottery model of writing – start by getting a nice big dollop of clay onto the working area and then set about moulding and shaping. This model may not work for everyone though. Zinsser (1983, p. 97) talks of feeling that he writes rather like a bricklayer. His thoughts, written at the time by someone who had just discovered the value of the word processor, are worth seeing in full:

My particular hang-up as a writer is that I have to get every paragraph as nearly right as possible before I go on to the next one. I'm like a bricklayer. I build very slowly, not adding a new row until I feel that the foundation is solid enough to hold up the house. I'm the exact opposite of the writer who dashes off his entire first draft, not caring how sloppy it looks or how badly it's written. His only objective at this early stage is to let his creative motor run the full course at full speed; repairs can always be made later. I envy this writer and would like to have his metabolism. But I'm stuck with the one I've got.

Towards the final stages of editing and revising, a piece of advice given by Harry Wolcott (1990) seems very helpful. He tells of how the idea came to him when he was assembling a new wheelbarrow from a kit: 'Make sure all parts are properly in place before tightening'. Before you start tightening your writing, he argues: 'Take a look at how the whole thing is coming together. Do you have everything you need? And do you need everything you have?' (p. 48).

His list of necessary parts includes a statement of our own viewpoints and opinions. We may prefer not to or simply not be willing to, but he believes this will be construed as a 'typical academic cop-out' – a failure to answer the question 'so what?'.

We may prefer not to be pressed for our personal reactions and opinions, but we must be prepared to offer them. It is not unreasonable to expect researchers to have something to contribute as a result of their studied detachment and inquiry-oriented perspective. (Wolcott, 1990, p. 49)

In completing a doctorate, people should be expected to voice their own views and draw out the 'so what?' implications. They can do this with due modesty and deference to past literature and research, but without overdoing the usual statement of humility and inadequacy. Wolcott (1990, p. 69) even argues that a study of even a single case should lead to some judgement and opinion. In answer to the sceptic who challenges 'What can we learn from one case?' Wolcott gives the answer 'All we can'.

Watching every word and sentence

I have made this letter longer than usual because I lacked the time to make it short. (Blaise Pascal, Lettres provinciales, letter 16, 1657)

A good old-fashioned guide by Bett (1952) gives simple advice: 'the essence of style is the avoidance of (1) wind (2) obscurity. In your scientific writing be simple, accurate and interesting. Avoid like the plague 'as to whether' and 'having regard to', beloved of the drawers-up of legal documents. Avoid 'tired' words. Avoid 'slang' (p. 18).

One of the old clichés, which is a tired one but does have some truth in it, is 'make every word work for a living'. Zinsser (1983, p. 98) offers one practical way of removing what he calls 'clutter'. He suggests reading the text and putting brackets round every word, phrase or sentence that 'was not doing some kind of work'. It may be a preposition that can be chopped out (as in 'free up', 'try out',' 'start up', 'report back'); it may be an adverb that is already in the verb (as in 'shout loudly' or 'clench tightly'); it may be an unnecessary adjective (as in 'smooth marble'). Brackets could also be put round the kinds of qualifiers that academics and politicians tend to use, such as 'tend to', 'in a sense', 'so to speak', or 'in the present author's view' (the latter is also circumlocution). Entire sentences could be bracketed if they repeat something already said (unless it really needs reinforcing) or add irrelevant detail (too much information perhaps). By bracketing the words or sentences as opposed to crossing them out, the reader/editor or writer can then see whether the text can really do without them – if so, then delete.

Incidentally, Zinsser (1983, p. 103) also emphasises the value of short sentences. He talks of how, in writing his own book:

> *I divided all troublesome long sentences into two short sentences, or even three. It always gave me great pleasure. Not only is it the fastest way for a writer to get out of a quagmire that there seems no getting out of; I also like short sentences for their own sake. There's almost no more beautiful sight than a simple declarative sentence.*

Haynes (2001, p. 93–6) gives excellent and witty advice on circumlocution. He identifies common examples such as 'at this moment in time' (meaning 'now'), 'until such time as' (meaning 'until'), 'is supportive of' (meaning 'supports') and 'is protective of' (meaning 'protects'). He suggests that two common causes of circumlocution are the use of euphemisms (for example, 'going to meet their maker' instead of 'dying') and *pomposity*. There is no shortage of the latter in academic writing. Authors may attempt to impress their audience with a pompous tone and choice of words. They perhaps hope to appear knowledgeable and 'academic'. The end result is often the use of inappropriate and pretentious language. Haynes suggests that this may happen when authors 'feel superior to their audience', but also occurs when 'authors feel insecure either because they are short of material or they do not have a secure grasp of the subject' (p. 94). It is certainly something to beware of, either as a reader or a writer. Every sentence, in a book or article or thesis, should make sense.

Proofreading and presentation

Spellcheckers are marvellous things but they need to be handled with care:

Candidate for a Pullet Surprise

I have a spelling checker
It came with my PC
It plane lee marks four my revue
Miss steaks aye can knot sea

Eye ran this poem through it
Your sure reel glad two no
Its vary polished in its weigh
My checker tolled me sew
(Dr Jerrold H. Zar, 1992)

Spellcheckers are no substitute for human proofreaders, especially if that human is *not* the writer. In my experience of writing and reading, the five more common areas where vigilant proofreading is needed are:

1. Missing apostrophes, for example, 'The pupils book was a complete mess. Its true to say that apostrophes are a problem'.
2. Unwanted apostrophes, for example, 'The pupil's made a complete mess.' It's bone was a source of amusement'. (The use of 'it's' for 'its', and vice versa, is a common mistake.) The bestselling book by Lynne Truss is an excellent and witty guide to punctuation: *Eats, Shoots and Leaves*, London: Profile Books, 2003.
3. Referencing: referring to items in the text which are not listed in the list of references at the end, and vice versa, that is, listing references which are not included in the text.
4. Commonly misused words: effect/affect; criterion/criteria; phenomenon/ phenomena; their/there.
5. Sentences that do not make sense. There is a danger, particularly for new writers who are striving to display their initiation into academic discourse, of 'shooting from the hip' with newly acquired buzzwords. Jargon can be valuable; terms such as 'ontology', 'epistemology', 'paradigm', 'triangulation' and 'validity', can all refer to important concepts, but they can easily be strung together to form a grammatical but totally meaningless sentence.

Presentation is no substitute for substance, but it is a *necessary* prerequisite for a positive reception (though not a *sufficient* one).

Many editors suggest proofreading from the bottom upwards, to avoid getting carried away by the content and flow of the text you are reading. Many people talk of testing your written sentences by ear: how do they sound and feel? Read aloud, read upwards from the bottom, line by line.

Tools of the trade and sources of guidance

McCallum (1997) suggests that the two main tools for a writer are a 'big fat dictionary' and a good thesaurus. A copy of the the the *Shorter Oxford English Dictionary* (it comes in two large volumes or some prefer the electronic version on disc). The writer also needs a good word processor and a healthily sized screen, although some writers genuinely still prefer a pen and notepad for composing.

Other guides and sources of information can be useful and many can be found on the World Wide Web. In seeking advice on English usage, *The King's English* by H.W. Fowler, originally published by Clarendon Press in Oxford in 1908, is now on the web through Bartleby of New York (www.bartleby.com). A paper equivalent (almost) is *MHRA Style Book*, from the Modern Humanities Research Association in London. This is a guide of about 80 pages on style, spelling, referencing, indexing, proofreading – indeed almost anything to do with preparing articles, papers or books for publication. One specific issue that comes up frequently is e-referencing, that is, referring to electronic sources. One of the best guides on this comes from the University of Bournemouth. They have an excellent site on referencing in general with a good section on how to refer to e-journals, personal electronic communications, CD-ROMs, and so on (www.bournemouth.ac.uk/using_the_library).

Approaches, styles and formats

Traditionally, within the social sciences, academic writing, particularly as represented in theses and dissertations, but also in peer reviewed journal articles and monographs and edited collections, has tended and been expected, to follow a basic format, with certain variations being acceptable for specific genre conventions (see, for example, Van Maanen, 1988, on ethnographic styles). To some extent, within this chapter so far, what we have had to say about writing has assumed this format which, essentially, consists of:

- an abstract;
- an introduction;
- a literature review;
- a justification for the methodology and methods;
- a description of the research setting/context/population;
- the presentation of findings;
- discussion of those findings;
- a conclusion;
- appendices where relevant (copies of questionnaires, interview schedules, transcripts and so on); and
- a list of references presented in a specific manner, usually according to the Harvard system.

All formats and styles of writing reflect understandings about the nature of knowledge. Thus, this traditional form, arising from the positivist paradigm, demands that social scientific writing be 'objective', realistic, neutral and unbiased and requires that the writer/researcher should not be personally present in the text, for fear of contaminating it with their subjectivity. However, we agree with the views expressed by Roland Barthes and Maggie MacLure, that: 'the writing of realism is far from being neutral, it is, on the contrary loaded with the most spectacular signs of fabrication' (Barthes, 1967, p. 73); and that, 'texts are often at their most persuasive when they don't seem at all rhetorical, but rather pass themselves off as fact or realistic description' (MacLure, 2003, pp. 80–1). What we are saying here is that all words and vocabularies are socially and politically located and value laden. Choosing one word over another, this style in preference to that, involves and implicates deep and far reaching meanings. It is not just a matter of tinkering with the surface.

Taking this view involves acknowledging that it is difficult, if not impossible to disembody or disassociate the writer from the text since at the least they will be writing in a style by and with which they want to be identified. It also means accepting that the traditional style of academic writing is just one form of narrative, one way of telling the story. Such a stance opens up a range of possibilities for those (postmodernists, poststructualists, whatever) who feel that different narrative structures seem more appropriate for communicating their understandings and accounts of their research because they fit better with their epistemological, ontological, ethical and value positioning.

The beginning of the twenty-first century is an exciting place for researchers to be because, providing they are unequivocally explicit to their readers about what they are doing and why and are able to justify their approach, and if they have supportive supervisors there are a host of what Laurel Richardson calls 'creative analytic practices' (2000, pp. 929–36) to make use of. Getting the support of your supervisor and also enlisting sympathetic examiners is crucial if you are going to adopt what might be termed as 'alternative' (that is, to the traditional) approaches.

Essentially, these 'creative analytic practices' are produced as academic scholarship, as legitimate ways of presenting social science research, thinking and theorising, and they have extended the boundaries of understanding primarily by acknowledging and, where appropriate, privileging subjectivities and the place of the affect and emotion in all aspects of social life. Narrative forms that evoke identification and/or empathy, and hence promote understanding, do seem to be highly appropriate in social research when human experience is the focus. The aim is to re-present subjective experiences and perceptions and, starting from the premise that all re-presentations are just that, not actual life as lived because that can never be completely and accurately captured, these 'alternative approaches' sometimes take explicitly fictional or poetic forms. Usually, however, they will come with some form of analytic introduction, commentary or discussion that relates the story to theory. And they should, in our view and as we have already noted, always make their 'fictionality' explicit.

Alternative approaches include: autoethnography, ethnographic fiction, performance ethnography, and poetry (for a range of examples see Banks and Banks, 1998; Brady, 2000; Clough, 2002; Ellis and Bochner, 1996; Richardson, 1997; 2000; Wolcott, 2002).

AUTOETHNOGRAPHY

Autoethnographies are accounts in which writers/researchers tell stories about their own lived experiences, relating these to broader contexts and understandings in much the same way as life historians analyse life stories in the light of historical, sociological or/and psychological theories and perspectives. In some cases autoethnographies focus on aspects of the research process, for instance, reflecting on the writing process or on the researcher's experiences in the field. In most cases, autoethnographers will employ literary devices in order to evoke identification and emotion.

ETHNOGRAPHIC FICTION

Ethnographic fiction (see Banks and Banks, 1998; Clough, 2002) is a narrative form in which fictional stories, which could be true, are told within an accurate cultural/social framework. In many respects this is much what novels do, with the difference lying in the intention. Novels are written to entertain and maybe to educate; ethnographic fictions are written as scholarship and are intended to further understanding of aspects of social life. They frequently, but not always, come with some form of analytic introduction, commentary or discussion that relates the story to theory. Some writers have used fictional forms in order to protect and preserve the anonymity of their informants and research settings, in other cases elements of different 'real' characters and/or contexts have been combined to create a composite.

POETRY

Some writers use poetic forms to re-present interview transcripts because they believe poetry comes closer to speech patterns and rhythms: others choose it for its power to reflect emotions. Poems rarely stand alone.

DRAMATIC PRESENTATIONS

Performance ethnography is an attempt to re-present an experience without losing the experience. In some cases there will be a script, in others the actors improvise around themes. Inevitably it raises all sorts of questions about the nature of social science. How it is actually presented varies. Sometimes it will be prefaced or followed by discussion, on occasion it may be undertaken in order to give others the opportunity to 'experience' particular situations and emotions.

MIXED GENRES

Mixed genre work can be considered as a form of triangulation in which scholars take from literary, artistic and scientific genres in order to try to give as rich a picture of the situation they are concerned with as possible. Mixed genres can make it easier to re-present the multifaceted nature and the multiple realities there are in any area of social life. Research into children's experiences of their first few weeks in secondary school might, for instance, include poems, pictures, photographs, essays, journal entries, autoethnographic writing by the researcher, the school prospectus and other documents as well as theoretical analysis. Some writers may adopt a mixed genre approach in order to 'hedge their bets' and increase the likelihood of their work gaining acceptability and publication.

ALTERNATIVE STYLES: IN CONCLUSION

That all writing is narrative writing is widely accepted. However, in the context of research, 'narrative' is generally understood to refer to qualitative research that uses and tells stories. Many people who use explicitly narrative approaches do so, at least partly, out of a political conviction that social research should be accessible and interesting, because they believe that it should seek to capture something of the sense of life as it is lived, and because they want to avoid the negative ethical and power consequences of assuming the sort of authoritative voice that denies the possibility of multiple realities. Having said this it is important to reiterate that it is only possible to re-present, not re-create experiences, perceptions and emotions.

Researchers and writers who want to go further in pushing the boundaries of what is regarded as legitimate scholarship often experience tension between writing as they want to and getting their work into the public domain. Bill Tierney suggests that we should,

> refrain from the temptation of either placing our work in relation to traditions or offering a defensive response. I increase my capacity neither for understanding nor originality by a defensive posture. To seek new epistemological and methodological avenues demands that we chart new paths rather than constantly return to well-worn roads and point out that they will not take us where we want to go. (1998, p. 68)

This is a courageous view. However it is important that narrative research, whatever form it takes, should be able to demonstrate both its scholarliness and its honesty.

In summary: some useful guidelines on writing

As a final section, we have collected together 16 pieces of advice on writing. They have been distilled from a variety of sources:

1. Do not procrastinate by waiting for the 'perfect opportunity', or the 'ideal writing conditions' such as a free day or a period of study leave, before you start writing. They may never come.
2. Read lots of different styles of writing. The more you read, the more you pick up, the wider your vocabulary will become and your own personal literary style-bank will increase. Anything that you may read can give you ideas for writing. Do not limit your reading to academic authors. Writers of fiction

use a vast range of styles and techniques that you can adopt and adapt to make your writing more interesting and, hence, more likely to be read!

3. Do not edit as you write that is, as you go along. Wait until later. Composing and revising/editing are different activities (like growing and cooking: Elbow, 1973).

4. Treat writing as a form of thinking. Writing does not proceed by having preset thoughts which are then transformed onto paper. Instead, thoughts are created and developed by the process of writing. Writing up your work is an excellent, albeit slightly painful, way of thinking through and making sense of what you have done or what you are doing. This is a good reason for not leaving writing until the end; writing should begin immediately.

5. Break a large piece of writing down into manageable chunks or pieces which will gradually fit together. We call this the 'jigsaw puzzle' approach – but an overall plan is still needed to fit all the pieces together. The pieces will also require linking together. The job of writing link sentences and link paragraphs joining section to section and chapter to chapter, is vital for coherence and fluency.

6. Share your writing with a trusted friend – find a reader/colleague whom you can rely upon to be reliable and just, but critical. Look for somebody else, perhaps someone with no expertise in the area, to read your writing and comment on it. They, and you, should ask: Is it clear? Is it readable? Is it well-structured? In other words use other people, use books, for example style manuals, books on writing. Do your own proofreading, but always ask someone else to cast an external eye.

7. Draft and redraft; write and rewrite – and do not either expect or try to get it right first time. Writing should not be treated as a 'once and for all' activity. Getting the first draft on to paper is just the first stage. Then 'put it in the ice box and let it cool' (Delton, 1985, p. 19).

8. Remove unnecessary words; make each word work for a living. After the first draft is on paper go back and check for excess baggage, that is, redundant words and circumlocution.

9. Avoid tired and hackneyed metaphors; watch out for overdoses of idioms such as 'horses for courses' or 'wood from the trees'.

10. Think carefully about when you should use an *active* voice in your sentences and when a *passive* voice may or may not be appropriate. The passive voice can be a useful way of depersonalising sentences but sometimes naming the 'active agent' helps clarity and gives more information.

11. Be honest with your reader. Feel free to admit, in writing, that you found it hard to decide on the 'right way' to, for example, organise your material, decide on a structure, get started, write the conclusion, and so on. Do not be afraid to say this in the text (Becker, 1986).

12. Vary sentence length. Use a few really short ones now and again, for example, four words. These can have impact.

13. Edit 'by ear'; make sure it sounds right and feels right. Treat writing as somewhat like talking to someone except that now you are communicating with the written word. Unlike talking, the reader only has what is on paper. Readers, unlike listeners, do not have body language, tone of voice or any knowledge of you, your background or your thoughts. Writers cannot make the assumptions and short cuts that can be made between talkers and listeners. Have your readers in mind especially in the later stages of drafting. Better still, visualise one *particular* reader. What will they make of this sentence?

14. Readers need guidance, especially to a long thesis but equally with an article. In the early pages, brief the readers on what they are about to receive. Provide a map to help them navigate through it.

15. Above all, get it 'out of the door' (Becker, 1986) for your 'critical friend' reader to look at. Do not sit on it for months, 'polishing' it. Get it off your desk, give it to someone to read (including your supervisor), then work on it again when it comes back.

16. Finally, two of the most common obstacles to writing are (a) getting started and (b) writing the abstract and introduction. You can avoid the former by not trying to find the 'one right way' first time round (Becker, 1986), and the latter by leaving the introduction and abstract until last. Writing with a word processor helps to ease both.

We hope that this chapter has offered some guidance, reassurance and insight to those who read it. Our parting messages are: the writing process is a complex one; it is in some senses a struggle for many people; reflecting on our own writing processes is a valuable activity; it is enjoyable and helpful to share these reflections with peers; there is a range of styles and approaches to planning and composing – but there is no one right way of writing. In the next chapter we go on to consider, in a more procedural style, the production of the actual thesis and the 'production values' inherent in that process.

Cameo: Me and my writing process

Kathryn Roberts

Getting started

You've searched the literature, you've carried out your primary research, you've read everything you can find about your subject, you just can't put it off any longer – you HAVE to start writing …

The very thought of writing at doctoral level can be daunting. There's a self-imposed pressure to get every chapter, every paragraph and every sentence, completely perfect, first time, every time. But that's not going to happen. It didn't happen for Shakespeare – why would it happen for you?

I like writing. I get a tremendous sense of achievement when I commit another 1,000 words to paper, and get another 1,000 words closer to my target. But for some reason – and I know I'm not alone in this – I will sometimes do *anything* to avoid sitting at my desk and putting pen to paper. When faced with the prospect of doing some more work on my doctorate, I'd often find that the most mundane of household tasks would take on irresistible and urgent proportions – I *must* do the dusting (I hate dusting), I really *must* clean the oven (an awful job), it really *is* time I cleared the garage out (I hate spiders) – anything, just to put off the evil moment for a bit longer.

And it's not just the mundane which distracts you. At times, you'll be over-whelmed by a sense of indignance: why should I sit at my desk when everyone else is getting on with their lives? I need a life too. Yes, of course I want my doctorate, but I mustn't lose touch with my friends, family, and the landlord of my local, must I? The landlord needs me to keep him in business. And what about the Imps? Lincoln City FC NEED my support on a Saturday afternoon, I'd be letting them down if I didn't go to the match, and that fresh air is better for me than sitting at my desk, right?

The list of distractions is endless, but if we're honest, it's only as endless as we allow it to be. Sooner or later, you realise that no one is going to come along and write your thesis for you, so you have no choice (because your pride won't let you give up) but to just get on with it.

Where to work

It's important to create a suitable environment to work in – preferably somewhere where you can leave mountains of paper, 'arranged' no doubt, in an order which is a mystery to everyone but yourself – so that you can pick up where you left off with the minimum of ceremony.

When to work

You'll know as well, what time of day is likely to be your most productive. For me, that was, and still is, between around 10.00 p.m. and 2.00 a.m. – later if I don't have work the next day. Why? Probably because the quality of TV programmes takes a noticeable nosedive between those times (although if you trawl through the cable channels carefully enough, you can usually find something to watch … No! Stop it! You're allowing yourself to be distracted again!).

Getting into intense writing mode is so rewarding – your brain works overtime and you wonder if you'll be able to switch it off, but the satisfaction derived from committing a few more thousand words to paper, and getting a few more thousand words nearer to your goal, makes the effort worthwhile.

Pen or keyboard?

In the early stages of my doctoral studies, I made the mistake of thinking that I should be able to write straight on to the computer. I'm more than competent on the keyboard, and I assumed that that would be the most efficient way of writing. However, I soon discovered that the quality of my writing was not as good when I tried to work in this way, so I reverted to writing everything in longhand first.

On the face of it, this might seem to be a more time-consuming approach, but this isn't necessarily so. Once I accepted the fact that I was unable to express myself effectively by composing straight on to the PC [personal computer], I developed a routine of writing a section, or chapter, in longhand, writing probably 15–20 pages, before attempting to commit it to electronic format. This meant that when I did come to type up what I'd written, I'd developed a better feel for what I was trying to say in that particular section, and the typing up process became the main editing process. I've spoken with fellow doctoral students who've told me about the 10–12 drafts of their theses which they've produced along the way – that, to me, is enough to put anyone off embarking on this particular journey. By editing my handwritten words during the typing up stage, I found that rewrites were rarely necessary. My handwritten paragraphs were nearly always full of crossings out and arrows, indicating where various sentences or sections should be moved to and from, as it's almost impossible to write perfectly first time, so by the time I came to write up my work, I could concentrate on improving my sentence structure, and ensuring that what I'd written flowed well.

So, don't feel inadequate if you're unable to write straight on to the PC, and don't assume that writing longhand is ultimately a more time-consuming first stage. If it eliminates the need for multiple drafts and redrafts, it can actually *save* time.

The bibliography

If you leave the bibliography until the end of the writing process, it'll turn into a monstrously large task. You can spend hours searching for the full reference relating to a quote which really *must* stay in your thesis.

But you can avoid this scenario quite easily by creating a bibliography file when you first start writing. For each text, article and website I used, I didn't just make a note somewhere, I recorded it in detail, in the correct format and sequence, in a separate bibliography file on the computer. I'm convinced that this saved me a huge amount of time in the long run. As the editing process progresses, you'll almost certainly want to discard some quotes which you initially considered to be vital to your message, but these can easily be deleted in the latter stages – you just need to run a check on the author's name or a keyword, using the 'Find' facility and remove from the bibliography file, any reference to sources which haven't made the final draft.

In conclusion

Now I have completed my doctorate, I consider myself to be a leading authority on 'how to avoid your doctorate' – maybe there's another thesis in there somewhere ...? If you're more disciplined than I am, congratulations! But if you examine your own situation and recognise the propensity to stray from the task, take heart – you can still get there.

9 Production Values in the Doctoral Thesis

CHAPTER CONTENTS

In Chapter 8, we discussed the writing process and looked at different styles of writing and presenting. In this chapter, we discuss the values associated with the production of the doctoral thesis. This is partly a matter of coming to terms with the qualities to be expected of a thesis at doctoral level, as opposed to those of a Masters dissertation for example. It also relates to the structure of the thesis, which includes the balance or proportion of the different components of the work. Furthermore, it involves issues of presentation at a technical level. Together, these considerations contribute to sound production values in the putting together of the thesis and submitting it for examination.

The distinctive qualities of a doctoral thesis

It is common to talk of 'doctoral quality', but often it is less clear exactly what this means. In the production of the thesis, there are a number of qualities that would be expected, many of which would also be found in a good Masters dissertation. The distinctive challenge at doctoral level is to put together a long and sustained piece of work. The PhD thesis is normally 80,000 to 100,000 words, and so four to five times the length of a Masters dissertation which is generally about 20,000 words long. The thesis for a taught doctorate is usually at least 40,000 words in length, and often 50,000 words, and this is also a significantly greater challenge in terms of the process of production than is the Masters dissertation.

The greater length available at doctoral level affords more opportunity to exhibit skills and insights related to the topic of the work. It allows for sustained discussion and argument. It permits detailed engagement with existing literature to show the strengths and limitations of previous work. It gives scope for a thorough examination of the methods to be developed, and the advantages of one research strategy over another. It makes it possible to develop both depth and breadth in pursuing a research topic – depth in detail and focus, breadth in range and scope. It offers a large enough canvas to create a significant contribution to the field being studied. A Masters dissertation may be able to develop some of these features, but it is very difficult for it to exhibit them all and it would not be expected to do so. In part this is because of the greater time that the doctoral thesis takes to complete, and therefore the opportunity for more reading, thinking and fieldwork. It is also because of the more substantial character of the final product. And yet, although this qualitative difference is inherent in the nature of the exercise, the production of the final thesis is vital to making the most of the opportunity that is available at this level.

Structuring the thesis

Producing the thesis as a sustained and coherent piece of work requires the author to have a clear sense of its various constituent parts and of how they should fit together. No two theses are exactly the same, and we would not want to give the impression that there is a single blueprint for a good piece of work, and still less for success in the final outcome. Nevertheless, there is such a thing as a conventional thesis structure, and this may be helpful as a starting point towards conceptualising how to develop the work as a whole. As with other aspects of the research project, moreover, this is rarely a straightforward or linear process, but tends to take place in an untidy fashion.

This process is well conveyed by one of our students who recalls the decisions made on the structuring of his thesis and how this related to the production in general. He makes a clear connection between the idea that there was an overall 'tale to tell', and the planning of the structure of the thesis. He notes that the decision was taken to produce a thesis with a 'conventional structure' because 'the tale could effectively be conveyed by that form'. According to this student,

> In its turn this meant that the thesis acquired a whole shape, something that I captured as a big messy cartoon on the study wall. This allowed the linkages to be plotted, identified the research, the things not known and the word length of each section. It sustained two years' work!

Moreover, he adds, this process had no particular order, indeed it was fundamentally disorderly in its character:

The approach made it possible to simultaneously write and research – with starts being made in two or three places, the methodology, the background, and the research itself. Some sections of the thesis done in this way were repeatedly changed by later work, but needed to be written in the first place. The opening chapters were the best examples of this, being drafted and re-drafted many times as the rest of the thesis developed. The last chapter to be completed was chapter one!

In other words, working with 'bits of thesis' meant also having 'times when it was seen as a whole'. It was crucial to have a sense of both aspects, the parts and the whole, in order to develop either.

With these points in view, let us try to examine what would be involved in a 'conventional structure' for a thesis, and what might generally be included in each section. Such a basic structure would comprise the following parts:

- Introduction.
- Theoretical framework/literature review.
- Method.
- Fieldwork (presentation and discussion).
- Conclusion.

This kind of template, with minor variations, is familiar in thesis production. It suggests overall a movement from a discussion of general issues to a focus on a particular research problem. Addressing or elucidating the research problem leads in turn to a deeper and fuller understanding of the general issues. The component parts of this general scenario might be conceptualised as follows.

INTRODUCTION

The introductory section to a thesis sets the scene for the thesis as a whole and should give the reader a clear sense of what to expect in the rest of the thesis. It should not attempt to provide substantive details or prolonged discussion of particular aspects, but simply to introduce and form a basis for what follows. The points that need to be made here are along the following lines:

- area of study;
- focus of study;
- key research questions;

- the bounds of the research;
- personal and professional commitment to the research;
- type of study;
- how to set about it;
- the significance of the study in relation to the existing literature;
- theoretical considerations; and
- the structure or format of the thesis.

We have encountered most of these issues already in the current work and here we are beginning to knit them together. There is a certain logic in the ordering of these constituent parts; basically it allows you to say *what* you are trying to do, then *how* you propose to set about it, and then *why* you think it is important, interesting and generally significant. These are the three key aspects to the research that need to be established from the outset.

It is helpful to clarify the area of study, focus of study and research questions in the first few pages of the introduction. This gives a clear purpose to the work. Often this may be developed further by noting the boundaries of the research. While you are trying to map out the territory in which you will be asserting your expertise, you also explain the related areas that you will not be pursuing in your work. There should be an intellectual basis for these decisions, which you can discuss in brief at this point. This is useful in helping to pre-empt a potential criticism that you have not looked at a particular set of issues in your research. If you explain the reasoning underlying your work as soon as you can, you are effectively forestalling this kind of criticism.

Often the introduction can also be used to explain why you have been interested in the topic of research that you are addressing in your thesis. This may be framed in terms of personal commitment or experience, for example in relation to issues that you have encountered in your own personal development or within your family. It may also be conceived in terms of professional relevance, for example the aims of your own work institution. Such issues may be elaborated further later in the thesis, perhaps in the methodology chapter, but rehearsing them here can help to explain the underlying assumptions and aims of the work.

The next set of issues tackled in the introduction often concern *how* you are going to set about addressing the topic and in particular the research questions that you have defined. This means first of all clarifying the method or methods that you have chosen for the study, and the kinds of sources that you will be drawing upon. It also entails declaring the kind of study that you are setting out to write. Is it a history? Or a case study? Or an ethnography? If so, of what kind? Often it is difficult to categorise the study neatly. If so, it might be seen as a combination or mixture of different types. Again, it can be helpful to try to define this as clearly as possible in order to give the reader an early understanding of the nature of the work.

The introduction may then proceed to explaining *why* you see the work as constituting a significant contribution to the topic and the field to which it belongs. A useful way of achieving this, without developing a full or extended discussion, can be to pick out two or three key works that are relevant to the topic. These can be surveyed briefly to explain how they suggest certain findings and assumptions in the field, and also to indicate gaps or other limitations that you are wanting to address through your own research. This is the starting point of grounding your thesis in the existing literature, and can be followed through in more detail in subsequent chapters. You may see the significance of the study partly at least in terms of its theoretical implications, perhaps confirming or modifying a particular body of theory, or approaching a topic through a specific and defined theoretical perspective. This can also be raised at this stage.

THEORETICAL FRAMEWORK/LITERATURE REVIEW

On a conventional pattern for a doctoral thesis, the next section would deal with the general background considerations within which your research is operating. Here there is a further qualitative difference in relation to the general run of Masters dissertations that should be taken into account. At the Masters level, it is appropriate to talk in terms of a 'literature review' that surveys the existing literature in relation to the chosen topic, which will probably be very small. At the doctoral level, it is not sufficient to survey the related literature; you should be engaging critically with the literature to discuss its strengths and limitations for the purposes of your research. This purpose may be conveyed more clearly by the development of a 'theoretical framework' for the research, using published literature to generate such a framework. The key aim of this section is to relate your research project to the issues raised in previous work, in such a fashion as to demonstrate the need for and importance of your contribution.

As part of this discussion, it can be very helpful to develop key themes identified from the literature that are relevant to your topic. It is important to do so in a focused way that raises questions to which you will seek to contribute through your research. Many doctoral theses include a rather indiscriminate account of previous work in the area that has little or no clear leverage on the topic of the research, but this is best avoided as it leads to irrelevance and also potentially excessive length that looks like 'padding'. A useful guideline here is, never raise a question that you do not mean to answer through your research.

This section can also be framed fully or partly as a historical introduction to the topic of the research, explaining the general historical background and development of the issues involved. Some historical dimension, however brief, is helpful in a very wide range of research topics even if the major preoccupation is with issues that appear to be purely contemporary. Again, care should be taken to frame this kind of discussion in terms of providing leverage or explanatory power for your research. A long list of dates and events, on its own, does not provide the kind of historical introduction that is required at this level.

METHOD AND METHODOLOGY

The method chapter is de rigueur for the modern doctoral thesis. It is important to use this to explain in as detailed a way as possible the steps that you have taken at every stage in your research process. You should also explain why you have developed one set of strategies rather than another – the methodology of your research as distinct from the method. There is a large and growing literature available on research method and methodology, and your discussion should be grounded in this to exhibit an informed and thoughtful approach to your research. The ethical dimensions of the research should also be rehearsed. It is increasingly common to develop a discussion of the problems and wrong turnings of the research project, or as it is often expressed a 'reflexive' approach to the experience of the research, although there is some debate over whether doctoral theses should spend time and space in dwelling on these (see, for example, Walford 1998).

FIELDWORK

The fieldwork section should document in full detail the research conducted to address the themes of the project. It needs to provide appropriate evidence to support an extended discussion of what you have found out about the topic. Much of this may be descriptive in the sense that you are reporting on findings, for example from a questionnaire survey. It should also provide commentary and argument about the implications of these findings. Some theses have separate sections on the description and discussion of findings. Such an approach should be treated with care, as it can become repetitive, but it acts as a reminder that it is important to both *present* and *discuss* data, and not do one without the other. In many ways, the presentation and discussion of original (fieldwork) data form the heart of the thesis, the most important part, which are based on your own research and will be found nowhere else, so special attention should be paid to developing this section clearly and fully.

CONCLUSION

The conclusion is often written quite hastily as an afterthought, but in fact it is another very important section that deserves careful preparation. It should not be used to develop substantive new material, but is an opportunity to emphasise what has been shown through the research and discussion in the work as a whole. This might well be done by returning to the key research questions raised in the introduction, in order to discuss how they have been addressed, and how our understanding of them has been extended and deepened. The overall argument developed in the thesis may also be elaborated in the conclusion to make sure that it is completely clear to the reader. It can be useful to explain briefly what you have learned about the research process during your doctoral project, and if there are any outstanding issues that arise from your findings you might like to point to further research that would be useful for other researchers to take up.

Proportion and length

In discussing the different sections of the thesis we have not paid any attention to their relative lengths and the overall proportions that should be kept in view. On the basis of a thesis comprising 80,000 words, the following guidelines may be helpful for each of the sections:

- **Introduction: 5,000 words.**
- **Theoretical framework: 10,000–15,000 words.**
- **Method: 10,000–15,000 words.**
- **Fieldwork: 40,000–50,000 words.**
- **Conclusion: 5,000 words.**

From this it can be seen that the fieldwork section might well take up one-half or more of the content of the thesis, or the equivalent of three or four substantial chapters. Here again there is an important difference in relation to the majority of Masters dissertations. The latter might give more or less equal space to an introduction, a literature review, a methods chapter, a fieldwork chapter, and a conclusion. In a doctoral thesis, while it is vital still to provide detail and discussion on other matters, the fieldwork takes pride of place and occupies a large amount of space. If one were to depict the structure in terms of word length and proportion, therefore, it might look something like this:

- Introduction.
- Theoretical framework.
- Methods.
- Fieldwork I.
- Fieldwork II.
- Fieldwork III.
- Fieldwork IV.
- Conclusions.

In order to sustain such a structured account, there will need to be a large amount of data or evidence generated from the fieldwork, and the analysis of this data will be closely related to the way in which the fieldwork chapters are divided up.

Many students are anxious, especially early on in their research, about the prospect of having to write 80,000 words. The size of the task seems highly daunting. And yet in practice it is comparatively rare to find that a draft thesis is too short. In the majority of cases the manuscript is too long, and sometimes even double the appropriate length, and has to be cut back quite severely. This can be for a number of reasons. First, the focus may not be defined clearly enough, and so the work becomes diffuse and potentially rambling in nature. Second, there may be too much material on background theory, literature and history. In some cases the reader may be waiting with increasing impatience well past page 100 to find some actual fieldwork or data against which to relate the background discussion. Third, there may be such a richness of data that to restrict discussion and documentation is difficult. This is often especially the case where interview evidence is used, because it tends to generate rich testimony that can be quoted extensively, and also because the researcher is anxious to do justice to the human stories that they have been entrusted with to pass on to the reader. Fourth, the approach taken by the author may be too descriptive, so that pages may be taken up in relaying ideas and issues that might only require a few lines of discussion.

In many cases it can be relatively straightforward to cut back on the content of the material, although there can be no doubt that it is often very painful to do so. Often where the material is obviously repetitive there may be clear decisions to be made. If possible, it is usually preferable to retain the detail and discussion of the fieldwork chapters, which as we have said are original to the thesis. For this reason, where length is excessive, the early chapters of the thesis might be reviewed with particular care to see where cuts can usefully be made. Finally, if all else fails, the focus of the thesis might be reassessed and if necessary made narrower so as to exclude some of the data and discussion from the account.

Quite often in the final drafting of the thesis, material needs to be moved around from chapter to chapter so that optimum use can be made of it. This happens frequently with fieldwork material, which might be deployed to support different stages of the discussion and a choice needs to be made about where best to put it. A key quotation might be moved from the middle of a chapter, where it may be buried, to a more prominent position perhaps in the introduction. These are all strategic decisions about how best to tell the story that you are aiming to put across to the reader in the clearest possible way.

Presentation

The final presentation of the thesis involves a number of technical exercises which although tedious are nevertheless very important for their contribution to the success of the research project. Often, theses which are the product of years of hard work can be let down by failure to pay attention to presentational issues at the final stage. These include the formal requirement of the thesis abstract. They also relate to the presentation of the references and the bibliography of the work as a whole, and the avoidance of typographical errors in the text of the thesis.

The abstract is normally included at the very front of the thesis, but is usually the last item to be written. It is basically a summary of the thesis, and again should not be treated lightly because it has a key strategic role for the work as a whole. It articulates the general argument of the work, and describes briefly the methods, key findings and main significance of the study. It should not be more than one page in length, and should not include references and quotes. It should be consistent with the discussion developed in the thesis itself – this should hardly need saying, but a surprising number of thesis abstracts fail to meet this test. It should be clear and straightforward in its summary of the work. In combination with the introductory chapter, the abstract should leave the reader with no doubt as to what the thesis is trying to achieve and how it is setting about it.

Sometimes the abstract sets the author of the thesis a difficult challenge. In some cases, the argument or significance seems elusive; in others, the work cannot be summarised in less than three pages. Where these problems arise it is often a warning of a larger difficulty about the thesis itself – the argument is indistinct, the focus is unclear or the significance is not articulated. It may be a warning to the author to go back to the text of the thesis as a whole and to rewrite and develop it further to make sure that these points are clearly covered.

A further task in the final stages of preparing the thesis is to check all of the references and the bibliography at the end of the work. Again, it is surprising how often the bibliography is left incomplete. All works referred to in the text of the thesis should be included in the bibliography; also, works that are not referred to in the text should not be included in the bibliography. Lapses can occur especially when references are added in the final stages of preparing the thesis. Items can easily go missing in these circumstances. Also page numbers should be included for chapters and journal articles, and the date of the work should be shown. Quite often the date on the reference in the text is not consistent with that shown for the item in the bibliography; this again should be checked systematically.

Finally, the work as a whole should be thoroughly proofread for typographical errors. It is very rare for a thesis to have no errors of this kind, as some will evade even the most exhaustive search. Nevertheless, a significant number of typographical errors will attract attention and will mar the work as a whole. It is unwise to depend on a spellcheck on the computer as many typographical errors will still slip through.

It may seem surprising and depressing that we set such store by these matters of presentation which may seem trivial alongside the major issues that you have addressed in the thesis. We make no apology for this, and would merely say that faulty presentation is regularly highlighted in examiners' criticisms of doctoral work. This seems to us unnecessary as it is so easy, if tedious, to set right. Also, once examiners start to recommend presentational changes they are more likely to begin insisting that minor changes relating to the content of the thesis should be made at the same time. And this takes us conveniently to the topic of our next two chapters, which focus on what happens after your work is finally submitted.

Cameo: Writing the thesis – a personal account from which it might be hard to generalise much

Paul Machon

What surprises, only 18 months after the completion of the thesis, is how untroubled the memory of the work has become, a view supported by the fat and shiny copy of the thesis that sits just in view, parts of which already seem to have been written by someone else. Only the research diaries, the lack of holidays and comments from others who endured the experience prod memories of the work's trials and the way it seeped into everything. Against uncertain memories it feels risky and presumptuous to offer a personal account of how the thesis was written; risky because one's account could be too polished and presumptuous because there's no certainty that one person's experience can be extended to others – hence the title. But let's try, and when any reader has completed their own thesis they will be the best judge of what's here.

The single greatest piece of help I had came when there was – clearly – a tale to tell. Elements of that tale, big elements too, had been rehearsed in discussion, in limited papers and had been supported by evidence that was initially collected. But somewhere near the start of the two year research and writing period one story, suddenly, came together from, perhaps because of, these earlier efforts. At that point planning the structure of the thesis became straightforward and big decisions were made about the work to be done. First amongst these decisions was to produce a thesis that would have a conventional structure because the tale could effectively be conveyed by that form. In its turn this meant that the thesis acquired a whole shape, something that I captured as a big messy cartoon on the study wall. This allowed the linkages to be plotted, identified the research, the things not known and the word length of each section. It sustained two years' work! The approach made it possible to simultaneously write *and* research – with starts being made in two or three places, the methodology, the background and the research itself. Some sections of the thesis done in this way were repeatedly changed by later work, but needed to be written in the first place. The opening chapters were the best examples of this, being drafted and redrafted many times as the rest of the thesis developed. The last chapter to be completed was chapter one! Having lots of writing and research under way at once allowed the thesis to be a constant companion. If demands at work were considerable a single and 'easy' section could be whittled at. When things were easier sustained time could be put into the research itself, the documents and interviews – but it seemed important to always be doing something.

Implicit in the last comment was knowledge of how I work best, and then planning to work in a way that played to that understanding. I can't write quickly, can't write to a fixed number of words in one go and so wasn't able to stop fiddling with what had already been done. Having something to do at all times suited me because I could prune those over-long sections – or write them for the first time, and work on the databases, graphs and tables that were part of my thesis. Working this way was slow, and slowed more as the thesis neared completion; I was never able to write a later part of a chapter without reading the opening section, and sometimes related chapters. Towards the end, this initial reading outweighed writing by huge amounts. Saying when something would have to do – was finished – always turned out to be difficult. This was one of a range of places where my supervisor was such an important and critical (in all senses) friend. Working with bits of thesis required times when it was seen as a whole; these all-through readings took time, but were important as they revealed both duplication (easy to deal with) and gaps (tougher – and on a couple of occasions requiring significant changes). As the research developed its outcomes were first fed into the core chapters and then rippled through the remainder. This was time-consuming but was worth it, and spectacularly for the two eureka moments when the research results just clicked into the narrative as though niches were made for them – for then the tale *had* to be right!

Like a shadow to the planning was the computing that supported it. I was determined that this would not be another enemy to fight but an ally in support of completing the work. Alongside the planning cartoon I developed architecture of directories and files with taxonomy of their own. This planning was done before I wrote a word and extended to a default font and page set-up. I was also determined not to lose anything, and so copied and re-copied files, backing-up onto a Zip® drive, the network at college, and e-mailing files to myself as attachments.

Lost in this short story is the enjoyment of being able to expose, from widely scattered data, a single tale being told for the first time. Missing too is any sense of the others who were involved in the production of the thesis. What I hope is not lost is a sharp sense that it was worthwhile, and that after it's over things seem different.

Part 5
Presenting and Sharing Research

10 Presenting your Work at the Viva

CHAPTER CONTENTS

Many doctoral students, especially those who are 'researching professionals', will be experienced at presenting orally during their own working lives. But presenting in the viva situation is likely to be a new experience and to offer a new challenge. For every doctoral candidate the oral examination is an important matter. For some it is a cause of anxiety and concern. As Tinkler and Jackson (2002) put it, the examination by viva voce (live voice) is of critical importance for two reasons: first, it is a site of decision-making and, second, the viva experience has an important influence on students' perceptions of academia. Research reported later on the viva show that it is not always a positive experience for students, even when they are successful. This chapter reports on the purposes and conduct of the oral examination, and discusses some of the contentious issues that surround it, from different perspectives. We also present some of the general questions that are likely to be posed in a viva, and offer suggestions for preparing for them and answering them in the 'live' situation.

The purposes of the viva

Written regulations from universities should state the purpose of the viva. Common statements include: to test the candidate's knowledge of his or her research and subject area; to allow examiners to clarify any queries that may have arisen when reading the thesis; to judge whether the candidate has developed research skills appropriate to doctoral level; to give the candidate the opportunity to 'defend' the thesis in person; to establish whether candidates fully understand the implications of their work. Some university regulations state explicitly that one of the main purposes is to ascertain whether the work is the candidate's own.

Many regulations inform us (that is, the student, the supervisor and the examiners) that the viva is an integral part of the examination of the degree – in other words, the oral is actually part of the examining process, not (say) a confirmation of any pre-determined judgement. It is not a rubber-stamping exercise. Students, supervisors and examiners perhaps need to remind themselves of this – the examination as a whole involves more than just a judgement of the written work, that is, the written and oral elements of the examination for a doctorate complement each other. For many universities, the written thesis is only 'part fulfilment' of the requirements for a doctorate.

From a more negative perspective, if a thesis does not meet the necessary criteria, some university regulations state that one purpose of the oral is to ascertain reasons why a student's work is *not deemed to* attain doctoral standard. This might lead to questions about supervision, research training, resources or any mitigating personal circumstances.

Conduct

Normally, the oral examination or viva should be arranged within a set time period from receipt of the thesis by the examiners. This might be 10 weeks or even 12 weeks – regulations should be checked for this. The internal examiner or the supervisor (regulations vary) will have responsibility for arranging the date of the oral with the external – this date should then be confirmed with the student, at the very least two weeks prior to the suggested date. A suitable venue is arranged, usually on the campus of the awarding university.

Both examiners should normally complete a preliminary report on the thesis independently and then arrange to confer prior to the oral. This liaison or meeting should be used to exchange and discuss their preliminary reports (these reports are not seen by the student or supervisor). The two examiners should also decide on the procedure and content of the viva, that is, what will be asked, who will be asking what and in what order. A good oral should have some sort of structure with prearranged questions and issues, and a predetermined order. However, an oral should be viewed rather like a semi-structured interview – the discussion, if it is a good one, may lead on to other questions and sub-questions, and deviate from the plan (see later).

In many universities, the external examiner will be expected and invited to chair the oral. However, it is still the internal examiner's responsibility to check that procedures are followed correctly. In some cases (described as 'exceptional' in some university regulations) the supervisor may be present at the oral – but he or she should certainly not play a part in the actual discussion. Our view is that the student should confer with the supervisor on this issue and make the request between them. For example, one student might feel that the supervisor's presence could give them support and confidence. A supervisor's presence may also be valuable when it comes to making notes, especially if revisions are ultimately required. Another might feel that the supervisor could be a distraction or an impediment to a full discussion. In all cases, if the supervisor is present, eye contact between student and supervisor seems best avoided (a suitable arrangement of chairs could ensure this).

Issues and concerns

There are numerous issues around the viva, its conduct and its purpose:

- **the wide variation between vivas, not only between institutions but within them;**
- **the lack of 'transparency' in the conduct of orals; and**
- **the lack of 'quality assurance' procedures involved.**

We raise and discuss some of those here, and give pointers to some very useful and insightful further reading on this issue.

Variability in the conduct and content of vivas is widely acknowledged (Cryer, 2000; Tinkler and Jackson, 2002; and many others). This variability is discussed shortly, but it is worth noting that the 'variations in vivas' (Morley et al., 2002) makes it difficult and dangerous to attempt to provide definitive guidelines and 'tips' to students. It also implies that a mock or practice viva should be treated with care – no guarantee can be made that it prepares or predicts with any success.

Several aspects of variability in policy and practice should be highlighted. Some useful research by Jackson and Tinkler (2001) showed that even institutional policy and written regulations showed great variation. In a sample of 20 universities they found that seven did not require examiners to produce independent reports prior to the viva. At the other extreme, one university actually stipulated that examiners should make a definite recommendation prior to the viva, implying that the oral is not really an integral part of the examination process.

The general view of recent research is that there is a great lack of clarity and transparency in the conduct and content of the actual viva. This is especially true in the UK where the oral is conducted behind closed doors, between consenting adults. One author has called the viva the 'best kept secret in higher education' (Burnham, 1994), while Morley et al. (2002) talk of variation and 'mystification'. The response to this lack of clarity has been interesting. One extreme suggestion has been to argue for the abolition of the viva, for example Noble (1994, p. 67) described it as 'an anachronism that can be traced back to the middle ages'. More commonly, calls have been made for the oral to be more public (similar to the situation in the USA and Scandinavia). In the past, the viva has been subject to very little regulation, accountability and quality assurance, in sharp contrast to other aspects of higher education. Calls have been made for transparency, clear guidelines and even nationally agreed standards (Morley et al., 2002).

Jackson and Tinkler (2001) argue that the essential step required, before such guidelines and recommendations can be made, is to clarify the purposes of the viva. Their research concluded that there is 'no consensus regarding the roles of the viva in the PhD examination process' (p. 364). This lack of agreed role and purpose may also apply to the 'professional doctorate', although there is a shortage of reported research in this area. The academics (supervisors and examiners) responding to their survey mentioned a range of roles for the viva that included: ensuring authenticity; checking the student's understanding and research ability; clarifying areas of weakness; testing knowledge of the literature; assessing oral skills; and checking that students can defend their thesis. Perhaps the most important finding is that for many academics, the purpose of the viva varies according to the quality of the written thesis that examiners read before the viva. Thus some academics view the viva following a strong thesis as a way of discussing and developing ideas with that student, and even offering advice on publication. For a weaker or borderline thesis, the viva might be used as a forum for giving constructive feedback and guidance – though some respondents saw it as an opportunity for the student to defend her or his work. In extreme cases of a weaker thesis, some academics commented that little could be done in a viva for the student to redeem himself or herself, describing it as a 'painful ritual' (p. 360).

One finding from Jackson and Tinkler's sample of academics is that 74 per cent of their respondents felt that the viva merely confirmed the examiner's prior opinion. One remarked that in over 50 vivas he or she did not know of an examiner changing his or her mind about the result (p. 361). This resonates with another surprising finding from the survey that 47 per cent of candidates in the arts, humanities and social sciences were informed of the examiners' decision at the start of the viva (c.f. only

15 per cent in the natural sciences). This seems astonishing, given that many university regulations explicitly forbid this and argue that the viva is an integral part of the examination. The above finding would suggest either that many examiners in this survey were not reading regulations or that they were ignoring them.

Students' perspectives and experiences

A number of interesting, if occasionally worrying, studies have been conducted on the student's view of the viva. Again, the focus has been largely on the PhD experience rather than the professional doctorate. Prior to the viva, most studies unsurprisingly report that students vary from being confident to anxious to extremely anxious (Hartley and Jory, 2000), in some cases saying they feel 'sick' or 'terrified'.

Following the viva, reported student experiences vary (predictably) according to the outcome. Thus the successful students in Hartley and Jory's study of psychology graduates (the passers) were most likely to report a boost in their morale and self-esteem, although one passer felt that his self-esteem had been reduced. The majority, whether passing or otherwise, seemed to find the experience 'draining'. The time allotted to the vivas experienced in this study ranged from 45 minutes to 4.25 hours. The vast majority of the students surveyed felt that the viva had been fair, especially the passers. In response to an open question about ideas for improvement to the viva, a significant number suggested the need for standardisation (for example, on length and guidelines) and less variability. The research by Jackson and Tinkler (2001) reported more negative experiences than Hartley and Jory, even amongst the passers. Some of the responses spoke of 'misery and humiliation, harassment and suffering' (p. 362). From 88 respondents, 20 per cent described the tone of their viva as 'hostile', 'sarcastic' or 'insulting' – although 60 per cent were more positive using adjectives such as 'relaxed', 'friendly' and 'enjoyable'. One of the interesting points to note is that an important number of candidates reported that their perceptions of 'academic competence' had decreased as a result of the viva, as had their desire to work within academia (even one-tenth of the passers expressed this negative view).

THE VIVA IN THE PROFESSIONAL DOCTORATE

Again, it must be emphasised that this research did not cover the professional doctorate, where the desire to enter academia may be less relevant. It should also be noted that there is a high probability that the examiners and supervisors of doctorates (whether professional or otherwise) do not themselves have a professional doctorate. There is a dearth of research on the assessment process, especially the viva, in the professional doctorate. It seems likely that the variability, inconsistency, unpredictability, privacy and lack of transparency will be as prevalent here as in the traditional PhD context.

One of the criteria for the assessment of a professional doctorate as opposed to a traditional PhD relates to our discussion earlier in this book, on the nature of different doctorates. The former can be seen (rather glibly) as producing 'researching professionals', with the latter aiming to prepare 'professional researchers' and some sort of entry or initiation into academia following 'live' peer review (though some might term it vivisection). These different conceptions should be reflected in the viva in the different contexts, though in reality this may not always happen and the actual event will depend (as always) on the two examiners and the way they work together.

Content

The 'content' of an oral examination will inevitably vary from one thesis to another, one field to another and between disciplines. However, there are certain general procedures for 'good practice' that are likely to be followed, and indeed many University regulations insist that they are followed. We outline some of these shortly. Later, we list questions that we know have been, and still are, actually used in vivas.

GOOD PRACTICE

Students should expect certain aspects of 'good practice' to be followed for the viva, although reality may fall short in some respects. The responsibility for ensuring good practice should fall on both the internal and external examiners. The venue for the viva may be someone's office or it could be a seminar or meetings room. The room for the viva should be suitably laid out with seating organised so that eye contact can be made between student and examiners (if the supervisor is present, he or she should literally take more of a back seat). The viva should start with polite introductions all round, led by the external examiner if he or she is the chair. The chair should explain what the viva is for, that is, a focused discussion (not an interrogation), with others who know the field, which gives the student a chance to 'defend' the thesis. Most regulations do not permit examiners to tell students whether they have passed or failed at the start of the viva – this seems perfectly logical given that the viva is an integral part of the examination. No specific recommendations (regarding pass, fail, minor amend-ments, re-submission) should be made at all during the course of the viva – they should be conveyed clearly after the examiners have conferred when the viva has finished. However, it seems civilised and conducive to a good discussion, to put the student at ease with a comment such as 'we have enjoyed reading your thesis, we found it very interesting and it raises some important issues'.

For most candidates, this will be their first viva (and possibly the last) so examiners should explain the process and procedures to them (in brief) – again with the aim of making them less nervous. It would seem to be good practice to start with a relatively easy, 'warm-up' question: 'tell us in brief what your thesis is about'; 'why did you choose this topic to research? What surprised you most in doing this study?' Specific questions will then follow, not all of which should have been pre-planned.

QUESTIONS THAT MIGHT BE ASKED IN A VIVA FOR A DOCTORATE (THOUGH PROBABLY NOT IN THIS ORDER)

General

Motivation: what made you do this piece of research? Why did you choose this topic? Why do think it is important?

Position: what is your own position (professional or personal) in relation to this field and these research questions? What prior conceptions and/or experiences did you bring to this study? How did your own position/background/bias affect your data analysis and your data collection?

Contribution: please could you summarise your thesis? What are the main findings of your research? What would somebody from this field learn from reading your thesis that they did not know before? What did you learn from doing it? What original contribution to knowledge do you feel that you have made?

Publication: which elements of your work do you feel are worthy of publication and/or presentation at a conference? What plans do you have for publication and dissemination? Has any of the work been published or presented already? (Note that the practice of disseminating some of the work via [say] a conference presenta-tion or a journal paper is within the regulations of most universities – check your regulations on this.)

Theories and theoretical frameworks

Please talk us through the main research questions that you were trying to address in your work. What was the origin of these questions?

What theories/theoretical frameworks/perspectives have you drawn upon in your research?

Which theories did your study illuminate, if any?

Literature review

What shaped or guided your literature review? Why did it cover the areas that it did? (And not others?) Why did you/did you not include the work of X in your study?

On methodology and analysis of data

Methodology: why did you employ the methods you used? Why not others, for example X? What informed your choice of methods? What would you do differently, with hindsight?

The sample: why did you select this sample? Can you see any problems with it? If it is a small-scale study, can you justify why so few were involved? (Note that these questions would only apply with certain types of research.)

Data analysis: did anything surprise you in the data ('hit you in the face')? Any anomalies? How did you analyse your data? How did you categorise/filter the data? Did themes emerge from your data (a posteriori) or did you 'bring them to the data' (a priori)? Why did you analyse it in this way? Could it have been done in another way?

Further work: which aspects of the work could be taken further? How?

Generalisability and key messages

How far do think you can generalise from your work? What lessons can be learnt from it by practitioners/ policy-makers/ other researchers? The 'so what' question: what are its key messages and implications?

Open forum

Reflections on the thesis: what are its strengths? And its limitations or weaknesses (with hindsight)? Is there anything else you would like to say or discuss that we have not asked you about?

GOOD PRACTICE IN ASKING QUESTIONS

Some university regulations actually give general guidance on good practice in asking questions. The University of Newcastle Handbook for Examiners of Research Degrees (2001) is particularly helpful here. The bullet points below are adapted from that handbook (pp. 7–8). Examiners should:

- **ask questions in a constructive and positive way, as opposed to negative and confrontational, for example, 'why did you use method X?' as opposed to 'why on Earth did you decide to do Y?';**
- **use a range of questioning techniques, that is, closed and open, specific and general;**
- **allow candidates time to reflect and to answer and encourage them to do this, that is, not to rush but to take time and reflect before answering;**
- **praise good answers, for example, if they are insightful, incisive or really help to clarify an issue or argument in the thesis; and**
- **give candidates the opportunity to recover from a poor answer that may be a result of nerves or misunderstanding. Examiners may rephrase a question and pose it in a different way, thus helping not only to clarify it but also to allow the student some recovery time.**

Some of these points are particularly important when English is an additional language for the student. The candidate may be far more adept with written English than with oral situations. The onus is on examiners to speak clearly, to pose questions that are brief, clear and actually make sense, and to give students time to answer – indeed, this is good practice whatever the student's first language.

BAD PRACTICE AND STRANGE BEHAVIOUR IN THE CONDUCT OF VIVAS

We have personally witnessed, and heard many malicious rumours about, some of the poor practice and unusual behaviours that can take place in an oral examination. Fortunately, our estimate is that these happen very rarely.

Some examiners seem to arrive with a bee, or several bees, in their bonnets. They have rigid views on what or whose writing should be included in a thesis. Very often, such people will expect the student to have cited this examiner's own work or to have read their latest book or web page. Others will 'show off' in the viva, in an attempt to impress the student, the internal examiner and the supervisor, if the latter is present. They will spend more time talking about themselves and their own work than the student's. Some will come with, to use the vernacular, a 'set of baggage' or a life story that they carry with them. Others, and fortunately this breed seems to be nearing extinction, seem intent on giving the student a 'hard time' during the viva. It is seen as something to be endured, not enjoyed. Their attitude is reminiscent of the advocates of caning and flogging – 'well, it never did me any harm'. Such examiners present the student with a series of hoops and obstacles to be jumped through, possibly because it gives them a sense of power ('I'll take this student down a peg or two'), or perhaps they may want the student to struggle or suffer a little; but commonly it is a case of 'it happened to me in my viva, so I'll make sure that it happens to you'. This is perhaps more likely to happen when the viva is the external examiner's first.

There may even be cases where the internal examiner behaves in some of these strange ways, and the external examiner is perfectly civilised.

An excellent summary of poor practice in oral examinations was given by Partington et al. (1993, p. 78). They gave labels to certain types, for example:

The inquisitor: this person acts like a hostile television interviewer, firing questions from the hip, often interrupting and scoring points. This can lead to anger and confrontation as opposed to reasoned discussion. The student is intimidated rather than engaged.

The committee person: the examiner takes the thesis page by page, questioning each point as it arises, thereby avoiding the important, key questions about the contribution of the thesis and its main messages.

The kite flyer: this examiner has a predetermined view of what the thesis is about and what it is linked to. The examiner explores this link at length, effectively examining a thesis that the student did not write or ever want to write.

The reminiscer: this person bores those present at the viva with stories of his or her own past research and publications, leaving no time for an exploration of the student's work.

The hobby-horse rider: this examiner is rather like the person above with a bee in the bonnet. They keep coming back to one theme or question, ad nauseam, often with prejudices about certain areas or research studies.

The proofreader: worse than the committee person, the examiner takes the student through the thesis line by line, pointing out minor errors and grammatical mistakes.

A university department with strong experience of selecting examiners will usually have good knowledge of whom to avoid and whom to choose. As a result, the viva should be a positive yet demanding experience for a student. The other important decision for a department is to select the right combination of internal and external examiners. There can sometimes be power struggles in this relationship – one should not dominate the other; they should be seen as equal partners in the process, whatever their status. Ideally, an external should be chosen who knows the field, will explore all aspects of the thesis fully, will engage the candidate in a fair and demanding discussion but will not intimidate, confront or attempt to impress those present (including the internal examiner).

Preparing for the viva

From the discussions earlier about the viva, its conduct and its perceived purposes it can be concluded that the key variables affecting the nature of a student's oral examination are likely to be:

- the written thesis itself;
- the regulations of the awarding university; and
- the examiners: their views on the thesis, whether they have read and will follow regulations, their 'personal agendas' and the likely 'chemistry' or interpersonal interactions between them and between the student and the examiners.

The first two are relatively clear, at least in the sense that they are written documents, in a way in the public domain. However, the manner in which they have been read and interpreted, alongside the variability in examiners and their personal characteristics, are certainly not clear and are undoubtedly difficult to predict. For those reasons it can be said that every viva is different – however, that is not a logical justification for not preparing for a viva. Preparation is vital. From our own experience, and from a reading of the literature in this area, we would make several general suggestions as a means of preparing for a viva:

- know your thesis inside out.
- have a mock viva, more to practise general oral skills, that is, the ability to talk about the thesis and respond to challenges, than to attempt to predict specific questions or to rehearse 'stock' answers.

- Talk to a range of others who have experienced vivas recently, but avoid horror stories.
- Be prepared to be criticised and challenged.
- Be prepared to defend your thesis and argue the case for what you have written.
- Be prepared to be asked to make (at the very least) minor amendments and possibly more fundamental changes to the written thesis.

This is probably the best general advice that can be given. On a more specific level, it is worth considering the list of possible questions above. There is a small possibility that none of those will be asked but a high probability that some of them will.

Several authors have given useful advice on the viva and how to prepare for it (Cryer, 2000; Phillips and Pugh, 2000, for example). It is worth reading at least some of their advice, although it does relate to our own. Murray (2003), for example, gives useful practical advice on 'how to survive the viva', arguing that students should not simply accept the viva as something with 'mystique' and just wait to see what happens. She suggests a range of 'don'ts' that include: don't be defensive, don't get angry, don't throw questions back at examiners and don't show reluctance to engage in debate. Murray also gives a range of ideas for preparing for the viva: practise answering difficult questions, including the 'two-minute answer'; practise the oral skills with different people, such as fellow students and colleagues; 'highlight the highlights' in the thesis and commit these to memory.

Giving answers: the 'oral thesis'

By preparing for the viva, students can actually improve the quality of their answers. Students can then communicate and convey their thesis orally as well as in writing.

The written thesis should act as the foundation and source of your oral answers (Murray, 2003, p. 89) so you should have it to hand and look for your answers 'therein'. But good answers can clarify and extend points made in writing and can therefore often reduce the requirement for amendments after the viva. Equally, however, our experience is that in some viva situations students actually explain things or express things more clearly than they did in writing – furthermore, they may even add or extend new important points, arguments or messages that did not appear fully in writing at all. This is perhaps one of the ironies in a good viva performance – the oral communication may extend and enhance the written thesis, and therefore lead to a request that this enrichment be added to the written thesis.

Preparing for the viva, and of course writing the thesis, means learning the language. As Murray (2003, p. 90) puts it, you should be able 'to speak the language of your discipline fluently'. As with any language acquisition, this needs prior practice. It involves learning the key terms in your field and being able to define and explain them. If you are using words like 'epistemology', 'ontology', constructivism or paradigm, then be prepared to explain them. Do not throw them in (via writing or in speech) if you cannot explain their meaning in your context. Equally, the best and most testing way to find out if someone really knows the meaning of an abstract term or an item of jargon is to ask them to give concrete examples, illustrations or instances. Be prepared for this.

Another useful tip is to be specific when answering, partly (as Murray, 2003, p. 92, puts it) to show off. If you mention an item of literature, give the detailed reference, right down to the author, date and page.

In answering the inevitable question about your 'original contribution', be upbeat without being arrogant. Rather than claiming world-shattering originality or paradigm revolution, you might lay claim to a 'fresh approach', a new perspective, different interpretation, modified theory or alternative model.

You will probably need to answer a call to reflect on the strengths and weaknesses in your work. Reflecting on its strengths will require some sort of claim for originality, as discussed above. We would suggest looking at weaknesses in terms of *limitations*. Everyone's work is limited in some way, even (perhaps especially in some circumstances) well-funded research. All researchers are limited in some way by time, resources, access to research sites and other constraining factors. Also, real-life research is messy and unpredictable – it is often the art of the possible. We suggest that students reflect on the limitations well in advance of the viva (including, of course, a section in the written thesis) and then present them in the viva in a positive light. For example, the need to *focus* on certain aspects of the literature or certain sites for data collection imposes limits. Difficult decisions have to be made in planning research and these lead to limitations and focus. The additional point to make in reflecting on the limits of your own work is that it points clearly to areas and imperatives for further research – and these pointers should be one of the strengths of your own thesis.

Finally, you should be asked whether there are any further points you would like to make that you have not expressed fully thus far in the viva. Be prepared for this, even if you feel that you do not need to speak further in your defence. You may be asked if you would like to pose any questions to the examiners. Again, be prepared for this. You might, if the viva has gone well, ask for ideas or possible outlets for publication of your research.

Outcomes and action

Each institution will have some variations in the written regulations, but the outcomes are likely to fall into one of the following categories.

PASS

This is the unusual outcome when a thesis is accepted exactly as it stands, without any need for minor changes or corrections to typos. If the examiners have found absolutely no typographical errors then either yours is the 'cleanest' thesis ever presented or they have not read it word for word.

MINOR AMENDMENTS

The thesis is passed, subject to minor amendments. The nature and extent of these can vary – small alterations, correction of typing errors, or making small revisions to sentences or paragraphs without major changes in the thesis underlying the thesis or the substance of the work. Examiners may also specify a *small* quantity of additional material to be added, for example, a strengthening or a more explicit statement of the key messages perhaps, or suggestions for further research. There is often a fine line between this recommendation and the next. Many universities give a time limit of one month (maximum) for this and, indeed, some may define the category of 'minor amendments' as those that can realistically be done in a month. Often, the changes will need to be approved only by the internal examiner.

RE-SUBMISSION

Again, this can vary enormously from relatively minor amounts of rewriting, for example, additions or amendments to the concluding chapter, to fairly major requests, such as changing the data analysis and discussion. In one case in our experience, the external examiner even asked the student to go out and collect further data. The maximum time allowed for a re-submission is usually one year.

Students can be asked to re-submit without the need for a further viva, provided the revised thesis is seen and approved by (in most cases) both examiners. In exceptional cases, when the oral has been very unsatisfactory, the recommendation may be for a re-submission followed by another viva. Finally, there may be a requirement for the candidate to undergo another oral examination without modification of the form or content of the written thesis, though this too is unusual.

FAIL

This is a very uncommon decision, which should not occur if the thesis has been carefully supervised and the student has taken and followed advice.

APPROVAL FOR MPHIL STATUS

Again, this is unlikely in our experience, but it has happened. The doctorate is not awarded but the examiners recommend that the thesis be accepted at Masters level, subject only to necessary changes to the title and cover.

The most likely outcome is some version of 'pass subject to revisions', in some form or other depending on the exact regulations. Following a viva, most students are asked to wait outside (hopefully in the supervisor's room rather than a corridor) so that examiners can reach an agreed decision. This may take some time, especially if the examiners cannot immediately reach a consensus. For example, they may need to debate whether the thesis requires minor amendments or should be classed as needing a re-submission.

When the feedback and the decision are given, we strongly advise that your supervisor is present (even if she or he was not there during the viva). If amendments are asked for, students should take great care to become crystal clear about the points being made and to clarify exactly what they need to do and to write. It is advisable to take notes, ask your supervisor to take notes and request the examiners to put their suggestions for amendment in writing (this should be their duty anyway, according to most regulations). If you are not clear, ask for clarification on the action you are being asked to take.

By way of summary, Table 10.1 spells out some 'dos and don'ts' that might be helpful in preparing for, and conducting yourself in, the oral examination.

Table 10.1 Dos and don'ts before and during the viva

Don't	Do
Be dogmatic	Be thoughtful and reflective
Be defensive	Be honest
Be rude	Direct, but not rude
Be long-winded	Be concise (but do not give one-word answers)
Try to please examiners by contriving to include their work in the references	Carry out some 'homework' on the examiners and their work
Demand certain examiners, for example, for being the 'expert' in your field	Have some involvement in discussing and choosing the examiners
Be 'laid back' and blasé	Be prepared, but not over-prepared, for example, by trying to predict questions
Be apologetic for what you have done	Be confident (but not overconfident)

In summary

One of the key messages of this chapter on the viva is that students should make themselves ready for it – treat it as something that can be 'researched' and prepared for. Do not treat it as a black box.

Our own experience and research indicates that: practice varies across institutions, so your own written regulations should be examined carefully; certain questions do recur, so it is worth preparing for the more general, commonly asked questions; there are guidelines and there is some consensus on 'good practice' for the viva, but not all of these will be followed all of the time. (See Murray, 2003, p. 7, and Tinkler and Jackson, 2004, for recent research on the viva.) Doing a doctorate requires a high level of written skill and academic literacy – but succeeding in a viva requires an equal level of oral ability and academic oracy. Both need to be practised and prepared for – either in seminar sessions, conference presentations or mock vivas. The viva is an integral part of a doctoral examination, not an add-on or a rubber-stamping exercise. There are two elements to a doctoral thesis: the written and the spoken.

The viva and the written thesis are important ways of presenting your doctoral work and making them public, especially once the thesis is housed and catalogued in the university library. In the final chapter of the book we present and discuss ways of disseminating your work more widely.

Cameo: Surviving the viva

Maxine Burton

After a sleepless night, the day of the viva has dawned. Getting the thesis completed for submission was hard enough. But this is the leap into the unknown. You have already run through every horror scenario in your head, you have even had viva nightmares, you have endlessly rehearsed all those problem areas you hope they don't pick up on (in my case, I was intent on appearing more knowledgeable than I felt on modernism and postmodernism, structuralism and poststructuralism!).

I dressed carefully in a smart suit, to demonstrate an efficiency I certainly didn't feel. I had already checked where the room was, in case I couldn't cope with navigation in addition to all the other anxieties. I had been told it was a 'very nice room', as if there might be some sympathetic magic in that. My supervisor had arranged to meet me beforehand. He tried to talk me through some possible questions, but one look at my face convinced him that I was beyond help – 'I'm just making it worse, aren't I?' So then he tried to be soothing, telling me I had done a good piece of work, but warning me that you could never tell what the examiners might want in the viva. Enough – I'd read my fill of how the only predictable thing about the viva was its unpredictability!

And suddenly we are outside the 'very nice room'. Doing a runner crosses my mind, but before I can act on this impulse, I am ushered in. Introductions are made, the examiners smile encouragingly and we're off. The first question is a general one, asking me to summarise the importance of my research. I start cautiously, find my voice has degenerated into a feeble croak, take a gulp of water and find my hands are shaking too. The examiners continue to smile and nod. Keep going … the questions come at me and there's nothing too off-putting yet. I allow myself to relax a little and try to think of it just as a discussion with people who are interested in hearing what I have to say. Before I realise, this is just what it has become, and we're talking about other research in my area, about possibilities for turning my work into a book. It occurs to me that they like my thesis and it's going to be alright. And then comes the stinker of a question, a question to which I have no idea of possible answers, having totally failed to anticipate it. By now I am confident enough to allow myself the luxury of saying that it's a difficult question, and asking the examiner to clarify what she means. I'm not sure that even then I manage to answer it. But an hour has slipped by, and they decide to put me out of my misery. I'm through – some minor corrections only.

I was told afterwards that I looked 'shell-shocked'. The imaginary scenarios I had run through did include a tentative one in which I 'got through', but it was still hard to believe. I have no idea if it really was a 'very nice room' – but the champagne tasted good afterwards!

In the 'viva literature' there was very little I had read that I found useful preparation, so I will offer some pointers as to what proved helpful for me.

Before:

- **Avoid reading or listening to the 'horror' stories which abound, unless you wish to increase your anxiety. For instance, hearing that the friendly, laid-back professor you have met at conferences can turn into the examiner from hell is not helpful.**
- **I did not have a mock viva, so cannot comment on them, but what I did find useful were the opportunities to present different aspects of my work in progress at conferences and at the EdD weekends. It was a valuable way of practising in front of a live audience, dealing with comments and thinking on one's feet.**
- **Generally, practise verbalising. If you cannot find willing peers/friends/family to indulge you, ask yourself questions and talk through the answers. It is all too easy to get locked into fine-tuning your written skills for the thesis and to forget how to talk about it. Never mind that much of what you prepare may never come up (and no, I wasn't asked about structuralism and modernism), it is a valuable skill you are practising.**
- **Make sure you know exactly what you have written and where in your thesis. There can be a long time between submission and viva (in my case, over two months). It's quite good to 'forget' about it for a time, as it means you come to it with fresh eyes. But it is what you've written that is being examined.**

◆ This re-acquaintance with your thesis is also the opportunity to spot all those errors that have 'slipped through' your proofreading. Make sure you know what they are, but do not offer them up to the examiners, unless they raise them first!

On the day:

◆ Avoid travelling on the day itself if you are coming any distance. It is better to stay the night somewhere near. You may still not sleep much, but at least you won't be worrying about traffic or delayed trains.

◆ When you get a topic you are happy with, keep going. The more *you* talk, the less opportunity there will be for other questions

◆ If you are asked a difficult question, do not jump straight in and expect to be able to dig yourself out. Take your time, ask for clarification, discuss alternative interpretations and ask if that is what they mean. Appearing 'thoughtful' is no bad thing.

11 Whatever Next? Spreading the Word and Becoming Part of the Research Community

CHAPTER CONTENTS

What should you do with your thesis after having your (probably) first and (hopefully) last ever viva? For many students, there can be a feeling of anti-climax after finishing their thesis and submitting it. This can be felt even more deeply after the viva is over and any necessary rewriting has been completed. One possible antidote to this is to consider producing either one or more conference papers or journal articles from it, or possibly a book with a commercial publisher – after all, two of the key criteria for the award of a doctorate are that it should make a contribution to knowledge in an area, and that at least some of it should be publishable. This chapter discusses some of the possibilities for disseminating your work, either during your doctoral programme or after completing your thesis. As 'researching professionals' or as 'professional researchers', students have a duty to disseminate their work to a wider audience – whether they be fellow researchers, practitioners or policy-makers.

Disseminating: before, during or after?

One of the dilemmas that students face is whether to present, disseminate or publish any of their work *before* the doctoral thesis has been submitted. There are no hard and fast rules on this. As supervisors and internal or external examiners we have seen many doctoral students present and publish aspects of their work (occasionally co-authored with their supervisor, which raises other issues) before the thesis has been examined. There is a range of possibilities for disseminating and presenting work in progress or work completed: some will involve spoken presentations, probably using visual aids; some will involve writing for conference proceedings, journals or book publishers; dissemination may involve a combination of spoken and written forms.

Most doctoral students will and should be encouraged to present their work internally, for example at departmental seminars or internally organised conferences. Another forum is the workshop or presentation session at a research association conference such as AERA or BERA (the American and British educational research associations respectively). At the other extreme, a student presenting to his or her peers can be a valuable experience for both presenter and audience. Another audience is fellow practitioners, certainly for the researching professional. All or any of these modes of presentation can be used either during or after your doctoral programme, that is, to present 'work in progress' or 'work completed'.

Our own personal experience of actually publishing in a written form (for example, journal article or book chapter) before submission of the thesis is that this has not presented a problem for examiners, but we strongly suggest to students that they discuss this carefully with their supervisor before going ahead. Provided the writing of the article/paper is seen as an aid or a complement to writing the thesis, then it can be beneficial to a doctoral student to mould their work for a journal before the thesis is submitted. It can also be a valuable way of receiving feedback on one's work, either from referees or from participants at a conference, depending on the mode of publication.

Converting the thesis to a 'publication'

For many students, the last thing they feel like doing after the examination process is complete is to return to their thesis and start to 'chop it up' and 'mould' it into some other form or forms. But this is exactly what is required. Perhaps the best tactic is to ignore it for several weeks, putting some time and distance between you and it, and then to return to it with the explicit aim of disseminating your work and 'getting published'. You may wish to be the sole author, which is fine, but the act of getting started is best done in collaboration with someone else, preferably your supervisor or a colleague who has experience of writing for journals or book publishers.

The first task is to set some goals. The thesis may contain different papers for different audiences: for example, there may be an important article to be written from the thesis on the methodology or even the specific methods used. This might be targeted (see later) on one journal. Another article might be written on the findings and their implications for practice – this might be geared at a more 'professional' journal, aimed at practitioners such as teachers or lecturers. Thirdly, within the thesis there might be an article that can contribute to thinking and theory within an area; and finally, between the two poles of practice and theory, there might be important messages for policy-makers and planners, and this might be targeted at a refereed journal on policy or a more 'professional' journal for policy-makers.

If the goal is to be a book, then it might contain a combination of all the above. However, commercial book publishers will want a clear statement of the potential market for the book and this is discussed shortly.

Going for journal articles

Books are written for markets – journal articles are written for peers. Different rules of engagement apply. We do not have the space in this book to explore fully the intricacies of writing, refereeing and editing journals (for a fuller account see Wellington, 2003, ch. 4). All we can do here is sum up some of the key tips for new writers (Box 11.1) and indicate some of the things 'not to do' (Box 11.2).

We suggest that you should have a clear target journal in mind *before* you write your article, not after. This means that your first job is to identify all the possible journals in your field that are potential targets. You should also be aware of the following: there will be considerable time lags between submission and receiving referees' comments – and between acceptance and actual appearance in print (in the region of two years in some cases); peer review can be difficult to accept, but you should view it positively, that is, as 'free feedback' and a way of making your article better; do expect to have to make at least some revisions to your first submission; you may be rejected by one journal – if so, improve your first version and send it to another journal as soon as possible. The main message is that you should not be discouraged by letters that say you need to make changes (this is to be expected, not feared) – make the changes and that journal will often publish the revised version.

Finally, there is one definite '*Don't*' with journal articles (incidentally, this is not as clear-cut with book proposals). It is now an accepted ethical code in most fields (written in some cases, tacit in others) that authors should never submit to more than one journal concurrently. In other words, submit in series, not parallel, even though this takes time.

Box 11.1: Writing for journals: tips for improving acceptance chances

- ◆ Select a journal and familiarise yourself with it, that is, select your target journal carefully and tailor your manuscript to suit it and its intended audience.
- ◆ Look for recurring topics, debates and themes.
- ◆ Decide on the type of journal and who it is for, that is, wide ranging or specialist? Professional or academic? Refereed or non-refereed?
- ◆ Read a good number of back issues and shape your article accordingly.
- ◆ Look for traits/characteristics in a journal and attempt to 'model' them.
- ◆ Try to make a unique contribution, however small.
- ◆ Try to write clearly and coherently.
- ◆ Have a clear 'argument' or thesis running through it.
- ◆ Include a 'so what?' section.
- ◆ Keep to the word length.
- ◆ Follow the journal's guidelines to authors, especially on citation style and referencing.
- ◆ Observe how past authors have structured their writing.
- ◆ Check journal style and past practice on headings and sub-headings.
- ◆ Ask a critical friend to read it before sending it off.

Box 11.2: Writing for journals: common mistakes

1. Lack of familiarity with the journal, its style and its readership.
2. Wrong style, wrong formatting and so on.
3. Wrong length.
4. Poor presentation, for example grammatical errors, typos.
5. No substance – 'much ado about nothing'.
6. Unreadability, that is, writing is unclear, turgid or does not make sense.
7. Manuscript not checked and proofread.

The book?

Commercial publishers will not publish books that people are unlikely to buy. No commercial book publisher will ever accept a traditional thesis exactly as it stands and 'convert' it straight into a book. (See Wellington, 2003, ch. 5, for evidence to support this trend.) The conversion is your job – but the task of converting a thesis into a book is no small one. It involves radical changes to the content, including much chopping down. It will need a new title, agreeable to the publisher. The audience and therefore the style of writing will be different. In short, it requires severe editing, extensive rewriting and certainly a large element of 'repackaging' or remoulding.

No one should ever write a book before seeking and finding a publisher, having one's proposal scrutinised and advised upon, and then receiving a contract safely in hand. Book proposals require considerable thought partly because, unlike theses, books have to be sold, meaning that somebody must want to buy them. Usually, a proposal will consist of a synopsis of the book and one or two sample chapters. But what else should a typical proposal contain? There is a fair measure of agreement amongst different publishers on the sections that should be covered in a good book proposal. These are summarised in Box 11.3.

Box 11.3: The key elements in a book proposal

- **The provisional title of the book.**
- **Its proposed contents: what will the book be about?**
- **A synopsis.**
- **The market, the intended readership: who is going to buy it?**
- **The competition: how will it compare with, compete with or complement existing books?**
- **Who is the author?**
- **The timescale and writing plan: when will the script be ready?**
- **Production requirements: how long will it be (the extent); how many tables, illustrations and so on will it contain?**
- **Sample material: one, or at most two, draft chapters.**
- **Potential referees for this proposal.**

If anyone would like full details and further insight, based on interviews with publishers, the business of writing a book proposal and publishers' criteria for acceptance are discussed at length in Wellington (2003, pp. 81–95). In addition, most commercial publishers provide their own guidelines and proforma.

Our own experience with publishers and their commissioning editors is that they are extremely helpful and will often support a good idea even if it will not result in the sale of tens of thousands of books. However, one point is worth bearing in mind from a career point of view: authors who intend to go into 'academia' after their doctorate will be subject to research assessment exercises – hence, they need to be conscious of steering the right course between audience appeal and scholarly substance. A book with popular appeal may not always carry the same kudos as an article in a high-status journal.

Entering the community of scholars

For many established authors, their first academic book or journal article was a by-product of their Masters or doctoral thesis; many theses have the potential to be transformed into a book, a book chapter or an article or more. Our suggestion is to go for it. The article or book is unlikely to have the extensive data presentation, tables of results, comprehensive literature review, methodology discussion, terms of conditionality, appendices and plethora of references that would be expected in a doctoral thesis – but its central themes, its original contribution to knowledge and its innovative ideas and discussion are all likely to interest a book publisher or a journal editor. Everyone starts somewhere. The viva and the written thesis are the first steps to getting known and entering the 'community of scholars' that people talk about but that newcomers often find difficult to locate and become a part of. Conference presentations and posters, papers and journal articles, and books all play a part in feeling part of that community.

Cameo: The doctoral experience – bearing fruit

Marion Jones

I feel embarrassed to admit that, initially, my intention to obtain a doctorate was of a rather utilitarian nature, a means to an end. I believed that becoming a 'doctor' would strengthen my credibility as an academic in general and secure my position within the institution in which I worked. However, after the first residential weekend I noticed a change taking place, indicating a distinct shift from an extrinsic, product-oriented motivation to obtain a doctorate towards an intrinsic, genuine interest in the process of conducting educational research. Suddenly, I felt a strong desire to become a member of the wider academic community, and as such place myself in a position to share and contribute to the knowledge base underpinning teacher education.

In the course of completing my written assignments and subsequently writing the thesis, I acquired a theoretical knowledge and understanding of the research process, which I applied in tandem with conducting my college-based research. The dissemination of research findings in the form of journal articles and conference papers was addressed on our doctoral programme – but translating this knowledge into action was yet another challenge.

Fortunately, when I submitted my first article it was accepted requiring only minor amendments, giving me a sense of increased confidence and achievement. But the second and third article provoked a more critical response from the journal reviewers. In view of the harsh nature of some of the comments I became rather despondent, almost reaching a point of giving up. In this time of crisis it was invaluable to be able to seek the advice and emotional support of my personal tutor and peers. Following their encouragement I persevered with the required amendments, learning an important lesson. Submitting articles for publication can be a time-consuming, lonely business, but, equally, when resulting in success, it can be extremely rewarding and generate an enormous amount of new energy and motivation. My early articles are in print as:

Jones, M. 2000 'Becoming a secondary teacher in Germany', *European Journal of Teacher Education*, 23(1), pp. 65–76.
2000 'Trainee teachers' perceptions of school-based training in England and Germany with regard to their preparation for teaching, mentor support and assessment', *Mentoring and Tutoring*, 8(1), pp. 63–80.

2001 'Mentors' perceptions of their roles in school-based teacher training in England and Germany' *Journal of Education for Teaching*, 27(1), pp. 75–94.

By targeting different journals, I had realised that no one submission process is ever the same. Each time, the obstacles I had to overcome presented themselves in a different guise. For example, one reviewer expressed his disappointment at my having omitted reference to a key text, which I had considered out of date and of little relevance. On further investigation, I established that the author was none other than the reviewer, who also happened to be one of the two chief editors of the journal to which I had submitted my article. The lesson that I had learnt was that gaining some information on a journal's editorial board members may prove helpful in striking the right chords. In an attempt to achieve this goal I responded to the reviewer's advice by including the reference, upon which my article was accepted for publication.

Another point of frustration I had to learn to manage constructively was receiving and responding to conflicting feedback in relation to one article, which in one case involved four different referees. Similarly, journals differ in the way they expect articles to be presented in terms of content, structure and typing conventions. While some journals are highly academic in attaching great importance to theoretical aspects, such as epistemology and methodological considerations, others are more concerned with professional issues related to policy and practice. I had reached the conclusion that familiarising myself with a journal's academic orientation, preferred style of presentation and the members of the editorial board can increase the chances of success.

The presentation of my first conference paper, which happened to be at Worcester College, Oxford University, proved a rather daunting experience. Filled with trepidation I once again jumped in at the deep end and, to my relief, realised that I could swim. With every conference attendance my confidence grew, allowing me to not only deliver but also enjoy presenting my research findings to a captive audience. Furthermore, I learnt that conferences can provide an ideal forum for networking, establishing links with colleagues from other institutions and other countries. They can also facilitate contact with editors, who are on the look-out for suitable material for their journals or wish to recruit members for their editorial panels (both of which happened to me recently).

Looking back, my doctoral programme proved to be a highly stimulating and enjoyable experience. Since finishing it, my interest in research has not subsided. In this sense, rather than being perceived as the end point of an apprenticeship, the doctoral programme has opened up a multitude of avenues in terms of my academic, professional and personal development.

Further Reading

One of the more widely read books in the UK is Phillips and Pugh's text, *How to get a PhD* (Open University Press). This is very popular with students and is well written. Its first edition was published in 1987, with a third edition appearing in 2000. It is a helpful text but it contains very little on taught/professional doctorates.

A text with similar aims is Pat Cryer's *The Research Student's Guide to Success* (2000, Open University Press), now in its second edition.

Working for a Doctorate (Routledge, 1997) is an edited collection (Graves, N. and Varma, V.) of ten chapters of varying value. The chapter on writing (by Hartley) is excellent for doctoral students.

The collection of case studies by Phillida Salmon entitled *Achieving a PhD – Ten Students' Experience* (Trentham Books, 1992) is a valuable publication.

Two texts from USA authors complement our own book. Rita Brause's *Writing Your Doctoral Dissertation* (Falmer Press, 2000) has some excellent chapters but is very American in its language and approach. Equally, *Surviving Your Dissertation* (by Rudestam and Newton, published by Sage in 1992) is a very useful guide but is very much written for the USA context. Both publications are attractively presented and give an interesting contrast to the UK situation.

One book that deserves a mention is the research-based and superbly written *Supervising the PhD: A Guide to Success* (by Sara Delamont, Paul Atkinson and Odette Parry, 1997, Open University Press) but as the title suggests this is more valuable for staff than for students.

For a really detailed and insightful book based on research into the examination process, see Penny Tinkler and Carolyn Jackson's *The Doctoral Examination Process: A Handbook for Students, Examiners and Supervisors* (Open University Press, 2004). The book focuses mainly on the viva, preparing for it and the selection of examiners (looking mainly at the PhD).

Rowena Murray has produced two very valuable and well-written guide books for doctoral students: *How to Survive Your Viva* (2003) and *How to Write a Thesis* (2002). Both are published by Open University Press.

Gina Wisker's *The Postgraduate Research Handbook* (Palgrave, 2001) is very much a comprehensive how-to-do-it guide, covering everything from choosing the right supervisor to 'life after the research'.

Some other texts that our own students have found helpful are:

Burton, S. and Steane, P. (eds) (2004) *Surviving your thesis*. London: Routledge.
Dunleavy, P. (2003) *Authoring a PhD*. London: Palgrave Macmillan.
Scott, D., Brown, A., Lunt, I., and Thorne, L. (2004) *Professional Doctorates: Integrating Professional and Academic Knowledge*. London: Institute of Education.

Further reading on writing and publishing

For those who wish to continue writing and to publish their work at conferences, in journals or in book form, the following sources make a useful starting point:

Becker, H. (1986) *Writing for Social Scientists: how to start and finish your thesis, book or article*. Chicago, Il: University of Chicago Press.
Day, A. (1996) *How to Get Research Published in Journals*. Aldershot: Gower Press.
Eggleston, J. and Klein, G. (1997) *Achieving Publication in Education*. Stoke-on-Trent: Trentham Books.
Henson, K. (1999) *Writing for Professional Publication*. Boston, MA: Allyn and Bacon.
Richardson, L. (1990) *Writing Strategies: Reaching Diverse Audiences*. Newbury Park, CA: Sage.
Wellington, J. (2003) *Getting Published*. London: Routledge.
Woods, P. (1999) *Successful Writing for Qualitative Researchers*. London: Routledge.

Useful Organisations and Websites

1. National Postgraduate Committee

This is a useful organisation to keep in touch with, especially as it maintains a well kept and interesting website (http://www.npc.org.uk/) and a valuable folder of resources, with on-line access:

- **About Postgraduates, by Ewan Gillon and Jeremy Hoad;**
- **Supporting Postgraduates, by Ewan Gillon and Jeremy Hoad;**
- **Postgraduate Policy Responses, The NPC's responses to consultation documents and reports into higher education; and**
- **Postgraduate Publications, including the Guidelines series.**

According to their site: 'the National Postgraduate Committee (NPC), constituted in 1992, set out to tackle the many issues on board that have since come about'. It is the only organisation in the UK run by postgraduates in the interests of postgraduates including both taught and research. Their 'Mission Statement' is: 'to advance, in the public interest, the education of postgraduate students within the United Kingdom. We shall achieve this by democratically representing postgraduates, contributing to discussions, supporting postgraduate representatives and facilitating communication between stakeholders'.

The General Secretary of the NPC can be contacted at:

Tim Brown, General Secretary, National Postgraduate Committee
University of Surrey Students' Union, Union House, University of Surrey, Guildford, Surrey, GU2 7XH
Telephone: 01483 683921 and 07881 845833
Fax: 01483 534749
Email: npc@npc.org.uk

2. Education-line

An Internet medium through which authors can present early versions of their work and interested parties can keep abreast of topical issues in educational research. Focus is on texts which are relevant to the study, practice and administration of education at a professional level. Texts are supplied for addition to the collection by their authors, often as a result of conference presentations. Service allows for identification of texts on very specific topics or within general fields. Texts in the Education-line collection are also indexed in the British Education Index.

Freely available through a variety of search options at: http://leeds.ac.uk/educol

3. SCUTREA (Standing Conference on University Teaching and Research in the Education of Adults)

SCUTREA is a forum for all concerned with research into the education of adults and adults' learning; those involved with the development of adult education as a body of knowledge; and those who wish to reflect upon, in order to understand and articulate better, their own and others' practice of working with adults in a wide range of educational settings.

SCUTREA was established over 30 years ago with its membership initially drawn from academic staff working in Departments of Adult Education in British universities. It now draws on a much broader constituency and welcomes individual and institutional members from across the international educational community. It remains a focal point for research in adult education in the UK, both inside and outside the university sector, and maintains close and active links with sister organisations throughout the world. These include the Adult Education Research Conference, USA; the Adult Learning Association – Research Network, Australia; the Canadian Association for the Study of Adult Education; and the European Society for Research in Adult Education. SCUTREA regularly hosts a major international conference in conjunction with these organisations as well as enjoying the participation of international colleagues in its annual national conferences. The annual conference of SCUTREA is usually held in early July. In addition, smaller conferences, workshops and study days take place throughout the year, often in conjunction with other national organisations with interests in adults' learning and research and practice in the many forms of adult education. SCUTREA publishes a regular newsletter, *SCOOP*, to which all members are invited to contribute. Membership of SCUTREA is open to individuals and institutions who are accepted by Council as 'making a contribution to the study of, or research into, any aspect of learning, education or training in adulthood'. In recognition of the fact that some individual members wishing to conduct research may not be supported by an institution, SCUTREA operates a research bursary scheme. This is designed to assist with research expenses for a single study, over and above normal living costs, such as travel associated with the research and/or administrative and stationery costs. A maximum of two awards can be made annually, up to a value of £500 each. Small bursaries are also available to assist attendance at the annual conference by postgraduate students, and others who may not have full institutional support, whose papers are selected for presentation. The Michael Stephens Award is also open to postgraduate students who present a conference paper.

Further details of all the above may be found at: http://www.scutrea.ac.uk

4. The Informal Education Encyclopaedia and Archive

A useful and well-maintained site containing a wide range of information on all aspects of informal education for adults and young people. Contains specially commissioned papers on recent work as well as archive material.

Freely available at: http://www.infed.org.uk

5. Websites on computer software for data analysis

http://caqdas.soc.surrey.ac.uk/
This website is run by an ESRC-funded project, and provides support, training and information in the use of a range of software programs which have been designed to assist qualitative data analysis. This includes debate about the methodological and epistemological issues arising from the use of such software packages. This is not a commercial site.

http://www.scolari.co.uk/
This website is part of SAGE publications, who sell a wide range of research methods software. The site provides an overview of the packages they offer and comparisons of what different software can do.

http://www.qsrinternational.com/
QSR International produce qualitative data analysis software packages, including NUD*IST and Nvivo. The website provides information about their software. There are links to books and papers written about using software packages for research.

6. Electronic databases for social sciences and education

Bibliography of the Social Sciences (IBSS) at: http://www.lse.ac.uk/collections/IBSS/

IBSS is compiled at the London School of Economics. It covers the social science subjects Anthropology, Economics, Politics and Sociology. It can be accessed through BIDS at: http://www.bids.ac.uk/

British Education Index at http://www.leeds.ac.uk/bei/
BEI contains education articles and papers published in Britain.

ERIC at: http://www.eric.ed.gov/
ERIC is an international database containing articles and papers on education.

ProQuest at: http://www.proquest.com/
ProQuest offer a number of different education products.

Web of Knowledge at: http://wok.mimas.ac.uk/
This database includes the Social Sciences Citation Index.

Books in print at: www.booksinprint.com
This database contains American in print and out of print titles.

British Library Public Catalogue (BLPC) at: www.blpc.bl.uk
This catalogue provides access to the main British Library catalogues, describing over ten million items, which are held by the British Library.

COPAC at: http://www.copac.ac.uk/
COPAC allows you to carry out simultaneous searches of the catalogues of all members of the Consortium of University Research Libraries, including the British Library.

7. Research funding organisation websites

Arts and Humanities Research Board (AHRB) at: www.ahrb.ac.uk

Economic and Social Research Council (ESRC) at: www.esrc.ac.uk

Leverhulme Trust at: www.leverhulme.org.uk

Nuffield Foundation at: www.nuffieldfoundation.org

Joseph Rowntree Foundation at: www.jrf.org.uk

References

Acker, S. (1999) 'Students and supervisors: the ambiguous relationship. Perspectives on the supervisory process in Britain and Canada', in A. Holbrook and S. Johnston (eds), *Supervision of Postgraduate Research in Education. Review of Australian Research in Education*, no. 5: pp. 75–94.

Armstrong, P. (2001) 'Becoming and being a researcher: doing research as lifelong learning', in L. West, N. Miller, D. O'Reilly and R. Allen (eds), *Travellers' Tales: From Adult Education to Lifelong Learning and Beyond*. Proceedings of the 31st Annual Conference, SCUTREA, University of East London, pp. 30–3.

Attwood, M. (1996) *Alias Grace*. London: Bloomsbury.

Banks, A. and Banks, S. (1998) *Fiction and Social Research: By Ice or Fire*. Walnut Creek, CA: AltaMira.

Barnett, R. (1997) *Higher Education: A Critical Business*. Buckingham: SRHE/Open University Press.

Barthes, R. (1967) *Writing Degree Zero*. Trs A. Laver and C. Smith. London: Cape.

Becker, H. (1986) *Writing for Social Scientists: How to Start and Finish your Thesis, Book or Article*. Chicago, Il: University of Chicago Press.

Belenky, M.F., Clinchy, B., Goldberger, N. and Jarule, J. (1986) *Women's Ways of Knowing: The Development of Self, Voice and Mind*. New York: Basic Books.

Bernstein, B. (1977) *Class, Codes and Control; Volume 3: Towards a Theory of Educational Transmissions*. 2nd edn. London: Routledge and Kegan Paul.

Bernstein, B. (1990) *Class, Codes and Control; Volume 4: the Structuring of Pedagogic Discourse*. London: Routledge.

Bett, W.R. (1952) *The Preparation and Writing of Medical Papers for Publication*. London: Menley and James.

Bickenbach, J. and Davies, J. (1997) *Good Reasons for Better Arguments: An Introduction to the Skills and Values of Critical Thinking*. Hadleigh: Broadview Press.

Bloomer, M., Hodkinson, P. and Billett, S. (2004) 'The significance of ontogeny and habitus in constructing theories of learning', *Studies in Continuing Education*, 26(1): 19–43.

Boice, R. (1997) 'Strategies for enhancing scholarly productivity', in J.M. Moxley, (ed.), *Writing and Publishing for Academic Authors*. Lanham, MD: Rowman and Littlefield. pp. 19–34.

Boud, D., Keogh, R. and Walker, D. (eds) (1985) *Reflection: Turning Experience into Learning*. London: Kogan Page.

Bourner, T., Bowden, R. and Laing, S. (2000) 'Professional doctorates: the development of researching professionals', in T. Bourner, T. Katz and D. Watson (eds), *New Directions in Professional Higher Education*. Buckingham: SRHE/Open University Press,. pp. 214–25.

Brady, I. (2000) 'Anthropological poetics' in N. Denzin, and Y. Lincoln (eds), *The Handbook of Qualitative Research*: Second Edition. Thousand Oaks, CA: Sage. pp. 949–79.

Brande, D. (1983) *Becoming a writer*. London: Macmillan.

Brockbank, A. and McGill, I. (1998) *Facilitating Reflective Learning in Higher Education*, Buckingham: Open University Press.

Brookfield, S.D. (1995) *Becoming a Critically Reflective Teacher*. San Francisco, CA: Jossey-Bass.

Burgess, R. (1984) 'Keeping a research diary', in J. Bell, T. Bush, A. Fox and J. Goodey (eds), *Conducting Small Scale Investigations in Educational Management*. London: Harper and Row. pp. 198–205.

Burnham, P. (1994) 'Surviving the viva: unravelling the mysteries of the PhD oral', *Journal of Graduate Education*, 1(1): 30–4.

Capra, F. (1997) *The Web of Life: A New Synthesis of Mind and Matter*. London: Flamingo/HarperCollins.

Carr, W. (1995) *For Education: Towards Critical Educational Inquiry*. Buckingham: Open University Press.

Chamberlain, P., Bornat, J. and Wengraf, T. (2000) *The Turn to Biographical Methods in the Social Sciences*. London: Routledge.

Christians, C. (2000) 'Ethics and politics in qualitative research', in N. Denzin and Y. Lincoln (eds), *Handbook of Qualitative Research: Second Edition*. Thousand Oaks, CA: Sage. pp. 133–55.

Clough, P. (2002) *Narratives and Fictions in Educational Research*. Buckingham: Open University Press.

Cohen, L., Manion, L. and Morrison, K. (2000) *Research Methods in Education*. London: Routledge/Falmer.

Cryer, P (2000) *The Research Student's Guide to Success*. Buckingham: Open University Press.

Davies, C. and Birbili, M. (2000) 'What do people need to know about writing in order to write in their jobs?', *British Journal of Educational Studies*, 48(4): 429–45.

Day, A. (1996) *How to Get Research Published in Journals*. Aldershot: Gower.

Delton, J. (1985) *The 29 Most Common Writing Mistakes and How to Avoid Them*. Cincinnati, OH: Writer's Digest Books.

Denscombe, M. (2001) *The Good Research Guide for Small-Scale Social Research Projects*. Buckingham: Open University Press.

Didion, J. (1979) *The White Album*. New York: Simon and Schuster.

Durkheim, E. (1977) *The Evolution of Educational Thought*, London: Routledge and Kegan Paul.

Edwards, R., Nicoll, K. and Usher, R. (2004) *Rhetoric and Educational Discourse*. London: RoutledgeFalmer.

Egan, J. (2001) 'Insider out: an activist's journey from grassroots to academe', in L. West, N. Miller, D. O'Reilly and R. Allen (eds), *Travellers' Tales: From Adult Education to Lifelong Learning and Beyond*. Proceedings of the 31st Annual Conference, SCUTREA, University of East London, pp. 99–102.

Elbow, P. (1973) *Writing without Teachers*. Oxford: Oxford University Press.

Ellis, C. and Bochner, A. (eds) (1996) *Composing Ethnography: Alternative Forms of Qualitative Writing* Walnut Creek, CA: AltaMira.

Erben, M. (1998) Introduction in Erben, M. (ed.) *Biography and education: a reader*, London, Falmer Press, pp. 1–3.

Fine, M. (1992) 'Passion, politics and power', in M. Fine (ed.), *Disruptive Voices: The Possibilities of Feminist Research*. Ann Arbor, MI: University of Michigan Press.

Fine, M., Weiss, L., Wesen, S. and Wong, L. (2000) 'For whom? Qualitative research, representations and social responsibilities' in N. Denzin, and Y. Lincoln (eds), *Handbook of Qualitative Research: Second Edition*. Thousand Oaks, CA: Sage. pp. 107–32.

Flower, L. and Hayes, J. (1981) 'The pregnant pause: an inquiry into the nature of planning', *Research in the Teaching of English*, 15: 229–43.

Freedman, J. and Combs, G. (1996) *Narrative Therapy: The Social Construction of Preferred Realities*. New York: Norton.

Gallie, W. (1955) 'Essentially contested concepts', *Proceedings of the Aristotelian Society*, 56, pp. 167–98.

Gamson, J. (2000) 'Sexualities, queer theory and qualitative research', in N. Denzin, and Y. Lincoln (eds), *The Handbook of Qualitative Research: Second Edition*. Thousand Oaks, CA: Sage. pp. 347–65.

Gilligan, C. (1982) *In a Different Voice: Psychological Theory and Women's Development*. Cambridge, MA: Harvard University Press.

Goodson, I. (1992) 'Studying teachers' lives: an emergent field of inquiry', in I. Goodson (ed.), *Studying Teachers' Lives*. London: Routledge. pp. 1–17.

Goodson, I. and Sikes, P. (2001) *Life History in Educational Settings: Learning from Lives*. Buckingham: Open University Press.

Grabe, W. and Kaplan, R. (1996) *Theory and Practice of Writing*. New York: Longman.

Graham, H. (1994) 'Surveying through stories', in C. Bell and H. Roberts (eds), *Social Researching: Politics, Problems, Practice*. London: Routledge and Kegan Paul.

Greenhalgh, T. (1997) 'How to read a paper. Papers that summarise other papers (systematic reviews and meta-analyses)', *British Medical Journal*, 315: 7109, 13 September. At: http://bmj.bmjjournals.com/archive/7109/7109ed2.htm, accessed 12 January 2004.

Griffiths, M. (1998) *Educational Research For Social Justice: Getting Off the Fence*. Buckingham: Open University Press.

Haggis, T. (2001) 'Whose learning story? Differing pictures of "adult" learners in higher education', in L. West, N. Miller, D. O'Reilly and R. Allen (eds), *Travellers' Tales: from Adult Education to Lifelong Learning and Beyond*. Proceedings of the 31st Annual Conference, SCUTREA, University of East London, pp. 152–5.

Halpern, D. (1996) *Thought and Knowledge: An Introduction to Critical Thinking*. Mahwah, NJ: Lawrence Erlbaum.

Hargreaves, A. (1994) *Changing Teachers, Changing Times*, London: Cassell.

Hartley, J. (ed.) (1992) *Technology and Writing*. London: Jessica Kingsley.

Hartley, J. (1997) 'Writing the thesis', in N. Graves and V. Varma (eds), *Working for a doctorate*. London: Routledge. pp. 96–112.

Hartley, J. and Jory, S. (2000) 'Lifting the veil on the viva: the experiences of psychology PhD candidates in the UK', *Psychology Teaching Review*, 9,(2): 76–90.

Hayes, J. and Flower, L. (1986) 'Writing research and the writer', *American Psychologist*, 41(10): 1106–13.

Haynes, A. (2001) *Writing Successful Textbooks*. London: A. and C. Black.

Henson, K. (1999) *Writing for Professional Publication*. Boston, MA: Allyn and Bacon.

Heron, J. (1996) *Co-operative Inquiry: Research into the Human Condition*. London: Sage.

Hertz, R. (ed.) (1997) *Reflexivity and Voice*. Thousand Oaks, CA: Sage.

Holly, L. (1989) 'Reflective writing and the spirit of inquiry', *Cambridge Journal of Education*, 19(1): 71–80.

Hunt, C. (1999) '*In search of the abstract quality*'. PhD thesis, University of Sheffield.

Hunt, C. (2000) 'Wyrd questions: reframing adult/community education', in T. Sork, V.-L. Chapman and R. StClair (eds), *AERC 2000: An International Conference*. Proceedings of the 41st Annual Adult Education Research Conference, Vancouver, University of British Columbia, pp. 185–9.

Hunt, C. (2001) 'Climbing out of the void: from chaos to concepts in the presentation of a thesis', *Teaching in Higher Education*, 6(3): 351–67.

Inglis, F. (2003) 'Method and morality: practical politics and the science of human affairs', in P. Sikes, J. Nixon, and W. Carr (eds), *The Moral Foundations of Educational Research: Knowledge, Inquiry and Values*. Maidenhead: Open University Press/McGraw Hill Educational pp. 118–33.

Jackson, C. and Tinkler, P. (2001) 'Back to basics: a consideration of the purposes of the PhD viva', *Assessment and Evaluation in Higher Education*, 26(4): 355–66.

Jackson, G., Kezar, A., Kozi, M. and de las Alas, N. (2000) *Tools for Preparing Literature Reviews: A Webtorial*, Graduate School of Education and Human Development, George Washington University, at: http://www.gwu.edu/~litrev, accessed 12 January 2004.

Kelly, L., Regan, L. and Burton, S. (1995) 'Defending the indefensible? Quantitative methods and feminist research', in J. Holland and M. Blair, with S. Sheldon (eds), *Debates and Issues in Feminist Research and Pedagogy*. Clevedon: Multilingual Matters/Open University Press.

Kolb, D.A. (1984) *Experiential Learning*. Englewood Cliffs, NJ: Prentice-Hall.

Kuhn, T. (1962) *The Structure of Scientific Revolutions*. Chicago, Il: University of Chicago Press.

Lather, P. (1986) 'Research as praxis', *Harvard Educational Review*, 56(3): 257–77.

Lunt, I., Brown, A., Scott, D. and Thorne, L. (2003) 'Professional doctorates and their contribution to professional development and careers', paper given at Sheffield, October.

MacLure, M. (2003) *Discourse in Educational and Social Research*. Buckingham: Open University Press.

Marx, K. (1969 [1845]) *The Eighteenth Brumaire of Louis Bonaparte, Marx and Engels Selected Works Volume 1*. Moscow: Progress.

Maynard, M. (1994) 'Methods, practice and epistemology: the debate about feminism and research', in M. Maynard and J. Purvis (eds), *Researching Women's Lives from a Feminist Perspective*. London: Taylor and Francis.

McCallum, C. (1997) *Writing for Publication*. 4th edn. Oxford: How to Books.

McDrury, J. and Alterio, M. (2003) *Learning through Storytelling in Higher Education*. London: Kogan Page.

Medawar, P. (1963) 'Is the scientific paper a fraud?', *The Listener*, 70 (September).

Medawar, P. (1979) *Advice to a Young Scientist*. New York: Harper and Row.

Mezirow, J. (1981) 'A critical theory of adult learning and education', *Adult Education*, 32(1): 3–24.

Mezirow, J. (1991) *Transformative Dimensions of Adult Learning*. San Francisco, CA: Jossey-Bass.

Miller, N. (1993) *Personal Experience, Adult Learning and Social Research: developing a Sociological Imagination beyond the T-group*. Adelaide: University of South Australia/CRAEHD.

Miller, N. and Brimicombe, A. (2003) 'Disciplinary divides: finding a common language to chart research journeys', in I. Davidson, D. Murphy and B. Piette (eds), *Speaking in Tongues: Languages of Lifelong Learning*. Proceedings of the 33rd Annual Conference, SUTREA, University of Wales, Bangor, pp. 162–7.

Mills, C.W. (1959) *The Sociological Imagination*. Oxford: Oxford University Press.

Morley, L. Leonard, D. and David, M. (2002) 'Variations in vivas: quality and equality in British PhD assessments', *Studies in Higher Education*, 27(3): 263–73.

Moxley, J. (1997) 'If not now, when?', in J. Moxley and T. Taylor (eds), *Writing and Publishing for Academic Authors*. Lanham, MD: Rowman and Littlefield, pp. 6–19.

Murray, R. (2002) *How to Write a Thesis*. Buckingham: Open University Press, pp. 101–11.

Murray, R. (2003) *How to Survive your Viva*. Buckingham: Open University Press.

Needleman , J. (1983) *The Heart of Philosophy*. London: Routledge and Kegan Paul.

Noble, K (1994) *Changing Doctoral Degrees: An International Perspective*. Buckingham: Open University Press.

Olesen, V. (2000) 'Feminisms and qualitative research at and into the millenium', in N. Denzin, and Y. Lincoln (eds), *The Handbook of Qualitative Research: Second Edition*. Thousand Oaks, CA: Sage, pp. 215–56.

Partington, J., Brown, G. and Gordon, G. (1993) *Handbook for External Examiners in Higher Education*, Sheffield: CVCP.

Partridge, E. (1979) *Origins: A Short Etymological Dictionery of Modern English*. London: Routledge.

Phillips, E. and Pugh, D. (1987) *How to get a PhD*. Buckingham: Open University Press.

Phillips, E. and Pugh, D. (2000) *How to Get a PhD*. 3rd edn. Buckingham: Open University Press.

Polkinghorne, D. (1995) 'Narrative configuration in qualitative analysis' in J. Hatch and R. Wisniewski (eds), *Life History and Narrative*. Lewes: Falmer, pp. 5–23.

Pring, R. (2000) *Philosophy of Educational Research*. London, Continuum.

Punch, M. (1994) 'Politics and ethics in qualitative research' in N. Denzin and Y. Lincoln (eds), *The Handbook of Qualitative Research*. Thousand Oaks, CA: Sage. pp. 83–97.

Ramazanoglu, C. (1990) *Feminism and the Contradiction of Oppression*. London: Routledge.

Reinharz, S. (1992) *Feminist Methods in Social Research*. Oxford: Oxford University Press.

Ribbens, J. and Edwards, R. (1998) *Feminist Dilemmas in Qualitative Research*. London: Sage.

Richardson, L. (1990) *Writing Strategies: Reaching Diverse Audiences*. Newbury Park, CA: Sage.

Richardson, L. (1997) *Fields of Play: Constructing an Academic Life*. New Brunswick, NJ: Rutgers University Press.

Richardson, L. (1998) 'Writing: a method of inquiry', In N. Denzin, and Y. Lincoln (eds), *Collecting and Interpreting Qualitative Materials*. London: Sage.

Richardson, L. (2000) 'Writing: a method of inquiry' in N. Denzin and Y. Lincoln (eds), *The Handbook of Qualitative Research: Second Edition*. Thousand Oaks, CA: Sage.

Rosaldo, R. (1989) *Culture and Truth: The Remaking of Social Analysis*, Boston: Beacon Press.

Rudestam, K. and Newton, R. (1992) *Surviving Your Dissertation*. London: Sage.

Scardamalia, M. and Bereiter, C. (1987) 'Knowledge telling and knowledge transforming in written composition', in S. Rosenberg (ed.), *Reading, Writing and Language Learning*. Cambridge: Cambridge University Press.

Schön, D.A. (1983) *The Reflective Practitioner: How Professionals Think in Action*. New York: Basic Books.

Scott, D. (2000) *Reading Educational Research and Policy*, London: RoutledgeFalmer.

Scott, D., Brown, A., Lunt, I. and Thorne, L. (2004) *Professional Doctorates: Integrating Professional and Academic Knowledge*. Maidenhead: SRHE/Open University Press.

Sieber, J. (1993) 'The ethics and politics of sensitive research', in C. Renzetti and R. Lee (eds), *Researching Sensitive Topics*. London: Sage.

Sikes, P. and Goodson, I. (2003) 'Living research: thoughts on educational research as moral practice', in P. Sikes, J. Nixon and W. Carr (eds), *The Moral Foundations of Educational Research: Knowledge, Inquiry and Values*. Maidenhead: Open University Press.

Simpson, R. (1983) *How The PhD Came To Britain: a century of struggle for postgraduate education*, Buckingham: SRHE.

Smedley, C. (1993) *Getting your Book Published*. Thousand Oaks, CA: Sage.

Sprent, P. (1995) *Getting into Print*. London: E. and F.N. Spon.

Tierney, W. (1998) ' Life history's history: subject foretold', *Qualitative Inquiry*, 4(1): pp. 49–70.

The University of Newcastle (2001) *University Handbook for Examiners of Research Degrees*, Newcastle: University of Newcastle-upon-Tyne.

Thomas, G. (1987) 'The process of writing a scientific paper', in P. Hills (ed.), *Publish or Perish*. Ely: Peter Francis. pp. 93–117.

Tinkler, P. and Jackson, C. (2002) 'In the dark? Preparing for the PhD viva', *Quality Assurance in Education*, 10(2): 86–97.

Tinkler, P. and Jackson, C. (2004) *The Doctoral Examination Process: A Handbook for Students, Examiners and Supervisors*. Maidenhead: SRHE/Open University Press.

Tooley, J. with Darby, D. (1998) *Educational Research: A Critique*. London: Ofsted.

Torgerson, C. (2003) *Systematic Reviews*, London: Continuum.

Usher, R. and Bryant, I. (1993) 'Whose line is it anyway? The use of interview transcripts in researching reflective practice', in N. Miller and D. Jones (eds) *Research: Reflecting Practice*. Manchester: University of Manchester/SCUTREA.

Van Maanen, J. (1988) *Tales of the Field: On Writing Ethnography*. Chicago, Il: University of Chicago Press.

Van Manen, M. (1997) *Researching Lived Experience: Human Science for an Action Sensitive Pedagogy*. 2nd edn. London, Ontario: Althouse Press.

Van Manen, M. (2002) *Writing in the Dark*. London, Ontario: Althouse Press.

Walford, G. (ed.) (1998) *Doing Research about Education*. London: Falmer.

Walker, H. (2001) 'Two research journeys: genealogy and positionality', in L. West, N. Miller, D. O'Reilly and R. Allen (eds), *Travellers' Tales: From Adult Education to Lifelong Learning and Beyond*. Proceedings of the 31st Annual Conference, SCUTREA, University of East London, pp. 419–22.

Wallace, M. and Poulson, L. (2004) 'Becoming a critical consumer of the literature', in L. Poulson, and M. Wallace (eds), *Learning to Read Critically in Teaching and Learning*. London: Sage. pp. 3–36.

Wason, P. (1980) 'Specific thoughts on the writing process', in L. Gregg and E. Steinberg (eds) *Cognitive processes in writing*, pp. 129–37, Hillsdale, New Jersey: Erlbaum.

Webb, G. (1996) *Understanding Staff Development*. Buckingham: SRHE/Open University Press.

Webb, S. (2000) 'Feminist Methodologies for Social Researching', in D. Burton (ed.) *Research Training for Social Scientists: A Handbook for Postgraduate Researchers*, London: Sage. pp. 33–49.

Wellington, J. (2000) *Educational Research: Contemporary Issues and Practical Approaches*. London and New York: Continuum.

Wellington, J. (2003) *Getting Published*. London: RoutledgeFalmer.

West, L. (2001) 'Journeying into auto/biography: the changing subject of lifelong learning', in L. West, N. Miller, D. O'Reilly and R. Allen (eds), *Travellers' Tales: From Adult Education to Lifelong Learning and Beyond*. Proceedings of the 31st Annual Conference: SCUTREA, University of East London, pp. 427–30.

Wilber, K. (1998) Interview with Ken Wilber, *Network: The Scientific and Medical Network Review*, 67(August): 11–12.

Willis, P. (2004) 'Mentorship, transformative learning and nurture: adult education challenges in research supervision', in C. Hunt (ed.), *Whose story now? (Re)generating Research in Adult Learning and Teaching*. Proceedings of the 34th Annual Conference, University of Exeter/SCUTREA, pp. 319–26.

Willis, P. (1977) *Learning To Labour: How Working Class Kids Get Working Class Jobs*, Farnborough: Saxon House.

Wisker, G. (2001) *The Postgraduate Research Handbook*. London: Palgrave.

Wittgenstein, L. (1955) *Tractatus Logico-Philosophicus*. London: Routledge and Kegan Paul.

Wolcott, H. (1990) *Writing Up Qualitative Research*. Newbury Park, CA: Sage.

Wolcott, H. (2002) *Sneaky Kid and Its Aftermath: Ethics and Intimacy in Fieldwork*. Walnut Creek, CA: AltaMira.

Woods, P. (1999) *Successful Writing for Qualitative Researchers*. London: Routledge.

Woodwark, J. (1992) *How to Run a Paper Mill: Writing Technical Papers and Getting them Published*. Winchester: Information Geometers Ltd.

Zinsser, W. (1983) *Writing with a Word Processor*. New York: Harper and Row.

Index

Added to the page number 'f' denotes a figure and 't' denotes a table.

abstracts 173–4
'academic knowledge' 9
affective dimension of research 32, 34–5
area of research projects see general area of research
     projects
argument, text as 42
assessment
  forms of 10
  see also vivas
assignments and the use of learning journals 37–8
'authentic educator/student relationships' 118
auto/biographical approach to research 16–29, 116–19
  framework for a personal life history 23–4
  life history 19–21
  and reasons for enrolment 17–19
  research positionality see research
     positionality
autoethnographies 157

BERA (British Educational Research Association)
     104, 199
bibliographical databases see electronic bibliographical
     databases
bibliographies 164
  presentation 174
biographical research 116–17
books, converting theses into 14, 200, 202–3
boundaries of research 65

cameos
  Alan Hearsum 28–9
  Bernard Longden 106–10
  Carolyn Mason 68–71
  Jean Clarkson 24–7
  John O'Neill 88–91
  Kathryn Roberts 162–4
  Marion Jones 204–5
  Mark Vicars 131–3
  Maxine Burton 195–7
  Paul Machon 175–6
  Tracy Marshall 48–51
chapter structure 148
circumlocution 153

clarity in vivas 182
classification 59
coherence 101
cohort effect 10, 12
communities of practice 12
community, research see research community
community of scholars, entering 203
compositional stage of the writing process 151
conclusion of theses 171
connectives 148
consistency 101
constructed knowledge 128f, 129
cost of research 67
'creative analytic practices' 157
critical, being 83–6
  learning 41–3
  of theory 60
'critical friends' 42–3
  supervisors as 47
critical mind 85
critical reflection 40
critical thought 85–6
'critical transformation' 120, 130
criticality 84, 85–6

data
  access to 67
  relationship between theory and 61
data analysis
  questions in vivas on 186
  websites on computer software for 211–12
databases, electronic see electronic bibliographical
     databases
dialectic, concept of 118
diaries 35
discourse, text as 42
disorientation 33
dissemination of work 198–205
Doctor of Philosophy degrees see PhD degrees
doctoral research see research
doctoral students see research students
doctoral theses see theses

doctorate degrees 3–15
  changing concepts 7–8
  criteria 14–15
  description 3–7
  history 6–7
  implications of starting 18–19
  motivation for 10–11
  see also professional doctorates
doctorateness 3, 15
doctorates in education (EdDs) 6, 7, 9, 12, 18
DPhils 6
drafting and re-drafting 151–2, 160, 173
dramatic presentations 158
Durkheim, Emile 57

e-referencing 155
EdDs (doctorates in education) 6, 7, 9, 12, 18
editing 151–2, 160
  'by ear' 161
education 24
  electronic databases for social sciences   and 76–7,
    212
  theory in 57
Education-line 210
electronic bibliographical databases 76–7, 212
enchantment 119–20
enrolment for doctorates 17–19
epistemology 99, 101
  and assumptions concerning the bases of knowledge
    101–3
'espoused theories' 33
ethical considerations 104–6
  as a dimension of research proposals 66
ethical research, questions for 105–6
ethnographic fiction 157–8
examiners 180, 188–9
  changing their mind 182–3
  see also internal examiners
experiential knowledge 128f, 129
external examiners 180, 184, 189
'eye of flesh' 128f, 129
'eye of mind' 128f, 129
'eye of spirit' 128–9

fail in vivas 193
feminist research 102, 114–16
  see also 'womens' ways of knowing'
fieldwork section of theses 170–1, 172
focus 61–4, 74, 81–2, 168, 191
  changing or modifying 63–4
focusing 149f
framework for a personal life history 23–4
framing 149f
framing research 55–71
  design 64–7
  focus 61–4
  role of theory 56–61
'fringe thoughts' 39

general area of research projects 61, 62, 168
  changing or modifying 63–4
  links between focus, questions and 62–3
generative model of writing 138
'global planning' 145
global professionals 4
good practice in vivas 184–5
  in asking questions 187
'grand' theory 60

Hargreaves, A. 59
headings, levels 147
human nature and agency 97–8, 99, 103–4

identity 31–2, 126, 133
*In a Different Voice: Psychological Theory and Women's
    Development* 102
Informal Education Encyclopaedia and Archive 211
information
  storage 79
  text as 42
inquiry trails 73
'insiderness' in research 114–15
internal examiners 180, 184, 189
introductory section to theses 167–9
  length 171
'Is the scientific paper a fraud?' 107

'jigsaw puzzle' approach to writing 160
journals 35
  publishing in 14, 200–1
  see also learning journals

knowing, ways of 112, 127–30
knowledge
  epistemological assumptions concerning bases 97,
    101–3
  types 9

labelling 59
learning on the doctoral journey 30–51
  identity and uncertainty 31–5
  research as an aspect of lifelong
    learning 40–1
  study tips 43–4
  to be critical 41–3
learning journals 35–40
learning process, writing as 140
Learning to Labour 59
learning transformation 33, 120, 130
length of theses 171–3
life history 16, 19–21, 98
  see also framework for a personal life history
lifelong learning, research as an aspect 40–1
limitations of research 191
linking 149f
literary product, text as a 42

literature reviews 72–91
  being systematic 78–9
  getting started 74–5
  picturing 82
  'place' 86–7
  purpose 72–4
  questions in vivas on 186
  as a section of theses 169–70
  sources 75–8
    primary sources 75–6
  storing information, notes and references 79
  talking about 81
  when to stop 80–1
  writing about the literature 80, 81–3, 87
lived experience 34, 35, 112–33
  rationale 114–19
  speaking what we know 119–27
  ways of knowing 127–30
logs 35

M Phil status, approval for 193
male knowledge 102
Masters 5–6
Masters degrees 5–6
Masters dissertations 165, 166, 169, 171–2
Masters level, theses accepted at 193
Medawar, P. 107
metacognition 86
metaphor, use of 36, 130, 160
methods and methodologies 63, 95–110
  definition 96–8
  ethical considerations 104–6
  explanation 66
  questions in vivas on 186
  as a section of theses 170
    length 171
  selection 98–104
    influencing factors 99
Mills, C. Wright 38
mixed genre work 158
mock vivas 181, 189
models 57–8
  predictive power 58

narrative research 159
narratives 19
  see also storytelling
National Postgraduate Committee (NPC) 209
'new route' PhD programmes 8
notes, storage 79

ontology 99, 100
  and assumptions about social reality 100–1
oral examinations see vivas
oral readers 150
'oral theses' 190–2
'organic transformation' 120, 130

originality of doctorates 14
outcomes of vivas 185, 192–4
  approval for M Phil status 193
  fail 193
  pass 192
    subject to minor amendments 192, 193
  re-submission 192–3
outlines, provision of 47
outside readers 150

paragraphing 149–50
part-time doctorate degrees 7, 10, 32
pass in vivas 192
  subject to minor amendments 192, 193
PCHE (postgraduate certificate in higher education) 8
performance ethnography 158
personal life history, framework 23–4
PhD degrees 3–4
  criticisms 7
  distinction between professional doctorates and 9,
    14–15
  history 6
  reasons for choosing 13–14
  theses 165
  see also 'new route' PhD programmes
phrases, connecting 148
pictorial representations of literature   reviews 82
planning writing 139–40, 145
poetry 158
positionality 19, 21–2, 99
positivism 116
postgraduate certificate in higher education (PCHE) 8
practical knowledge 128f, 129
practicality of research 67
practice, communities of 12
practice vivas 181, 189
praxis 17
predictive power of models 58
presentation
  of theses 173–4
  of writing 154–5
presentational knowledge 128f, 129
primary sources 75–6
procedural knowledge 128f, 129
productive writers 144–5
professional doctorates 5, 8, 9–10
  distinction between PhD degrees
    and 9, 14–15
  reasons for choosing 11–12, 17–18
  vivas 182, 183–4
  see also EdDs (doctorates in education); taught
    doctorates
'professional knowledge' 9
professional researchers vii, 8, 9, 17, 184
progress reports 46
proofreading 154–5, 174
proportions of theses 171–3

propositional knowledge 128f, 129
'publications'
    conversion ot theses into 199–200
    see also books; journals
publishability of doctorates 14

qualitative research
    criticisms 21
    writing up 146–7
qualitative/quantitative dichotomy 97
quantitative research, rejection by feminist research
    115–16
questions, research *see* research questions
questions for ethical research 105–6
questions in vivas 185–9
    general 185
    on generalisability and key messages 186
    good practice 187
    on literature reviews 186
    on methodology and analysis of data 186
    open forum 186
    on theories and theoretical frameworks 186

re-submission of theses 192–3
reading
    connection between writing and 142–3
    see also oral readers; outside readers
reality, representations of 57–8
received knowledge 128f, 129
references 74
    presentation 174
    as sources 77
    storage 79
    see also e-referencing
reflection 36, 37, 38, 57
reflective practice 130
reflexivity 21, 112–13
    discussion in theses of 170
representations of reality 57–8
research
    as an aspect of lifelong learning 40–1
    auto/biographical approach see auto/biographical
        approach to research
    doing 95–110
    framing *see* framing research
    limitations 191
    as lived experience *see* lived experience
    personal and affective dimension 32, 34–5
    'writing up' 139
    see also feminist research; narrative research; qualita-
        tive research;   quantitative research; social
        sciences research
'research careers' 24
research community viii
    becoming part of 198–205
Research Councils 7
research diaries 35, 39–40

research funding organizations 77
research positionality 19, 21–2, 99
research proposals 64–7
research questions 62, 74, 168
    changing or modifying 63–4
    links between area, focus and 62–3
research relationship 118–19
    see also supervisory relationship
research students
    becoming 31–5
    learning and learning strategies 40–51
    views of vivas 183–4
research training programmes (RTPs) 8
researching professionals vii, 8, 9, 17, 179, 184
reviews of literature *see* literature reviews
risk analysis 66–7

schedules of work for research projects 67
SCUTREA (Standing Conference on University
        Teaching and Research in the Education of
        Adults) 210–11
secondary sources 75
secretarial stage of the writing process 151
sentences
    connecting 148
    style 152–3, 161
significance of research 63, 65
signposting 149
silence 128f, 129
skilled writers 144–6
    comparison with unskilled 145–6
social constructivism 59, 100
social reality, ontological assumptions 100–1
social sciences
    electronic databases for education and 76–7, 212
    models in 58
social sciences research 97–8, 112
    objectives 146
    use of biographical methods 116
    'the sociological imagination' 20
software
    for data analysis 211–12
    for referencing 79
sources
    for literature reviews 76–8
    for writing 155
    see also primary sources
spirituality 121, 127
    see also 'eye of spirit'
Standing Conference on University Teaching and
        Research in the Education of Adults
        (SCUTREA) 210–11
storage of information, notes and references 79
stories, literature reviews as 83
storytelling 116–19, 132
    see also narratives
students *see* research students

studying, practical tips 43–4
subjective knowledge 128f, 129
successful writing 146–7
supervisors
    management of 34
    presence at vivas 181, 193
    responsibilities 45–6, 180
supervisory relationship
    aspects 119–27
    practical tips 45–7
systematic, being 78–9
systematic reviews 78

talking about literature 81
taught doctorates
    theses 165
    values and principles associated with
        learning 41
    see also professional doctorates
teacher culture, forms 59
teaching, modes of 10
'telling stories' 116–19, 132
text 42
theoretical framework for theses 169–70
    length 171
    questions in vivas on 186
theory
    relationship between data and 61
    theorising 56–61
    transference 60
    see also 'espoused theories'
theses 119, 165–76, 180, 203
    accepted at Masters level 193
    conversion into books 200, 202–3
    conversion into 'publications' 14, 199–200
    presentation 173–4
    proportion and length 171–3
    qualities 165–6
    re-submission 192–3
    structuring 166–71
    see also 'oral theses'
thinking, writing and 137, 138–9, 140, 142, 160
time for writing 143–4
Tooley report (1998) 60
'transfer of skills' 4
transference of theory 60
transformation 120, 130
'transformative learning' 33
transparency in vivas 182
truth 101–2

uncertainty 32–5
'unitary transformation' 120, 130
unity of opposites 28–9
unskilled writers, comparison with skilled 145–6
USA, history of doctorate degrees 6, 7

variability in vivas 181
vivas 179–97, 198, 203
    concerns 181–3
    conduct 180–1
    content 184–9
        bad practice and strange behaviour 187–9
        good practice 184–5
        questions see questions in vivas
    dos and don'ts 194t
    guidance 196–7
    oral answers 190–2
    outcomes see outcomes of vivas
    preparing for 189–90
    purposes 179–80
        clarification 182
    students' views 183–4
vocational knowledge 9
voice 160
    giving people 115, 146
    of researchers 114, 115, 119, 120
Vygotsky, L. S. 59–60

ways of knowing 112, 127–30
websites
    on computer software for data analysis 211–12
    government and organizations' 78
    research funding organizations' 77
    see also Education-line; Informal Education
        Encyclopaedia and Archive
'whole-person' processes, education and research as
    118
'womens' ways of knowing' 128, 129
writers
    comparison of skilled and unskilled 145–6
    features of skilled, productive 144–5
writing 36, 137–64
    about the literature 80, 81–3
    approaches, styles and formats 155–9
    classical models 137–9
    difficulty in 140–2
    editing, drafting and redrafting 151–2, 160, 173
    exposing 150, 161
    getting started 142–3
    guidelines 159–61
    for journals 200–1
    managing time for 143–4
    planning before 139–40
    proofreading and presentation 154–5
    structuring 147–50
        strategies 149f
    successful 146–7
    and thinking 137, 138–9, 140, 142, 160
    tools and sources of guidance 155
    words and sentences 152–3

'zone of proximal development' (ZPD) 59–6